Informix Dynamic Server™ with Universal Data Option™

Best Practices

ISBN 0-13-911074-7

9 780139 110740

90000

Informix Dynamic Server™ with Universal Data Option™

Best Practices

Edited by
Angela Sanchez

Prentice Hall PTR
Upper Saddle River, New Jersey 07458
http://www.phptr.com

Library of Congress Cataloging-in-Publication Data
Informix dynamic server with universal data option : best practices / edited by Angela Sanchez.
    p.   cm.
   Includes index.
   ISBN 0-13-911074-7
   1. Database management. 2. Data warehousing. 3. Informix
–Universal server. I. Sanchez, Angela.
QA76.9.D3I53318   1998
005.75'6--dc21
                                           98-27471
                                         CIP

Editorial/Production Supervision: *Craig Little*
Acquisitions Editor: *John Anderson*
Buyer: *Alexis R. Heydt*
Cover Design: *Anthony Gemmellaro*
Cover Design Direction: *Jerry Votta*
Art Director: *Gail Cocker-Bogusz*
Series Design: *Claudia Durrell Design*
Marketing Manager: *Miles Williams*
Manager, Informix Press: *Judy Bowman*

© 1999 Prentice Hall PTR
Prentice-Hall, Inc.
A Simon & Schuster Company
Upper Saddle River, NJ 07458

Informix Press
Informix Software, Inc.
4100 Bohannon Drive
Menlo Park, CA 94025

The publisher offers discounts on this book when ordered in bulk quantities. For more information, call the Corporate Sales Department at 800-382-3419; FAX: 201-236-7141, email corpsales@prenhall.com or write Corporate Sales Department, Prentice Hall PTR, One Lake Street, Upper Saddle River, NJ 07458

   Prentice Hall books are widely used by corporations and government agencies for training, marketing, and resale.

   The following are worldwide trademarks of Informix Software, Inc., or its subsidiaries, registered in the United States of America as indicated by ®, and in numerous other counties worldwide:

   INFORMIX®, Informix {___} DataBlade® Module, Informix Dynamic Scalable Architecture™, Informix Illustra™ Server, InformixLink®, INFORMIX®-4GL, INFORMIX®-4GL Compiled, INFORMIX®-CLI, INFORMIX®-Connect, INFORMIX®-ESQL/C, INFORMIX®-MetaCube™, INFORMIX®-Mobile, INFORMIX®-NET, INFORMIX®-NewEra™ INFORMIX®-NewEra™ Viewpoint™, INFORMIX®-NewEra™ Viewpoint™ Pro, INFORMIX®-OnLine, INFORMIX® Dynamic Server™, INFORMIX®-OnLine Workgroup Server, INFORMIX®-OnLine Workstation, INFORMIX®-SE, INFORMIX®-SQL, INFORMIX-Superview™, INFORMIX®-Universal Server.

   All other product names mentioned herein are the trademarks or registered trademarks of their respective owners.

Printed in the United States of America

10 9 8 7 6 5 4 3 2 1

ISBN 0-13-911074-7

Prentice-Hall International (UK) Limited, *London*
Prentice-Hall of Australia Pty. Limited, *Sydney*
Prentice-Hall Canada Inc., *Toronto*
Prentice-Hall Hispanoamericana, S.A., *Mexico*
Prentice-Hall of India Private Limited, *New Delhi*
Prentice-Hall of Japan, Inc., *Tokyo*
Simon & Schuster Asia Pte. Ltd., *Singapore*
Editora Prentice-Hall do Brasil, Ltda., *Rio de Janeiro*

Contents

Chapter 3 Building Complex Decision-Support Models Using a Universal Warehouse

by Jacques Roy

Chapter 4 DataBlade Modules for the Informix Dynamic Server with Universal Data Option

Chapter 5 Using Custom DataBlades to Move Beyond a Three-Tier Architecture

Chapter 18 Informix Digital Media Solutions: The Emerging Industry Standard for Information Management

Foreword

by Michael Stonebraker

The Next Great Wave is beginning to take shape.

This book contains a collection of articles describing what it looks like, written by those involved in daily, hands-on work with object-relational database management systems.

A bit of background: the original motivation for extensible databases was born out of the frustration users felt in trying to apply relational technology to manage business data. From the first, the focus of object-relational research was to improve this situation by bringing business knowledge closer to where the data was stored. This meant creating a new database management system (DBMS) technology, one based on the best of existing technology, but with the added ability to accept new data types and methods.

In the short term, the object-relational DBMS will succeed simply because it is a better relational DBMS. And extensible technology is maturing rapidly—Informix is in the process of preparing the second release of its object-relational DBMS. Informix Dynamic Server with Universal Data Option, version 9.2, represents the complete integration of the relational DBMS with the extensible DBMS.

Which brings us back to this book. Several of the articles you'll find here are tutorials on how to create extensions to the basic database framework, and how to apply them to solve real-world problems. Others describe the experiences of developers who use Informix Dynamic Server with Universal Data Option to support Web site development, a traditionally strong market for the technology.

Beyond the Web, however, the book describes how organizations have used object-relational DBMS technology to change the way they do business, by allowing their employees to share libraries of rich content, and by providing groupware solutions for project management—all with high levels of performance and scalability. It also demonstrates how object-relational database features like user-defined aggregates are ideal for advanced decision-support systems.

Looking ahead, it is clear that object-relational databases will become the mainstream DBMS technology of choice within the next few years, if only because technically aggressive organizations view them as delivering strong competitive advantage. There exists an enormous, pent-up demand for applications such as digital image management ("Find all the photographs we took in Paris last April with the model wearing 'this' shirt."), geo-location ("Show me the nearest Italian restaurant."), e-commerce ("Compute the shipping costs to send my Hawaiian shirts to Toledo, Ohio, by air freight"), and digitizing X-rays and ultrasound ("Show me the difference between this X-ray and the last one."), to name just a few.

Over time, these are the kinds of applications that will drive the database market. Since the object-relational DBMS acts as a framework for integrating the components of the solution, there is no limit to the potential for innovation.

This book, for all of its depth, barely scratches the surface.

Dr. Michael Stonebraker
Chief Technology Officer
Informix Software, Inc.

Architectural Options for Object-Relational DBMSs

by Michael R. Stonebraker

This paper describes and evaluates the architectural options for evolving a relational database management system (RDBMS) towards the object-relational database management system (ORDBMS) paradigm. The goal of this evolution is to produce a single system possessing the benefits of both relational and object-oriented technology, namely:

- The functionality of a dynamic programming language like Structured Query Language (SQL) that understands objects— user-defined types and functions—in addition to simple datatypes (integers, characters, and dates).
- The scaleability and performance that is the result of two decades of research and development by RDBMS engine vendors and the academic community.

We explore this topic first by describing the technical alternatives database vendors have for achieving this goal, and second by examining how well these alternatives perform according to both of the criteria introduced above. Finally, we survey the commercial database (DBMS) marketplace, and show how each vendor is managing the change.

Introduction

Modern business is making increasing demands on data processing technology. First, this is because the environment within which modern industry operates is becoming increasingly complex. Today, managers need to incorporate geographic considerations into marketing, risk analysis, and supply chain management. They need to access textual reports based on the concepts that the reports discuss. They need to include digital photographs, audio data, and digitizations of items like checks and signatures. As object-oriented programming languages penetrate the mainstream, they need a DBMS technology with a philosophy closer to their client tools.

And there is no shortage of this kind of information. All of the datatypes we have described above are significantly larger than the types MIS is familiar with. One characteristic of this kind of data is that it is machine-generated. As fast as a user can type, electronic hardware can scan pages and perform optical character recognition thousands of times faster.

Yet even with all of these increasing demands there is unlikely to be a diminution of user expectations with respect to performance. This situation requires a DBMS capable of storing objects (and not simply as records) combined with support for new access methods, query processing algorithms, and storage management techniques with no degradation in the DBMS capability for traditional alphanumeric data processing.

One option is a pure object-oriented database management system (OODBMS) approach that allows developers to store and retrieve C++ and Smalltalk objects efficiently. However, OODBMSs do not, at this date, excel at processing relational fixed-form data. Conversely, a purely relational database does not make modeling complex situations easy. Any complexity cannot be handled within the system: it must be given special treatment externally. An ideal solution is one that combines the power of the object-oriented approach with the data management flexibility of the RDBMS.

The object-relational approach does this, as adopted by Informix in Informix Dynamic Server™ with Universal Data Option™. Universal Data Option merges the best of both worlds by combining the unmatched scaleability and performance of the Informix Dynamic Scaleable Architecture (DSA) with the object-relational features. This creates a single, integrated framework enabling businesses to manage all types of information efficiently: numbers and character strings, GIS data values, images from document scans and text data from OCRing these images, digital photographs, audio, and Web pages. Indeed, any datatype.

The achievement of building Universal Data Option is quite remarkable. The relational DBMS must be drastically altered to include object-relational (OR) functionality: user-defined types and functions, inheritance, and polymorphism. Certain relational DBMS vendors are either unable or unwilling to perform the required surgery, and instead have elected to pursue inferior strategies for achieving OR functionality.

This paper assesses the architectural options available to various vendors along two crucial dimensions:

1. Functionality—The desired functionality for an object-relational DBMS includes support for base type extension, complex objects, and inheritance within the SQL query language. Some vendors, such as Oracle 8.0 and the Oracle Networking Computing Architecture (NCA), do not remotely meet this test, and should not be called object-relational DBMSs. Others, such as the IBM DB2/6000 Common Server, come closer. Hence, there are a spectrum of capabilities offered in the marketplace.

2. Performance—There are two crucial decisions to make with respect to technical architecture for an ORDBMS. First, is the server extensibility achieved by *tight integration* of user-written code within the DBMS framework (for sorting, indexing and query processing), or *loose integration* which is achieved by creating a layer of wrapper logic that hosts the extension. Second, the server can call the extensions without needing to ask the operating system to intervene in the operation *tight*

coupling or employ a heavyweight mechanism like the remote procedure call (RPC) *loose coupling.* As we shall see, the performance implications of anything except server extensibility achieved by the tight integration of user code into the DBMS leads with a tightly coupled calling mechanism to disastrous performance.

After a detailed discussion of these two dimensions, the characteristics of the solutions proposed or implemented by the various database management system (DBMS) vendors will be discussed.

Functionality of an ORDBMS

To illustrate the required functionality of an ORDBMS, the following example table will be used.

```
create table Emp
     (name = Scottish_name,
     age = int,
     location = point,
     picture = image);
```

Here, *name* and *age* have the obvious interpretation. However, two additional fields have been added to a traditional Emp table: the location of the employee's home address, and the employee's picture. These fields are of the datatypes "point" and "image," respectively.

Following is a typical query to this table:

```
select name
   from Emp
where name < 'b'
   and age > 50
   and contains(location, circle ('(10,10)',1.5))
   and beard(picture) > 0.7
order by name ascending;
```

This query locates all employees whose name begins with an 'a', whose age is above 50, who live within a five-mile circle surrounding the point "10,10", and who also have beards.

This query, although simple and straightforward to the average reader, is impossible in a traditional relational database management system (RDBMS). First, in many countries outside the United States, names do not sort in strict ASCII order. In such places, the normal "collation sequence" of letters is complicated by case-sensitive rules. Scotland is one such example. In the Edinburgh phone book, the following names—all variants of the clan McTavish—are sorted together:

• McTavish
• MacTavish
• M'Tavish

As a result, one cannot use the varchar datatype found in SQL-89 because it supports a '<' operator which collates in ASCII order, and thereby generates an incorrect answer for many Scottish queries. In addition, one cannot perform any single character substitution algorithm, such as supported in SQL-92, since {a, c,'} are only "silent" if preceded by an 'M'. Instead, to perform the above query requires a new datatype, Scottish_name, with a type-specific notion of '<'.

Moreover, when the user requests the result of the query in ascending order, the system must generate the answer in Scottish_name order. Hence, sorting must be accomplished using the user-defined notion of '<'.

In addition, the third clause contains a pair of user-defined functions (*contains*, *location*) and a nonstandard datatype (*circle*), while the fourth clause contains a user-defined pattern recognition function (*beard*) that looks at an image and determines whether the person in the image has a beard. The user-defined functions (*beard*, *location*, and *contains*) must be writeable in SQL, a stored procedure language such as Informix's SPL, or in a third-generation language, such as C or Java. Since it is impossible to write the *beard* function in a stored procedure language, an object-relational DBMS must support coding functions in all of the three languages noted above.

As a result, this article defines basic object-relational functionality as the ability to construct the above table, register the above functions written in one of the three languages, and execute the query noted above.

Systems which provide this functionality include Informix Dynamic Server with Universal Data Option, and are termed fully object-relational. In contrast, other systems, such as Oracle 8.0 and Oracle NCA, have essentially no object-relational functionality. Finally, other systems, such as IBM's DB2/6000 Common Server, have some object-relational functionality but do not pass the functionality test.

As a result, systems will be classified along a functionality axis from no object-relational functionality to full object-relational functionality. In addition, Informix is collaborating on a benchmark with the University of Wisconsin which will more precisely and completely categorize object-relational functionality in the near future.

Performance

There are two critical functions that an object-relational DBMS must perform in order to offer high performance in an object-relational environmen; namely, it must tightly integrate object functionality into its engine and it must efficiently call user-written functions. These aspects will be discussed in turn.

Tight Integration

There are two options in the support of object-relational functionality. First, one can tightly integrate the functionality into an existing SQL engine. Alternately, one can implement functionality in a simulation layer above an unchanged core engine, as noted in Fig. 1–1.

To achieve high performance, a vendor must utilize the first approach, that of tightly integrating objects with its access methods, sort engine, and optimizer. The performance difference between the two choices will be explored using aspects of the previous sample query.

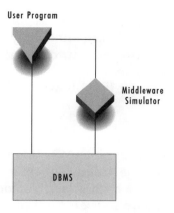

User Program

Middleware
Simulator

DBMS

Figure 1–1 *The architecture
of middleware simulators.*

Consider the clause:

```
where name < 'b'
```

which finds Scottish_names which begin with an 'a'. To provide
high performance on this clause, an engine must use a b-tree
index to identify the required names. Hence, b-tree code must
be extended to support the indexing of new datatypes, such as
Scottish_name, and must keep the indexed objects in sort
order, according to a type-specific notion of '<'. In other words,
the b-tree code must understand objects.

If a simulation layer is used, then the b-tree code will not
understand objects and cannot be used to process the above
clause; instead, a sequential scan will be required. The performance difference between an indexed scan and a sequential scan
is typically one or two orders of magnitude.

Now consider the following clause:

```
where contains(location, circle ('(10,10)',1.5))
```

This is a two-dimensional search that cannot be optimized
using a one-dimensional access method such as a b-tree. To perform such searches requires access methods particularized to
geographic data, such as r-trees, quad trees, or grid files. As a
result, an object-relational engine must be capable of supporting

additional access methods, including those written by third parties. If a simulation methodology is utilized, then there will be no fast access paths for nontraditional datatypes, and performance will gravely suffer.

Next, consider the following clause:

```
where beard (picture) > 0.7
```

It makes no sense for a DBMS to build a b-tree index on the bits in an image, because there is no inherent order that can be exploited by such an index. Instead, the above clause can be accelerated if an index is built on the result of the user-defined function, *beard*. As a result, a high-performance object-relational system must allow indexes to be defined on a *function of an attribute*. Again, a simulation layer cannot accelerate clauses of this kind.

Now, consider the following clause:

```
order by name ascending
```

If objects are tightly integrated into the sort engine in the DBMS, then the qualifying names can be efficiently sorted by the DBMS sort engine. Alternately, the sort must be performed in the simulation layer outside the core engine. The consequence of moving the sort farther from data storage is a severe performance hit.

Lastly, consider the following pair of clauses:

```
where, name < 'b'
and contains(location, circle ('(10,10)',1.5))
```

In the above example, the optimizer must decide whether to use a b-tree index on the first clause or an r-tree index on the second clause to solve the query. If the selectivity of the first clause is much finer than the selectivity of the second, then the b-tree approach should be selected. Otherwise, the r-tree choice should be executed. In addition, in certain circumstances it is desirable to use both access paths. If objects are tightly integrated into the optimizer, then these decisions can be easily made. Without tight integration, incorrect query execution plans are likely, and disastrous performance can result.

These examples have all indicated the severe performance consequences of *loose integration*, that is, implementing objects in a simulation layer, as compared to *tight integration*, implementing objects in the core engine. The performance degradation often approaches orders of magnitude in size.

Degree of Coupling

Whenever a user-defined function is used in a SQL query, the vendor must support one or more protocols to execute a call to the user-written routine. The choice of the calling protocol is motivated by performance and safety considerations.

In the previous example user query, there is an operator '<' which ascertains if a given Scottish_name collates before the letter 'b'. The function which supports '<' may have an execution path length of 100 usecs and is called once for each record evaluated in the query. As such, the performance of the call is a concern. If the overhead of the call is significant relative to 100 usecs, then overall query performance is adversely affected.

In addition, one must be concerned about the effect of bugs in user-written code and the damage that bugs can cause.

Table 1–1 indicates the performance of the various options in calling a user-defined routine.

One can call a user-defined procedure in the same address space as the DBMS, thereby obtaining the highest performance. The second option is to support the *fenced* execution of local procedures, whereby the DBMS is protected from errors in the user-written routine. Of course, the performance tax of this choice is dramatic, as noted in Table 1–1. A third option is to use the standard RPC system found in essentially all operating systems.

Table 1-1 *Calling characteristics.*

Calling protocol	Typical call overhead (usecs)
Local Procedure Call (LPC)	~1
Fenced LPC	~75
Remote Procedure Call (RPC)	~1000
CORBA	~10,000

However, the tax for this feature is another big increase in overhead. The last recourse is to use a protocol such as CORBA, that includes an Object Request Broker (ORB) which can locate the required user routine is a distributed computing system. Again, performance degrades by another order of magnitude.

Most extension systems, for example, Novell NLMs, CICS applications, VB controls, and Netscape plug-ins, offer only LPC, because the performance of the other options is unacceptably bad. Moreover, essentially all existing Illustra customers use LPC, although RPC is also available. Again, the motivating issue is achieving good performance. In short, the tight coupling of user routines is required to achieve good performance. Of course, loose coupling is desirable in certain circumstances, and should be provided in any complete system.

This article now focuses on three points about the safety of user-written functions. First, a bug in any program causes the address space in which it runs to fail. The functionality utilized is then unavailable until recovery is accomplished. Any program that is used as a plug-in to any framework will have this characteristic. As a result, good software practice includes a serious quality assurance program, and released code, either from a DBMS vendor or a third-party supplier of extension routines, must be tested thoroughly. The adequate testing of any software routines inserted into a production system is standard practice in the industry.

Second, either fenced execution or RPC is available at a huge performance penalty if a user does not feel confident in their routine.

Third, safety concerns are different for an interpreted language, such as Java, than for a compiled language, such as C or C++. In an interpreted language, the execution system will catch errors, and safety concerns are not an issue.

In this section we have indicated that the tight integration of object-relational capabilities into the underlying engine, as well as tight coupling to user-written routines, is required to achieve good object-relational performance. As such, the products of the various vendors offer performance that ranges from bad to good, depending on their choices in these two areas. The next section of this article discusses a collection of architectures that have been proposed and compares them on the basis of functionality and performance considerations.

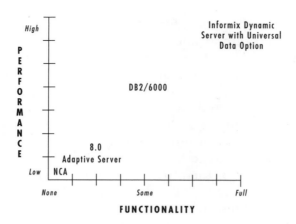

Figure 1-2 *Functionality versus performance for servers.*

Marketplace Architectures

In Fig. 1–2, five systems, Sybase's Adaptive Server, Oracle NCA, Oracle 8.0, IBM's DB/2 version 5, and Informix Dynamic Server with Universal Data Option, and Common Server, are placed on the functionality versus performance chart. Along the horizontal axis is the object-relational functionality provided, ranging from none to full. On the vertical axis is the degree of integration and degree of coupling provided, which determines performance, ranging from low to high.

Sybase Adaptive Server

Sybase were late-comers to the object-relational party. In fact, it is unclear today whether Sybase even intends to produce an ORDBMS at all or instead focus on marketing a middleware and connectivity product. Sybase's Adaptive Server provides a set of interfaces allowing developers to integrate data sources into a single query-able system: a technology superficially similar to Informix's Virtual Table Interface. In fact, Sybase has built a sophisticated wrapper layer around both Sybase's core SQL-92

RDBMS and whatever extensions developers add. The DBMS server itself is almost unchanged.

At the time of writing, users could integrate code written in the Java language or integrate data sources with 'C'. This means that it is not possible to pose our query to the Adaptive Server. Instead, each datatype must be integrated separately, and the code to run functions like `beard()` is hosted outside the DBMS, in the layer of wrapper code.

This makes Sybase a loosely coupled and loosely integrated ORDBMS. So far as their architecture is concerned, this implies mediocre performance (at best) for operations involving any one extension, and disastrous performance when they are combined. For example, in our sample query, each data source must be handled separately and the result of each operation "joined" in a final step. If the proportion of employees living in the specific circle is very high, but the number over fifty is relatively low, the system will still compute the `contain()` function for every emp and join the result set in the middle-ware.

Since so much effort is required to "extend" a relational engine to make it "object aware," some vendors use application middleware approaches to mimic this functionality. This is possible due to many application frameworks, such as the following:

- VB controls;
- Netscape plug-ins;
- Oracle cartridges;
- Novell Network Loadable Modules (NLMs); and
- The class library interface in most 4GLs.

These frameworks support the execution of user-written routines in a non-SQL context. Such frameworks allow one user program to make a function call to a second user program, thereby providing application-to-application connectivity.

However, this architecture has nothing to do with DBMS-type extension because it is not integrated with SQL. For example, Oracle NCA cannot run the example query unless a user writes an application program that implements this functionality. Middleware plug-ins do not constitute a true object-relational DBMS architecture at all; there is no server-managed integrity, no common query language, no single table view, and numerous other disadvantages.

As such, Oracle NCA is at the far left-hand side of the diagram of Fig. 1–2. In addition, NCA uses CORBA as its connection protocol, the slowest of the options. Hence, it is also at the bottom of the chart. NCA should never be confused with an object-relational DBMS.

Oracle 8.0

Oracle 8 was released in early 1997. According to the analysts, it was primarily a scaleability and performance release that included very few ORDBMS features. Such features, as it did have, were poorly integrated with the rest of the system—indicating that they were hasty, last minute additions to the product plan. Specifically, it contained an extension to the stored procedure facility of Oracle 7.3, whereby a stored procedure can appear in the WHERE clause of an SQL query. This is added functionality relative to Oracle 7.3, where stored procedures can only be executed. The arguments to an Oracle 8.0 stored procedure are the fields in a row in a table.

This capability is not helpful in generating the schema for the example data, which requires points, images, and Scottish_names. In addition, Oracle 8.0 functions can only be coded in PL/SQL. As noted earlier, none of the functions in our example query are easily written in PL/SQL.

In addition, Oracle 8.0 offers a limited form of inheritance, whereby tables can inherit data from other tables and can inherit functions in PL/SQL written for those tables. However, Oracle 8.0 does not support the overloading of function names, *polymorphism*, so it is impossible for a user to redefine the behavior of a subobject.

As such, Oracle 8.0 has minimal object capabilities and does not support user-defined base datatypes or sets, and does not support functions in a third-generation language.

In addition, user-defined functions are not integrated with the access methods, sort engine, or optimizer. Because Oracle 8.0 only supports loose integration, it is also near the lower left-hand corner of Fig. 1– 2.

Oracle 8.1 and 8.2

Oracle marketing talks extensively of the future notion that cartridges in the Oracle NCA can be plugged into either a middleware application layer or the DBMS engine. In fact, cartridges
are not part of Oracle 8.0, and they are unlikely to be supported
until Oracle 8.1 or even 8.2 (due in 1999).

Since this capability has yet to be designed, it is impossible to
place Oracle 8.1 or 8.2 in our diagram, because functionality
and degree of integration are not yet known.

IBM DB2/6000 Common Server

IBM DB2/6000 Common Server supports base-type extension and
can construct the schema indicated earlier. In addition, it can
almost run the example query; unfortunately, it is impossible to
have a type-specific notion of '<'. Hence, the following clause:

```
where name < 'b'
```

must be executed in user code. Also, DB2/6000 Common Server
does not support inheritance or complex objects. As such, it is to
the right of Oracle 8.0, but does not support full functionality.

In addition, the DB2/6000 optimizer is aware of objects, but
the access methods and sort engine are not; they work only on
SQL-89 datatypes. Furthermore, user-defined functions can be
written in C and are called using either LPC or RPC. Hence, the
IBM system offers better performance than the Oracle systems,
but there is still room for improvement.

Informix Dynamic Server with Universal Data Option

Informix Dynamic Server with Universal Data Option is the
result of a code merge of Informix's Dynamic Scalable
Architecture (DSA) with the Illustra Server. It preserves the scalability and alphanumeric performance of Informix DSA, while
also providing the Illustra data model and query language. As
such, it provides user-defined types, user-defined functions, complex objects, and inheritance. Moreover, it allows a user to over-
load all operators and functions. It is the only system which will

run the example query, and therefore, it is on the right-hand side of Fig. 1–2.

Moreover, it is a single engine with an object-aware optimizer, sort engine, and b-tree package. Lastly, it supports LPC. As such, it is the only system with both tight integration and tight coupling. As a result, it is positioned highest on the vertical axis.

Summary of Architectural Options

This article has discussed the six systems in the previous section. This section briefly reviews the characteristics of these systems.

Sybase Adaptive Server

This system is a loosely coupled and loosely integrated ORDBMS. Its architecture can at best provide mediocre performance for operations involving any single extension, and this performance worsens when extensions are combined.

Oracle NCA

This is not an object-relational engine, but rather an application middleware system. The possibility of inserting "cartridges" in either middleware or the server will not be available until 1998 or 1999. Informix has this capability.

Oracle 8.0

This system can be described as Oracle 7.3 with a limited notion of inheritance and extensions to stored procedures. Basically, it is a scalability release with minimal object capabilities.

Oracle 8.1 and 8.2

Better object support is expected in version 8.1 or 8.2 with the support of cartridges.

IBM DB2/6000 Common Server

This is an engine with support for base-type extension, but not inheritance or complex objects. Object support is tightly integrated into the engine and extensions are tightly coupled, thereby offering good performance.

Informix Dynamic Server with Universal Data Option

This is an engine with support for all object-relational concepts, offering both tight integration and tight coupling. It is considered the best of the current breed of products.

Chapter 2

Informix's Universal Data Option: A Platform for the Universal Warehouse

by Malcolm Colton

Overview

Data warehousing is engaged in deriving new information from collections of historical data. It attempts to answer such questions as "How are we doing? How did we get here? What can we do better?" Often these warehoused data collections are very large, and require special hardware and software for their management. Often the data is summarized and restructured from the operational data stores, and complex algorithms must run against the data warehouse to derive the required information. Increasingly, corporations want to warehouse data that is intrinsically more complex than traditional alphanumeric data. An object-relational database management system (ORDBMS) like Informix Dynamic Server™ with Universal Data Option™[1]

---

[1] For general information about object-relational technology, see *Object-Relational, The Next Great Wave*, by Michael Stonebraker (Addison-Wesley, 1996). For information about the Informix Dynamic Server with Universal Data Option, see documentation on Informix's Web site at www.informix.com

proves to be an ideal platform for warehousing data of any degree of complexity that is manipulated by very complex algorithms. This paper discusses major data management issues in data warehousing, and suggests how object-relational technology can be applied to solving the issues.

Basic DBMS Aspects of Data Warehousing

Building and maintaining a data warehouse is a complex exercise, and most aspects are beyond the scope of this paper. This paper focuses only on the issues related to the data warehouse's data store and how to build the applications that surround it. Within this context, several elements require attention in managing the data in a warehouse:

- Data structures;
- Algorithms;
- Data visualization;
- Data and system management; and
- Legacy integration.

Data Structures

There are three major data structure requirements for a data warehouse platform:

- Flexible and comprehensive data models;
- The flexibility to easily change the model; and
- A broad range of indexes to support a variety of queries.

Fundamental to asking questions of data is organizing the data in such a way that it supports the questions. A wide variety of knowledge and areas of interest dictate a wide range of possible data structures. Thus, for a data management platform to be useful for a wide variety of data warehousing tasks, it must be incredibly flexible in its ability to efficiently model data. Classical relational databases, which are limited in the kinds of data structures and the complexity of the algorithms they support, are unsuited to many data warehousing tasks. Examples include:

• Demographics;
• Time series;
• Geodetic data; and
• Images, video, sound, and other rich media.

A data warehouse platform must also be flexible, not only in modeling the structure of the data, but also in providing index data structures that deliver high-speed shared access to the data. While proprietary, closed, special-purpose systems were used initially for data warehousing, companies are increasingly building their data warehouses on a relational DBMS (an architecture often called relational on-line analytical processing, or ROLAP). Current relational database management systems (RDBMSs) typically provide b-trees, hash, and bitmap indexes. As we will see, an ORDBMS is much more flexible in this area.

A business may grow by mergers and acquisitions, it may divest itself of divisions or subsidiary companies, or it may simply change focus as market conditions shift beneath it. As a company transforms itself in response to changing market conditions, the intrinsic meaning of historical data changes, and data warehouses must change to reflect this new understanding. For example, the state of California recently suffered a number of drought years. Climate researchers wishing to examine historical records of drought turned to the photographic archives kept by the state. However, even though the collection contained photographs of value in assessing the effect of drought in the past, the photos were often not categorized in a useful way, because the photograph was not taken to show drought effects. A more useful search of the archive requires a restructuring based on the automatic recognition of photographs that relate to drought by the direct analysis of the images' content.

Current technology dictates that the data warehouse remain separate from the transactional data used to run the business, since they require different optimizations. A transactional data store is usually highly normalized, meaning that data is stored once and only once in the simplest possible way. Great care is also taken to minimize the number of indexes down to only those which are required to run the production applications. This makes modification highly efficient, but entails complex, expensive queries. The data in the warehouse, on the other hand, is often highly structured, summarized, and multiply indexed, rendering modification very expensive, but queries very efficient. One consequence of this division between operational and historical data is that it is much harder, or even impossible, to ask data warehouse questions of operational data, so analysis always trails operational data by some time interval that can be measured in days or even weeks. A more flexible platform holds out the tantalizing possibility that a single data store can be used for on-line transaction processing (OLTP), as well as data warehousing—provided that neither form of processing pushes the performance envelope too hard.

Algorithms

Data structures exist to support the analytical algorithms that extract meaning from the data. The real value of the warehouse comes from the analysis performed by the algorithms, so it is vital that the data management platform supports a flexible way to define algorithms. While, in principle, there are a number of possible locations to store and manage the data processing algorithms, the DBMS is a good choice for several reasons:

- It locates the algorithms in close proximity to the data, minimizing data movement;
- It provides a central point of access for the algorithms, enabling a single copy to be shared efficiently between multiple applications. This simplifies maintenance, since the single copy can be modified once, and the new version is then instantly available to all applications; and
- The DBMS is a sophisticated platform that provides parallel operation, shared data management, and a number of other features that simplify the task of creating high-performance systems.

An RDBMS provides only stored procedures written in the SQL language, which severely limits its functionality as a data warehouse platform. SQL is an incomplete programming language which lacks many of the constructs of a general purpose programming language like C or C++. Furthermore, it is interpreted, and this makes it very slow as compared to a compiled language like C or C++.

As companies move into the world of complex, highly structured data—such as images, maps, and time series—SQL shows another of its rigidities. The SQL language of an RDBMS is based on the SQL-92 standard, which defines only a handful of alphanumeric datatypes. More complex data which does not fit into these datatypes is stored as a binary large object (BLOB). The SQL language has no constructs for manipulating the internal content of BLOBs, and forces the application to export BLOBs to another application for processing. In the case of a data warehouse—where the data store is very large—this massive movement of data is impractical, and severely limits the utility of an RDBMS to support warehouses of complex data. A more flexible platform can support the running of complex algorithms against simple alphanumeric data, as well as newer, complex data.

Visualization

Ultimately, the output of a data warehouse query must be analyzed by humans, who require some visualization of the data. This can be as simple as a spreadsheet or a printed report, or as complex as a virtual reality display. Much creativity often goes into delivering the information in an evocative way which renders it easy for people to grasp patterns and connections in the data, and leverages the pattern recognition "wetware" of the human brain. This is an area of intensive research, with much to be learned about how the human brain interprets visual information and the formatting of data so that it elicits the brain's attention.

Increasingly, the World Wide Web (Web) is used as a delivery mechanism on corporate intranets. Therefore, a good data warehouse platform must provide excellent support for both the delivery of pre-planned and ad-hoc visualization of data across the Web.

Data and System Management

Managing any database system can comprise a significant fraction of the total cost of system ownership, so a data warehouse database, like all others, must be easy to manage using the vendor's tools and/or third-party tools. But the size and complexity of data warehouses makes additional demands which require special treatment.

Database size has a dramatic influence on the backup and restore strategy. With a database in the tens of gigabytes range, it is still credible to routinely dump the database and restore it— or better, the failed portion of the database—in the event of a hardware failure. A database measured in terabytes is a different matter—it is no longer feasible to backup or restore the entire database, and other strategies must be used to ensure that the system can recover from hardware failures. For example, a system can use RAID (Redundant Array of Independent Disks) technologies extensively, with the assumption that failures are rare enough to be tolerated and that the data will be rebuilt as required. Optimally, a data warehouse DBMS must rebuild fragments of indexes and tables, rather than require rebuilding the entire object.

To effectively run queries across such large data stores, the database must use hardware in parallel. Among other things, this means that the data must be spread over multiple disks and drives in a way that maximizes the parallelism available. To enable this, the DBMS must support a number of flexible options for partitioning the data—whether by round-robin, primary key, hashing, or user-defined algorithms.

Integrating Operational and Legacy Data

While the warehouse itself is the primary source of data for its applications, many applications also need access to operational data or data lying in unwarehoused legacy systems. A typical case is a decision-support system that analyzes the historical data from a data warehouse, merges it with the operational data that has not yet migrated into the warehouse, and yields an up-to-the-minute view of the data. This is often accomplished in stock trading support applications, where a historical analysis is combined with an analysis of the recent activity which is available from real-time data feeds.

There are two choices here: either the application or the DBMS can manage the data. Integrating data in the application makes use of the computing power of the client, rather than the server, which may be appropriate in many cases. However, it does complicate the client-side applications which, for a number of reasons, systems managers want to simplify as far as possible. On the other hand, data integration in the DBMS requires extending the DBMS to access the foreign data sources in an optimized way.

Data Warehousing in Practice

Scrubbing

Creating a data warehouse often forces a company to examine the definition of its terms in a vastly different way. Discrepancies are always found in the way that data of the same meaning is stored in different systems. What is the real meaning of *customer*, *discount*, *account*, or *account balance*? Sometimes data of very different meanings is intermingled together, and sometimes data with the same meaning is stored differently, or stored multiple times. The process of resolving all these data disputes is called *data scrubbing*, and the scrubbing typically occurs as the data is exported from legacy systems into the warehouse. If the warehouse is periodically refreshed, then scrubbing is a repetitive task. Scrubbing can be performed in middleware, but the warehouse database itself is the repository of data warehouse semantics, and seems the obvious platform for scrubbing.

Growth

There is rarely a good reason to remove data from a warehouse, since by definition, it is often a historical repository. The result is inexorable growth. This presents storage questions to the system manager, as well as new problems regarding the warehouse DBMS. Once the data is very large, statistical sampling techniques become vital. If a question can be answered with 95-percent accuracy by reading only a fraction of the data, this clearly represents a significant savings in processing time. Visualization also becomes more important as the amount of data overwhelms a person's ability to comprehend it in a less compelling form.

Data Liquidity

Data warehouses are usually created from operational data which, because of the stringent demands of high-performance transactional systems, often adheres to a very different structure than is optimal for a warehouse. While OLTP data from a relational DBMS may be hypernormalized, data in older legacy systems may not even be in a *first normal form*. Hence, data must be transformed as it enters the data warehouse. This transformation often involves summarization, so it is important that the DBMS can incrementally compute aggregates and other summaries as data is progressively loaded.

Of course, the data warehouse DBMS must also adequately index the data to provide a rapid response to a variety of questions. For example, it is important to consider bit-map indexing, indexing on the output of functions applied against the data, and the indexing of multidimensional and other complex data.

Data Marts

Subsets of the entire data warehouse are often extracted to form *data marts*—smaller data warehouses designed to be used by a particular department, or to answer specific questions. Maintaining the currency of the data marts is one of the ongoing management tasks for the data warehouse manager. The algorithms used to determine what data belongs to a particular mart are often complex, and it is important that the data warehouse platform can accept complex algorithms to create the data mart extracts. The requirements of the data mart's data management platform are very similar to those of the warehouse itself, with the exception that the requirements for managing large amounts of data are somewhat less. Note, however, that one customer may create a 100 GB data mart from a terabyte data warehouse, where the entire data warehouse of another customer may occupy less than 100 GB: *mart* and *warehouse* are relative, and not absolute terms.

DSA Support for Data Warehousing

Informix database managers are built on the same foundation: Dynamic Scalable Architecture (DSA). This recently built architecture provides a number of critical features which ensure robust scalable operation across large machines, user communities, and data sets. Some of its more important features are described below.

Multithreading

DSA provides a robust and highly efficient threading model that supports large numbers of concurrent database processes, thus minimizing the cost of context switching between the threads. This provides maximum throughput for applications with very large numbers of users. Originally designed for the demands of large OLTP applications, this feature also enables a large community of knowledge workers to share the same data warehouse.

Asynchronous I/O and Shared Data Cache

Using the threading mechanism, DSA servers automatically retrieve data in parallel across multiple disks and channels. This optimizes the throughput for applications against large data stores. Of course, data retrieved from disk is held in the shared server cache, and is available to other applications which need the same data. The server automatically adjusts the size of this cache according to demand.

Parallel Operations

Taking advantage of the threading mechanism, DSA is able to allocate tasks across a number of "virtual processors" so that it can divide a single insert, update, or delete across several CPUs at the same time on a symmetric multiprocessing (SMP) machine. DSA takes this further and can also allocate multiple threads to a sort or merge—significantly decreasing response time for queries that involve sorting, summarization, or aggregation.

Similarly, DSA provides parallel operations for index creation, backup, and restore. Because of the very large size of many data warehouses, parallel operations are required to complete such operations in a reasonable time.

Informix's Universal Data Option for Data Warehousing

Built on Dynamic Scalable Architecture, Informix Dynamic Server with Universal Data Option has all the features of DSA that make it a powerful data management platform. In addition, it offers a number of object-relational features which support data warehousing:

- The ability to store and manage complex structured data;
- The ability to execute algorithms of any degree of complexity in the server against simple or complex data;
- The ability to define indexes based on the output of complex functions;
- The ability to define multiple index types for the management of different data domains;
- The availability of plug-in datatype and function extensions from data experts; and
- A built-in gateway kit for the integration of foreign data stores.

Complex Datatypes

Since Informix Dynamic Server with Universal Data Option is an object-relational DBMS, it is able to present an open interface to developers who wish to model complex data. This interface, which is consistent with the emerging direction of the SQL-3 standard, enables a developer to create new datatypes that are managed within the server with the same rich functionality as the more familiar alphanumeric datatypes defined by the earlier SQL-92 standard. Unlike relational DBMSs, which are forced to store complex structures as unstructured BLOBs, an ORDBMS can "see" inside the structure of a complex datatype and provide full relational functionality against it: manipulation and modification of subcomponents, content-based queries, comparison, and indexing.

There are a number of options for creating new datatypes within Informix Dynamic Server with Universal Data Option:

- Datatypes based on other datatypes, which inherit their structure and behavior; and
- Complex datatypes made up of other datatypes.

A new datatype is defined on top of Informix Dynamic Server with Universal Data Option's smart BLOB object, which provides the necessary underlying database functionality, including the incremental logging of changes to subcomponents. The server provides constructors for sets, multisets, and lists as part of the datatype definition. Every object within Informix Dynamic Server with Universal Data Option can have a unique 64-bit object identifier (OID), and these OIDs can be used to create structures based on pointer references.

Because Informix Dynamic Server with Universal Data Option supports inheritance, a developer can create a datatype definition based on an existing datatype. A wide variety of structural and behavioral information can be inherited. Inheritance is one of the major benefits of object-oriented modeling; designers find it very intuitive to define data models based on full or partial inheritance from super-classes.

Composite datatypes can be constructed from simpler preexisting types as building blocks to create increasingly complex structures. This is one way to implement a *star schema*, in which allied data elements are linked to a central coordinating entity. For example, a number of customer activities may be linked into a "star" which is clustered around the basic customer record.

Once a datatype is defined, it can be used to create a table or a column within a table. Tables also support inheritance, so it is possible to create a table hierarchy that matches part of a data class hierarchy. Complex structured columns act normally in the SQL language, with their subcomponents defined using "extended dot" notation. For instance, a developer can create an address_t type that contains street_t and city_t types, and then create a column which holds a complex address:

```
create type address_t
   (street street_t,
   city   city_t);
create table customers
   (name name_t,
   address address_t);
```

A developer can then access the city part of a customers row using the following SQL:

```
select c.address.city
from customers c
where <some condition>
```

Or the developer can choose to retrieve the whole structured address with the following simple SQL:

```
select address
from customers
where <some condition>
```

This example restructures normal alphanumeric data, and many data warehousing tasks can benefit from this functionality. Increasingly, however, customers intend to warehouse more complex data, such as images, videos, maps, documents, etc. The extensibility of Informix Dynamic Server with Universal Data Option makes this possible for the first time, because a developer can define the structure of these complex datatypes within Informix Dynamic Server with Universal Data Option and provide full relational services against the complex data.

Casting

Informix Dynamic Server with Universal Data Option is a strongly typed system which ensures that different datatypes are mingled in inappropriate ways. For example, product volume sales may be measured in liters, pounds, dozens, and square meters. It makes no sense to add such disparate units together, and Informix Dynamic Server with the Universal Data Option can prevent such errors.

Where different datatypes must be compared or converted, Informix Dynamic Server with Universal Data Option provides the ability to define *casts*. Casts define the algorithms used to perform conversions. For example, a developer can create a cast that interconverts Italian lira and English pounds by looking up the current or a historical conversion rate. Once a cast is defined, Informix Dynamic Server with Universal Data Option can use it to automatically support queries that span multiple datatypes, and performs conversion as required between types. By storing casts in the DBMS, it is possible to locate them in an easily managed central point, and improves standardization by ensuring that all applications which use the database employ the same technique to perform the conversions, and reduce coding by providing easily reusable components.

Extending the Client

Of course, the DBMS is only part of the application environment. If the DBMS is to be extended to manage new and complex kinds of data, then so follows the client. In a classical client/server application, this presents serious problems, as multiple applications installed on a large number of client machines can require upgrading each time that the server is extended. However, new client-side developments—driven largely by the emergence of the World Wide Web—offer ways out.

Client-side architecture is moving rapidly towards a component model, where an extensible platform accepts plug-ins of various kinds—even at runtime—to support new kinds of data. A well-known example is the Netscape browser, which accepts plug-ins and applets to manage and display different kinds of data. For example, with the aid of a Real Audio™ plug-in, a Netscape browser can play Real Audio sound files through a PC's sound system. The browser also accepts Java applets, small applications written in Java which execute under the control of the browser and extend the browser's capabilities.

Informix Dynamic Server with Universal Data Option is an excellent repository for application components. Once such components are stored in the server, the DBMS can ensure that it returns to client applications not just the data they want, but also the application extensions to display and manipulate the data. For example, a document query can return Microsoft Word files, Adobe Acrobat Files, VRML scenes, and PowerPoint presentations. Informix Dynamic Server with Universal Data Option can ensure that it returns the components that client applications need to manage diverse datatypes.

Complex Functions

Data structures are an important part of defining a warehouse data model. Equally important are the algorithms that are used to manipulate the data. Legacy relational DBMSs limit server-side application code to stored procedures written in SQL—a slow, interpreted, clumsy, and incomplete language. Informix Dynamic Server with Universal Data Option, on the other hand, enables developers to write data manipulation code in any high-level language that generates a shared library (a DLL in Windows NT, or a .so file in UNIX).

Using a general-purpose language has a number of advantages over SQL or a proprietary query language:

- It executes much faster than SQL because it is compiled rather than interpreted;
- The general purpose language provides better programming facilities—both within the language and in the supporting development environment than is available for SQL, making it easier to write complicated algorithms and ensuring their correctness;

- Because such languages are so widely used, they are well-standardized and a huge population of expert programmers is available.

Routines are dynamically linked into Informix Dynamic Server with Universal Data Option as required at runtime, and become part of the normal SQL syntax. A client application developer using Informix Dynamic Server with Universal Data Option sees a DBMS filled with not just the required data, but also the behavior needed to support an application. Such developers typically call server-based routines when building their applications, instead of accessing the data directly. This *encapsulation* of the data by the routines insulates client application developers from implementation details, and frees system developers to modify the underlying data structures without requiring the modification of client applications. Such encapsulation also enables a developer to create *self-describing* data structures that respond to application questions about their structure and the functions defined on them, rendering it much simpler to integrate such data into a variety of applications.

For example, a developer using the customers table previously created can create a function called *proximity* that computes customers' distances from the nearest retail store. Once this function is created, it can be used by an application developer to find customers located close to stores and to compare their buying behaviors with those who live farther away, as follows:

```
select c.name, c.address, s.store_id
from customers c, stores s
where proximity(c.address, s.address) < 20;
```

Locating significant pieces of application code in the server rather than in the client supports the increasingly important *thin client* model of application development. This model seeks to minimize the cost of maintaining (possibly very large numbers of) clients by locating functionality in a smaller number of more easily maintained locations.

Typically, the thin client model is implemented by relocating functionality to middleware, but an ORDBMS also allows the code to be relocated into the server. The server offers significant performance superiority over middleware as a data management platform, as follows:

- The algorithms are located adjacent to the data, thus minimizing data movement overhead—a major concern when working with the large stores of data warehouses. Co-locating algorithm and data is critically important if the routine is used to qualify rows, because it removes the need to move enormous amounts of data to a middleware platform merely to determine if it should be retrieved.
- The cost of the invocation of a server-based routine is significantly less than that of a middleware routine—especially if the protocol used for the invocation is an expensive one like CORBA, and if the routine is invoked on a row-by-row basis.
- The ORDBMS provides a sophisticated platform for these routines. Without the need to write code to support specific features, it provides highly efficient shared data access with the asynchronous retrieval of data from multiple disks and drives, automatic parallelization, and transaction support. In middleware, these issues must be managed by the application itself, and require considerable complex code.
- Because the routines are typically only part of a query, locating them in the server enables the DBMS optimizer to select the optimal path to the data to satisfy the application query. The definition of an Informix Dynamic Server with Universal Data Option routine includes the information given to the optimizer to help it accomplish this task. If the routines are in middleware, there is no optimizer that has an overview of the entire system, and thus suboptimal query plans are all too possible. In large data warehouses, a poor query plan can mean that a query completes in days rather than seconds.

Note that this discussion is not meant to suggest that middleware is always a poor solution to an application problem. On the contrary, Informix Dynamic Server with Universal Data Option supports a number of middleware protocols which enable it to both call distributed objects and be called by them. However, these protocols are best used for the function for which they were designed: interprocess communication. They are unsuitable and inefficient as a data management architecture.

User-Defined Aggregates

A special kind of user-defined routine is a user-defined *aggregate*. As the name suggests, aggregates are routines that summarize data. The SQL-92 standard defines a handful of standard aggregates like average, sum, maximum, and minimum. Data warehousing applications often require much more sophisticated summarizations, and Informix Dynamic Server with Universal Data Option provides features that enable developers to create aggregates that run over a result set or complete table to summarize the information in a highly efficient way. A frequent requirement in data warehousing applications is to find the *top n* of some class: the top five selling products, the most valuable 100 customers, etc. *Top n* can be implemented as a user-defined aggregate

A major advantage of aggregating in the DBMS rather than in the client application is that less data flows over the client/server network connection, dramatically increasing the speed of the query.

Appropriate Indexing

Due to the large volume of data stored in data warehouses, optimizations for speed of access are critical. A DBMS contains data structures called *indexes* that speed access to the data. Without the right index, the only strategy available to a DBMS optimizer is to scan an entire table looking for the right rows. A useful analogy is the well-known phone book, which is ordered alphabetically. By this ordering, it is possible to find a phone number quickly. Without the ordering, it would be necessary to read the book from the beginning until encountering the required name.

Existing RDBMSs use b-trees as their primary access method, while some also support hash and bit-map indexing. Unfortunately, there are many classes of data for which these indexing methods are quite unsuitable in principle, for example, documents and maps. The RDBMS has two problems in dealing with such data:

• It is forced to store complex data as BLOBs, which it is unable to index;

- It is unable to create the right kind of index to support the data.

Informix Dynamic Server with Universal Data Option, on the other hand, is unlimited in its ability to create indexes on any kind of complex data, and developers can create new kinds of indexes that can plug into one of its open interfaces. These features enable Informix Dynamic Server with Universal Data Option to effectively index a wide variety of datatypes.

Effective access to complex data requires two additional Informix Dynamic Server with Universal Data Option features: functional indexing, and user-defined index operators.

Functional indexing enables the server to create an index on the output of a function applied to the data, rather than just on the raw data itself. For example, an index created on the bits of a collection of images has little utility. One created on the output of a function that extracts features from the image is much more useful, since it enables images to be accessed on the basis of their semantic content, for example, "find pictures that look like this one." The search for customers who are located some distance from stores, reproduced below, is best supported by an index created on the proximity function.

```
select c.name, c.address, s.store_id
from customers c, stores s
where proximity(c.address, s.address) < 20;
```

By using an index on the output of *proximity(customers.address, stores.address)*, Informix Dynamic Server with Universal Data Option is able to answer queries like the previous one efficiently.

User-defined operators enable a system developer to define the order of entries in the index to Informix Dynamic Server with Universal Data Option, in other words to define the semantic meaning of *greater than*. An example is the sorting Scottish names. In Scotland, MacTavish, M'Tavish, and McTavish are considered semantically equivalent, and sort next to one another. Without user-defined operators, it is impossible to create a system that sorts Scottish names correctly and simultaneously sorts other alphabetical information correctly. Another example is that of comparing faces. Face recognition software can analyze photographs to extract key features of faces, which can then be used to create an index that supports queries against facial similarity (for example, in an authentication system). But the similarity operator is more complex than just a numerical comparison of the output from a feature extraction algorithm. Full support for face recognition also requires the definition of the ordering of this output: user-defined comparison operators.

Integrating the Legacy

A data warehouse rarely stands alone; instead, applications access data from the warehouse and other systems. Informix Dynamic Server with Universal Data Option contains a "gateway kit" called the virtual table interface (VTI) which makes it easy for developers to create applications that perform an optimized integration of data from foreign systems of any kind, from relational to flat files, to data feeds.

To use the VTI, a developer creates an empty table that maps to the desired structure of the foreign data. Attached to the empty table are functions that define how to perform select, insert, update, and delete statements against the foreign data source. As far as an application developer is concerned, the table then acts like a normal table under Informix Dynamic Server with Universal Data Option, and can participate fully in any SQL data manipulation language (DML) statement. At runtime, Informix Dynamic Server with Universal Data Option automatically executes the functions attached to the table, and returns rows into the DML statement exactly as if the rows originated from a real table of data in Informix Dynamic Server with Universal Data Option. Because function developers can instruct the optimizer about the cost of functions, the optimizer can intelligently place access to a virtual table within a complex DML statement, thus enabling the creation of an optimized gateway.

If the foreign data source is structured differently than the local data (less summarized, for example), the VTI functions can reformat the data, and perform aggregation as required to prepare the data for loading into the universal warehouse. This is also a way to scrub data as it is imported, via reference to preexisting data within the Informix Dynamic Server with Universal Data Option data store. VTI can also be used in a batch import situation in which the Universal Warehouse is periodically refreshed with data that is imported, reformatted, and scrubbed from the operational systems.

DataBlade Solution Components

While Informix Dynamic Server with Universal Data Option can be extended by any customer to support new datatypes, functions, indexing schemes, and data integration through the VTI, one of its most appealing features is that many extensions are available from third parties who specialize in the management of particular kinds of data. These turnkey extensions are called DataBlade® modules and they provide ready-made application modules for complex data management.

A DataBlade module typically contains the new datatype definitions and functions needed to manipulate datatypes. In the case of new classes of data, they may also contain new indexing methods. Sometimes, they also contain table definitions and other database components. Multiple DataBlade modules can be used to solve a given data warehousing problem. DataBlade modules are open and allow a developer to:

- Create tables and columns that use the datatype definitions;
- Create new datatypes which inherit structure and behavior from the supplied definitions;
- Over-ride its function definitions; and
- Use its indexing schemes to create new indexes.

Informix's Universal Data Option in Data Warehousing

An object-relational DBMS offers much new functionality which is tremendously useful in managing a data warehouse, which is either made up of simple data accessed with complex algorithms, or where the data structure is also complex. It can act as an intelligent and optimized gateway to foreign data or as the repository for complex data, algorithms, and access methods.

This section examines how an object-relational DBMS like Informix Dynamic Server with Universal Data Option is an excellent data warehouse platform.

Universal Server as a Data Repository

With other technology, creating a data warehouse is an exercise in compromise. The data model must be mapped down onto the relatively primitive data management facilities of the DBMS, and inevitably there is some semantic loss during this mapping process. In many cases, this loss is so severe as to make the warehouse effectively impractical. An ORDBMS, on the other hand, is practically unlimited in its ability to model complex data structures and algorithms, enabling it to directly manage the data model and significantly reduce information loss between the model as designed and its implementation. This direct implementation of the model also makes it easier to build client applications, because the data and its behavior more closely mimic the structure and behavior of the modeled organization.

Performance

Because data warehouses are typically very large, with the largest warehouses comprised of the biggest databases ever created, extremely high performance is a fundamental requirement. Even fractional differences in performance can mean the difference between a warehouse which is usable or unusable, as they translate into minutes or hours of difference in response times. An ORDBMS offers a number of performance advantages over other implementations:

- For data stored in the ORDBMS, there is no time spent in extracting it into a middleware layer;
- Object-relational technology moves the algorithms to the data, rather than vice versa. This significantly reduces data movement overhead for large data stores;
- User-defined and functional indexing provide efficient access to even non-traditional data like maps, documents, and images; and

- Since the ORDBMS contains a query optimizer, complex queries—even those involving user-defined functions—are automatically executed in the most efficient way possible.

The first three of the above points may represent a performance advantage of more than 100 to 1 against a standard RDBMS. The fourth point, the optimizer, guarantees consistently efficient query plans.

Some Informix customers have implemented applications on RDBMS technology, found its performance to be unsatisfactory, and then reimplemented on Informix Dynamic Server with Universal Data Option. They have realized considerable savings in code, sometimes discovering that an ORDBMS implementation takes less than half as much code as an RDBMS implementation of the same application. This reduction in code, of course, means a reduction in development and maintenance time and cost. It stems partly from better code reuse in an ORDBMS, partly from the easier and more natural implementation of complex algorithms in a general purpose programming language, and partly from the availability of complex application components in the form of DataBlade modules.

DataBlade Modules for Data Warehousing

Some DataBlade modules which were useful in data warehousing at the time of writing are briefly described below. Note, however, that new DataBlade modules are becoming available almost daily. The Informix Web page at www.informix.com contains an up-to-date list of the DataBlade modules which are currently available.

Documents: Adobe, Excalibur, PLS, and Verity

The fastest emerging market for complex data warehouses is that of documents. Every corporation has a vast store of unmanaged documents which relate to its business. Examples include legal documents, design and manufacturing specifications, change orders, manuals, order forms, etc. Document management DataBlade modules offer the first chance to bring these document stores under digital control, providing the ability to rapidly perform a variety of text searches based on word stems, semantic networks (thesauri), or fuzzy matching.

Maps: Andyne, ESRI, Informix Geodetic, and MapInfo

Geospatial DataBlade modules enable companies to warehouse large collections of geographical data. Application examples include land-use planning, mining, pollution control, fleet management, analysis of demographic patterns, and computer-aided design (CAD) diagrams. Informix provides DataBlade modules to manage data even at the scale where the shape of the earth becomes significant, for example, mapping satellite imagery to the earth's surface. Other DataBlade modules provide the ability to transform a U.S. postal address into a latitude and longitude pair, and support spatial queries based on proximity. These DataBlade modules typically also include client components that simplify developing client viewers of the spatial data.

Statistics: FAME, StatSci, and TimeSeries

The analysis of large numeric warehouses almost always involves the statistical analysis of data. StatSci, a division of MathSoft, has created a general-purpose statistical library of DataBlade modules that implement over 100 statistical functions. Informix provides a Time Series DataBlade module that specializes in managing data whose time sequence is significant, such as stock price records or sales records. Fame, the leading time-series vendor on Wall Street, has extended this DataBlade module with its own algorithms to create a sophisticated library for managing and manipulating time-series data.

Data Scrubbing: Ecologic, and Electronic Digital Documents

Several companies are developing DataBlade module technology to assist in scrubbing a database. For example, this technology can be used in name and address scrubbing, and enables a company to easily remove duplicate names from its mailing list—even when names and addresses are differently phrased—or to discover orders among different companies for similar parts, and thus enabling a consolidation of buying power.

Data Mining: Angoss, and Neovista

Data mining tools examine data to discover new relationships between data elements. Because these data mining operations can run across large parts of the data warehouse, or even all of it, it is vital that the algorithms run very near to the data. Embedding data mining tools inside a DataBlade module ensures that data mining activities run as efficiently as possible.

Informix's Universal Data Option as Middleware

While it would be simpler if all warehouse data could reside in Informix Dynamic Server with Universal Data Option, this is an unrealistic assumption in the current world of multiple complex legacy systems, some of which are the core operational systems of the business. There are two ways of dealing with foreign data: import it into a central warehouse, possibly with periodical refreshes, or use middleware to connect the systems together in real time. Informix Dynamic Server with Universal Data Option offers important advantages in both scenarios.

As a data store, its advantages have been described. In addition, Informix Dynamic Server with Universal Data Option shares system management facilities and bulk load facilities with its Informix sister products built on the Dynamic Scalable Architecture.

Middleware provides a layer between the client and server that can transform data as it is retrieved from or updated to other data sources. Informix Dynamic Server with Universal Data Option provides a platform for building middleware that is infinitely extensible. It enables the management of any kind of protocol to connect to any kind of data source and apply any kind of manipulation to its data, while transforming it into an arbitrary new structure. All this is accomplished on a platform designed to scale over multiple disks, multiple CPUs, large memory, large data stores, and large numbers of users. It is secure, robust, and transactionally consistent, and it possesses sophisticated tools for backup and recovery.

Informix Dynamic Server with Universal Data Option presents a standard open interface to client application developers. The applications interact with data using SQL in a way that shields application developers from all the legacy complexity, while still providing highly efficient access. Application developers write as if all the data were resident in Informix Dynamic Server with Universal Data Option, a very simple and highly productive architecture.

Data Security

Much data warehouse information is very sensitive; it may be a company's best estimate of its past and current position, or confidential medical information, or it may be the collection of all of a company's contracts or design documentation. Securing access to this data is critical. The extensibility of Informix Dynamic Server with Universal Data Option carries over into the realm of security, where it delivers not only the standard RDBMS facilities, but also a programmable security interface.

Where the current RDBMSs provide excellent basic security by restricting user access to data or stored procedures, they lack the ability to easily implement more sophisticated methods, or security at other points in the system. Informix Dynamic Server with Universal Data Option routines can be attached to tables as triggers and execute at select, insert, update, or delete times. Because these routines are written in a general purpose language, they can implement additional security functionality of any kind, including dialog with other systems.

Data warehouse security provides some interesting challenges. For example, it is common to treat aggregate data as more or less confidential than single-item data. For example, epidemiological studies of a pattern of a particular disease are less sensitive than the individual medical records from which they were derived. On the other hand, while a doctor may have access to his or her patients' medical records, that does not carry the right to see summaries that show the performance of the HMO. A warehouse has to be careful not to allow inappropriate aggregation: after all, a single item is an aggregate of size one. In some cases, it is important to block access to a particular piece of data. In extreme cases, "cover stories" may be returned to those with insufficient access to know the real story. Informix Dynamic Server with Universal Data Option provides a platform on which to implement any security model.

In some areas, the level of sensitivity regarding information justifies the encryption of network traffic. The openness of the medium can play a part here as well: radio is a less secure medium than telephone. Because encryption and decryption can be performed in the ORDBMS itself rather than in another layer, the data is significantly less exposed to attack. For example, a DataBlade module that understands the SET security model enables Informix Dynamic Server with Universal Data Option to act as a trusted participant in electronic commerce applications, while completely shielding the data from unauthorized access.

Administration

Some studies suggest that system administration represents a significant fraction of the cost of DBMS ownership. Informix Dynamic Server with Universal Data Option has tools which simplify the management of the system.

Firstly, all the data within Informix Dynamic Server with Universal Data Option is backed up and restored as a unit. It is always transactionally consistent. As with all DSA products, Informix Dynamic Server with Universal Data Option can restore to a point in time, a single object, or a single disk. Informix Dynamic Server with Universal Data Option has a high-speed backup mechanism, and supports incremental backups, thus minimizing backup time. Its high-speed parallel restore reduces down time after a system failure. It can participate in replicated systems that reduce the risk to data through redundancy and distribution.

The Informix-Enterprise Command Center enables a system administrator to take charge of any number of distributed Informix servers from any point on the net. Such tools promote even "lights out" warehousing in a remote location. Informix Dynamic Server with Universal Data Option's open interfaces enable it to be managed by a number of SNMP-based, IIOP-compliant system management tools.

Web-Enabled Warehouse

The Web is an important delivery platform for applications which were once implemented using only classical client/server technology. Since the warehouse will be used for all kinds of research queries, it is important to note that it is easy to Web-publish ad-hoc information from the warehouse, since otherwise the cost of maintenance proves very high. As well, it should be easy to create turn-key, Web-delivered reports.

The Informix Web DataBlade module and Web development environment are designed to deliver "query dialtone" to any Web-connected device, and support the rapid and simple deployment of Informix Dynamic Server with Universal Data Option data onto the Web. The Web DataBlade module supports the concept of "application pages" which contain parameterized database queries as well as the standard HTML page layout information. Parameters from the user's query screen are dropped into the queries which Informix Dynamic Server with Universal Data Option executes, and it then formats the resulting data into HTML for display on the page. This "cyber-publishing" of the data simplifies the provision of general Web services to data warehouse information workers without incurring high maintenance costs. The Web DataBlade module also supports the concept of device-dependent rendering, and allows the server to create pages in the appropriate format and level of detail for a variety of devices. Using third-party DataBlade modules, developers can create applications that use the *push* model of information delivery; instead of waiting for users to browse their way to the required information, it is automatically delivered to them.

Because Informix Dynamic Server with Universal Data Option provides programmable access to the data returned across the Web, all the security features mentioned in the Data Security section also apply to Web applications, including participation in secure electronic commerce.

Visualization: Brio, Business Objects, Cognos, and Formida

While Informix Dynamic Server with Universal Data Option can deliver any kind of data or analytical product, the best use of the information requires that it is presented to its users in a visually compelling way. General-purpose data visualization tools are available in specific data areas, simplifying the delivery of information in a form that triggers the pattern-matching "wetware" of the human brain. Statistics and maps in two and three dimensions are well served with excellent tools. Increasingly, third-party tools, such as Brio, Business Objects, Cognos, and Formida, are appearing to simplify the creation of applications which deliver information in a visually compelling way.

Summary

Data warehousing is increasingly viewed as a vital part of conducting business. Without an examination and analysis of past events, a company is "flying blind" and risks failing to realize its maximum potential or losing its competitive edge. Current ROLAP solutions suffer from the severe compromises that must be made to model complexity in an essentially simple system. Informix Dynamic Server with Universal Data Option, together with its rapidly expanding suite of DataBlade modules, is an exciting new alternative that overcomes some of the critical limitations of the standard relational engines to deliver the high-performance modeling and manipulation of complex data and complex algorithms.

Building Complex Decision-Support Models Using a Universal Warehouse

by Jacques Roy

Introduction

This paper discusses the challenges of implementing a complex data warehouse and presents a solution using Informix Dynamic Server™ with Universal Data Option™.[1]

Database Background

In the early days, database technology was based on a hierarchical model. Application programs were closely tied to the physical representation and organization of the data. The

---

[1] This information was originally presented at the Informix Worldwide User Conference on July 25, 1997 by Brian Miezejewski of the Sabre Group and Jacques Roy of Informix Software, Inc.

introduction of the relational model was a significant improvement. The two major features introduced were the logical representation of data and a non-procedural language. By relying on the logical representation of the data, application programs required few changes, if any, in the event of database changes. Specifically, physical changes made to the database to improve performance required no application changes.

The object-relational model builds on the strength of the relational model and improves on it. By allowing developers to add new datatypes to the database server as first class types and manage as such, it elevates the logical representation of the data to a business representation. This facilitates communication between the domain experts and the computer experts. It also renders the applications less susceptible to changes—the interface to the business datatypes can remain constant even if business rules change.

A type is considered first class if it is fully managed by the database server. In brief, if the database server recognizes a type like any other base type (integer, decimal, character, etc.), it is then considered a first class type. It does not require interventions outside the server to be manipulated, and does not have additional restrictions, compared to the base types.

Informix Dynamic Server with Universal Data Option features have been grouped under the term "DataBlade module technology." This term is widely used in written and verbal communication as the solution to a variety of business problems.

What Is a DataBlade Module?

DataBlade modules are a set of user-defined types and manipulation functions which are packaged together to solve specific business problems. The user-defined types may identify a new datatype based on an existing one, a complex type representing a collection of values, or a new representation which is better suited to the problem at hand.

The server uses the manipulation functions to incorporate and support the needed functionality. They may include arithmetic

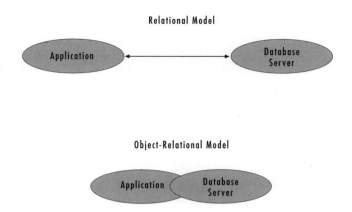

Figure 3–1 *The object-relational model provides for the integration of application business objects.*

operations, comparison operations, conversion operations, and business-specific operations. These manipulation functions can be written in C, Java, or the Stored Procedure Language (SPL). A set of functions may be implemented in SPL for proof-of-concept and later rewritten in C to improve performance.

DataBlade modules give the user access to the technology of a domain expert. When a company has a specific in-house expertise, it can as easily develop its own datatypes and manipulation functions, and package the expertise for internal use as a standard across databases and applications.

The end result of this technology is a better integration between an application and a database server. This leads to a more flexible design, which results in simplified application programming and better performance.

Informix Dynamic Server with Universal Data Option Features

In addition to the ability to extend the server to handle new datatypes, Informix Dynamic Server with Universal Data Option includes, among other things, the following useful features:

Table/Type Inheritance and Polymorphism

Table/type inheritance and polymorphism provides a smooth implementation of an object design. Table inheritance enables the use of polymorphic functions which provide different functionality based on the table that is processed. It also provides the added benefit of data partitioning to complement the implementation provided by the Dynamic Scalable Architecture (DSA).

Functional Index

It is now possible to create an index based on the result of a function. An obvious candidate for this kind of index is a date field. This eliminates the need to store a "quarter," or week number value, when it can be derived from the date through a simple function.

R-Tree Index

This kind of index is used to support spatial and other multi-dimensional queries. This index can also be used to index age and income relationship, for example.

Smart Large Objects

A smart large object can be read partially from any position within the data to reduce data movement. For example, operations on a time series access only the required data, instead of reading the entire large object as in a standard binary large object (BLOB) implementation.

Universal Data Warehouse: The Problem

The Sabre Group faced the challenge of creating a departmental decision-support system (DSS) data warehouse for a commercial airline.

A typical data warehouse uses multiple data sources. The Sabre Group's is no exception. It uses about 415 different data sources; over 200 of these sources are used regularly. The format of the data is not homogeneous because less than five percent of the data is controlled by Sabre. This raises several issues, as follows:

- **Heterogeneous Formats**
  The data is provided in different representations with different formatting.
- **Multiple Aggregation Levels**
  Some data represents monthly totals, other data is grouped by week, or is represented at the transaction level.
- **International Languages**
  Some sources are of international origin. Differences may be in the language and identification of the data.
- **Data Quality**
  There is no quality control over incoming data. Some sources may contain duplicate information, conflicting information, and even test data. The information may be incomplete or inaccurate.

To add to this complexity, the format of currently used data sources may change over time and new data sources may be created. The original sources are well over 10 terabytes (TB) in size.

The airline industry faces some challenges which limit the efficiency of relational databases and force a reliance on custom applications. To illustrate the problem, consider the following examples:

- **Datetime**
  Relational databases provide a datetime base type which assumes that all recorded activities occurred in one location. In the airline industry and in transportation in general, the location of the time needs to be considered, due to time zone issues. If a flight leaves Dallas at 8:00 and arrives in Denver at 9:00, we cannot assume that the flight took one hour. In extreme situations, flights arrive before they left.

    In addition to the time zone issues, an airline must consider the daylight savings time policy which applies at a specific location. Even in the United States, the daylight savings time policy is not consistent. The variation spans from no daylight savings time to different dates for the change and, in some cases, different policies are in effect at different locations within a state.

• **Flight Matching**

A specific flight leg may use different types of equipment on different days. The flight time may change, due to various considerations, yet it is still considered the same. Finally, the flight number may change and remain the same flight. This kind of "fuzzy" matching is virtually impossible to perform within a relational database.

First Try

Several years ago, The Sabre Group decided to attack this problem using state-of-the-art technologies, including object-oriented methodologies. The development was accomplished using the SmallTalk programming language, and accessing a relational database. The hardware was selected from "open system platforms" using commodity processors. A symmetric multi-processing (SMP) machine was employed to maximize the parallelism of SQL query processing.

The resulting two-tiered system provides two major benefits. It maximizes the parallelism of queries for optimal performance and provides the user with a business view of the information. All of the translation between the business model and the relational model is handled with business objects, which are included in the client application. The size of the database is approximately 120 gigabytes (GB).

The implementation of the original data warehouse uncovered several problems:

• **Object Mapping Was Slow**

The creation of the business objects involved much data movement. In many cases, the business rules could only be applied after transporting the data to the application. Furthermore, the business requests generated large, complex SQL queries.

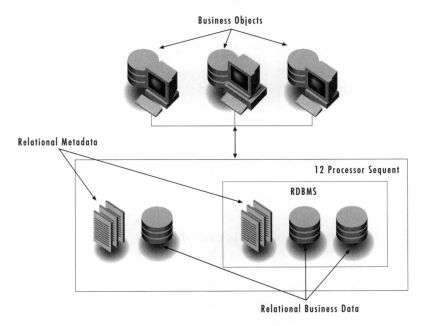

Figure 3–2 *The Sabre Group's system architecture.*

- **Data Was Not Integrated**
  The data warehouse handled only specific datasets. Many more datasets required attention. Because this data warehouse was not integrated, the business experts spent a considerable amount of time studying the data source before processing to obtain useful results. There was the potential that simple errors could generate erroneous results which could, in turn, result in disastrous business decisions.
- **Difficult to Maintain**
  The addition of new application code or the modification of old code often required additional modifications to SQL statements and stored procedures.
- **Multiple Technologies**
  The system was made up of SmallTalk code, SQL statements, stored procedure code, etc. This required a wide skillset which was difficult to find when hiring new employees.

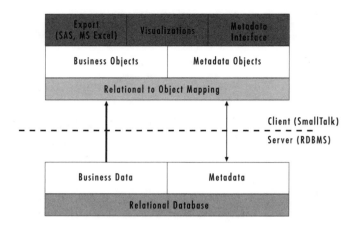

Figure 3–3 *The Sabre Group's application architecture.*

• **Client-Based Business Objects**

The business objects and, therefore, the business rules were tied to the client. They could only be reused in custom client applications. Because these custom applications must provide additional capabilities—such as report generation, printing, export facilities to other tools, etc.—the size of the application and development time are impacted, as well as overall responsiveness to user requirements for new functionality.

Clearly something needed to be done to handle the vast majority of the data that was still outside of the warehouse. However, the business model proved to be a success. The users were able to navigate through the data in business terms, which made it easier to use.

The Integrated Data Server

The integrated data server is the second generation of Sabre's decision-support system. It aims to provide a single point of contact with all of the different data sources. The goal is to create a multiterabyte object-oriented data warehouse. Both the design and implementation are object-oriented, from the business concepts to the data representation.

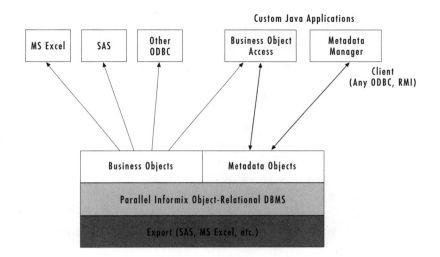

Figure 3–4 Integrated data server architecture.

Several database technologies have been evaluated, including the leading object databases. After several months of evaluation, the object databases were rejected for lack of scalability, among other reasons. The object-relational technology shows the most promise. It provides the object-oriented concepts of hierarchy and polymorphic dispatch, allows the creation of new datatypes, and retains the SQL language and scalability. Sabre selected Informix Dynamic Server with Universal Data Option because it is by far the most complete and mature implementation currently available on the market.

In the integrated data server, maximizing parallelism is crucial to providing the required response times. At the present time, the data warehouse is expected to grow to an estimated size of 3.5 TB. This raises an interesting issue that as the project is more successful, the demand for it will grow. Demand could necessitate duplicating the data warehouse on separate machines to provide the required computing power to an increasing number of users.

This new implementation will include data warehouse and business process metadata. The metadata will provide the means to adapt to changes in the data sources, without requiring modifications to the applications.

The airline industry has specific needs that cannot be met with the standard SQL datatypes. For example, an SQL datetime type cannot be used directly without additional information. Time zones and daylight savings time must be taken into consideration. Some regions do not use daylight savings time. Among those that do, some have different rules that govern the application of changes. By creating a new business type, it is possible to encapsulate the appropriate behavior. The new business type then becomes a first class type within the database server. Application programs can take advantage of the new functionality without the addition of new code. This benefit extends to common, off-the-shelf products like Excel, SAS, etc. The server-side implementation also has the additional benefit of providing a consistent implementation of business types. This extends also to the implementation of business rules. In this way, different applications won't provide different answers to the same questions.

Object-Oriented Design and Implementation

As mentioned earlier, the integrated data server makes use of the current object-oriented (OO) framework technology to render both the metadata object models and business object models extensible. The metadata models take advantage of the table inheritance feature of Informix Dynamic Server with Universal Data Option. Extending a model can be as simple as creating a new table under a hierarchy and adding a few functions to implement the additional functionality.

To preserve the object-oriented aspect of the implementation, all business types must be implemented as specific datatypes. This means that they must be either distinct datatypes of existing types, or implemented as opaque datatypes. The representation of an airport field must be of the "airport" type, not of the char(3) type. Similarly, revenue must have its own type, rather than the money SQL datatype.

The new business datatypes also incorporate the business rules, including rules on comparisons. For example, LG_PAX_CNT = LG_PAX_REV (passenger count versus passenger revenue) can be disallowed as part of the datatype definition. Comparison rules provide instant error detection of semantically incorrect statements, which prevents against the return of a result that may not be recognized as erroneous. The business rules also include conversion rules, in which monthly revenue can be compared to daily revenue to provide a valid result.

Using Strong Typing

The programming world gained a powerful tool when strong typing was adopted in the ANSI C language. The strong typing provided in function prototyping generates warnings when a function call appears to be misused. This identifies many potential problems in production code, leading to higher software quality.

The use of strong typing, in combination with precisely defined object operations, is essentially the same as teaching business rules to the Informix Dynamic Server with Universal Data Option. The integrated data server creates user-defined types (UDs) for each business types, including:

- **Identifiers**: AIRPORT, AIRLINE, EQUIPMENT, etc.
- **Counters:** PASSENGERS, MILES_FLOWN, etc.
- **Money:** REVENUE, COST, etc.

The operations are then implemented between these business datatypes. The operations obey the business rules. The goal is to implement rules such as COST that can be subtracted from REVENUE, but not vice-versa. Some rules may require explicit cast from one business datatype to another. Other rules may implement an implicit cast that allows for automatic conversion when manipulating monthly and weekly revenue, for example.

Type-Based Integrity Check

Relational database systems provide a way to validate columns so that they follow the specified rules. This implementation works at the column level, and not at the type level. This makes sense, considering that the relational model has a definite number of pre-defined datatypes. Integrity checking is already implemented in the database server for these datatypes—nothing more is required.

The implementation of integrity constraints in the business datatype eliminates the need to add the constraint in the database schema each time that the type is required. If business requirements change, the integrity check needs to be modified in only one location, for simplified maintenance.

The integrity check is implemented in a support function of the business type. It can be implemented using the C language, a fast compiled language that provides the performance required in modern data warehouse systems. The flexibility of compiled languages can be exploited to implement arbitrarily complex constraints with minimum overhead. Furthermore, small lookup tables can be cached in the server, for faster processing.

What Makes the Integrated Data Server Universal?

The integrated data server stores and manipulates a universal set of datatypes. By this, we mean that all the business datatypes are represented, and some build on other business datatypes. With the definition and behavior centralized in the database, universal reuse of the functionality is available through any of the interfaces. This results in universally open access to all stored data using either custom applications or common off-the-shelf products that access the repository through a standard database interface like Open Database Connectivity (ODBC).

Conclusion

Informix Dynamic Server with Universal Data Option provides new possibilities for data warehouses which must handle complex types such as a universal datetime or the difficult business rules that govern the matching of flights. Informix Dynamic Server with Universal Data Option is a perfect match for data warehouse applications. It is built on a mature technology that provides high performance through the parallel execution of SQL queries. Its object-relational features can be exploited to adapt the database to the business environment, instead of making the business model fit into a rigid framework. It also provides a smooth migration from object-oriented design to its implementation.

The implementation of business datatypes simplifies the formulation of queries by working at a higher level of abstraction. Applications that use these types are more stable, since they operate at the business level. The use of a stable interface to the business objects shields application code from revisions in the business rules; thus, applications are more resilient to change, providing lower maintenance costs and a faster response to new user requirements. The server-based objects provide additional performance benefits through compiled functions and a reduction in the data movement between the database server and the application program.

Informix Dynamic Server with Universal Data Option opens the door to new solutions for existing problems. It provides a set of capabilities that enables the use of more direct solutions, and enables businesses to be better equipped to maximize their performance.

About Sabre Technology Solutions

Sabre Technology Solutions (STS) is a division of the Sabre Group. The Sabre Group is a leader in the electronic distribution of travel-related products and services, and is a leading provider of IT solutions for the travel and transportation industry. They are headquartered in the Dallas-Fort Worth, Texas area.

For more information consult their web site at: http://www.sabre.com

DataBlade Modules for the Informix Dynamic Server with Universal Data Option

by Jim Panttaja

Overview

Following the introduction of the Informix Dynamic Server with Universal Data Option in December 1996, it has become critical for potential customers and analysts to identify the salient features of the product's architecture in order to differentiate it from other similar products. This article is a discussion of the product, with the goal of identifying those features. It also focuses on the primary extensible feature of the product: DataBlade Modules.

Introduction

The key features and attributes of the Informix Dynamic Server with Universal Data Option and DataBlade Modules are as follows:

Extensibility

- DataBlade technology allows the implementation of specific domain expertise, whether standard, purchased, or custom. This technology provides companies with an exceptional ability to leverage their domain expertise in the marketplace, while obtaining optimal performance from locally executed functionality (internal to the database server).
- Multiple domain-specific DataBlade modules can be used in a database or in a single table to customize the scope and intent of a corporate data repository.

Integration

- The datatypes and functions are fully recognized by the Informix Dynamic Server with Universal Data Option (the Universal Data Option) as internal components, and are indistinguishable from built-in datatypes and functions.
- The datatypes can be used and referenced in all table creation statements.
- DataBlade module functions integrate naturally with SQL-based application models since they can be referenced in SQL statements as part of the SELECT list, the WHERE clause, or an ORDER BY clause.

Performance

- In an SQL-based server, it is critical that the optimizer maintain autocratic control over all data. With the Universal Data Option, the cost-based optimizer can optimize queries that reference built-in and user-defined types effectively, taking advantage of domain-specific indexes which are built on the new types.
- The optimizer has the ability to take advantage of distribution statistics for a given column of a new type.
- The localization of the execution calls to the DataBlade functions—as internal calls in the Universal Data Option's kernel—provides the minimization of overhead and optimal performance.

Ease of development

- BladeSmith, a wizard-based tool, can generate the required SQL statements to create the datatype and the functions, to generate the C function definition, and the make files required to implement the functions.
- The definition of the DataBlade module is maintained in a form that can be used on subsequent releases to generate code in other languages, such as C++ or Java, and to support new access methods or changes in syntax or calling sequences.
- There is no need to provide any special coding to deal with concurrency, locking, logging, buffering, or recovery issues.

Informix Dynamic Server with Universal Data Option

The term "Universal Server" was introduced last year as a new server type—built on top of relational database technology—that allows new, complex datatypes to be integrated in a single database with the entirety of an enterprise's structured data. These datatypes represent specific domains which were not previously manageable in an RDBMS—text, video, images, maps, sound—or complex domains which can be represented with more meaning using an object model instead of a relational model.

The DataBlade module approach of the Informix Dynamic Server with Universal Data Option yields not just the integration of new datatypes into the database, but the integration itself is accomplished in a way that supports sets, lists, and other composite datatypes. This kind of integration allows the optimizer to make accurate decisions on the order of evaluation of various clauses. It also enables the optimizer to make accurate choices between various indexes, including b-tree, r-tree, or vendor-defined access methods. In short, the database application developer can treat this new datatype just as all existing datatypes, using the same SQL constructs to access the data.

What Are Data Blades?

A DataBlade module is a combination of the following elements:

- New datatypes declared via a CREATE TYPE statement, and recognized by the Universal Data Option. These can include new collection types (sets, arrays, or lists), new row types (composites), new distinct types based on an existing type, and user-defined types implemented in C, C++, or Java (in mid-1997).
- New functions declared via a CREATE FUNCTION statement. These may be written in Stored Procedure Language (SPL), Informix's SQL-based function language, C, C++, or Java (in mid-1997).
- Indexing schemes based on existing access methods (b-Tree or r-Tree) or on new access methods.
- New domain-specific application code which can run on a client machine. However, not all DataBlades modules provide this capability, although a video DataBlades modules might include an application to display the videos.

The datatypes and functions are fully recognized by the Universal Data Option, having been declared using SQL CREATE TYPE and CREATE FUNCTION statements. When a table is created, it can have columns of any new datatypes created by a DataBlade module developer, or purchased and installed. Specialized DataBlade modules can come from Informix or a third party with specific domain expertise. Functions can be referenced in SQL statements as part of the SELECT list, in the WHERE clause, or in an ORDER BY clause.

Not only are the new datatypes and functions recognized by the Universal Data Option, they are indistinguishable from the built-in datatypes and functions. The developer of datatypes and functions can provide costing information to the Universal Data Option's optimizer, so that the cost-based optimizer can effectively optimize queries which reference built-in and user-defined types. This costing information includes the relative expense of a function—including several different cost functions—and the ability to take advantage of distribution statistics on a given column.

Third Parties Can Enhance the Informix Dynamic Server with Universal Data Option

Third-party companies can create DataBlade modules to take advantage of the company's domain expertise. For example, a company with expertise in encryption techniques can provide a set of functions that encrypt data. Another company can provide new datatypes to efficiently store and manipulate mapping data. A third company can provide efficient indexing techniques for text data. In fact, several competing companies may have different indexing techniques for text data—each more suitable for a given problem domain. One may handle foreign language text well, while another may handle technical jargon better.

Each of these DataBlade modules may be selectively incorporated into the Universal Data Option for a given installation. Data based on the datatypes of these various DataBlades modules can then be used in tables, and in fact can be used in the same table. The optimizer efficiently chooses query plans based on the WHERE clause used in a given statement.

Note that an application development organization can use these same techniques to develop internal applications, as many companies currently do with the Illustra product. Several beta customers for the DataBlade Module Developer Kit are using DataBlade modules for internal application development.

The DataBlade Module Developers Kit

The DataBlade Module Developers Kit includes a set of three tools to facilitate the development of DataBlade modules. The three tools are BladeSmith, BladePack, and BladeManager.

BladeSmith is a wizard-based tool that allows a developer to define a new datatype, and specify the various operators and support functions desired. Based on this definition, BladeSmith generates the required SQL statements to create the datatype, the functions, generates the C function definition, and the make files required to implement the function. If the new datatype is based on a C structure, BladeSmith generates the C code required for many of the operators and support functions— including the writing of a first estimate of the code required to implement features such as equal, greater than, and less than operators, a compare function, and all of the operators and support functions needed to implement either a b-tree or r-tree.

After the C code and SQL statements are generated, the definition of the DataBlade Module is maintained in a form that can be used on subsequent releases to generate code in other languages, such as C++, or Java (in future releases), and to support new access methods or changes in syntax and calling sequences.

BladePack is a tool that takes the SQL scripts generated by BladeSmith, and the object modules built from the sources generated by BladeSmith, as well as other components which must be delivered to a customer, including help files, read-me files, application code, additional SQL-scripts, and prepares a distribution. The current release supports building a release directory, or using InstallShield to create a self-extracting installation file.

BladeManager is a tool that is used by the administrator at a customer site to install DataBlade modules into databases. It manages which DataBlade modules are located in which database. It also supports the deinstallation of DataBlade modules.

These tools simplify the task of writing DataBlade modules. There is no need to provide any special coding to deal with concurrency, locking, logging, buffering, or recovery issues. All of these functions are managed by the Universal Data Option.

DataBlade Modules for Application Development

DataBlade module development uses SQL statements, such as CREATE FUNCTION, CREATE TYPE, and an application programming interface (API)—based on the successful API from Illustra which has been available for three years—to develop the datatypes and functions. This interface is successfully used for application development as well as DataBlade module development by third parties, without causing damage to the kernel or to databases. It is quite simple for an application to encapsulate knowledge in datatypes that are specific to an application. This interface requires the expertise of a knowledgeable C programmer, but does not require systems programming experience. However, it may require a programmer with domain management expertise, which is, of course, what the DataBlade module represents.

To ensure the architecture and integrity of the commercial DataBlade modules developed by third parties, Informix has established a group of architects and developers to work with these third-party developers. This group also identifies tools, such as Purify, and creates other tools to validate the design and implementation of these DataBlade modules.

How Does This Compare to Oracle Data Cartridges?

Oracle has announced an architecture that will extend their products to include support for new datatypes and functions for those datatypes. This architecture is called Network Computer Architecture (NCA), and the component used to extend the database is called a "cartridge."

Some of the same third-party companies, which already announced the development of DataBlades for the Universal Data Option, have now announced that they will also develop Data Cartridges for the Oracle Universal Server.

Early releases of Oracle 8 will probably include some support for specific new datatypes which will be added to the server itself, although not through the Data Cartridge mechanism. Oracle has announced support for video, text, and image data.

The Data Cartridge architecture uses Inter-Cartridge Exchange (ICX) to communicate among other Data Cartridges, with CORBA services, clients, or servers. This is described by Oracle as an object bus which provides inter-component communication. This layer will be much less efficient than the communication mechanism utilized by the Informix Dynamic Server with Universal Data Option. Oracle claims to provide an extensible indexing API; however, it is difficult to imagine how an index implementation via an object bus architecture can provide efficient access to data via the SQL language.

The Informix Dynamic Server with Universal Data Option allows for customized or industry-specific domain functionality inside the server with optimal performance. Oracle plans limit the use of custom and third-party solutions to the less efficient mechanisms offered with ICX. The marketplace has shown a desire and preference to use proprietary technology that is based on special domain expertise. Companies that require this technology are on the forefront in the use of specially defined domains and need to leverage specific expertise in their manipulation of these domains. This support will be much less efficient, that is, slower, with Oracle Data Cartridges.

The Informix DataBlade Module interface allows new datatypes to be seamlessly integrated into the database. In contrast, the Oracle Cartridge architecture provides a seam that impedes communication among the components of the server, and the various cartridges.

The ORDBMS and DataBlade Modules: Technology of Tomorrow Here Today

One of the concerns that has been voiced in the trade press and by Informix's competitors is that it will be either impossible, or take a long time to integrate the object relational (and extensible) features of the Illustra product (Illustra Technologies and Informix merged in February 1996) with the high-performance engine delivered by Informix. On September 30, 1996, the Informix Dynamic Server with Universal Data Option was shipped to DataBlade Module developers on schedule, and the product version was delivered in December 1996, as promised at the time of the merger.

When Informix provides the Informix Dynamic Server with Universal Data Option benchmark numbers, and as DataBlade developers deliver even more DataBlade modules, Informix will have met its promises of February 1996, proving that you *can* meld two companies and technologies, and provide a Universal Server that is extensible and delivers performance comparable or better than the best relational database servers.

Using Custom DataBlades to Move Beyond a Three-Tier Architecture

by Bill Kelley

Introduction

The three-tier architecture has been a successful "standard" solution to high-performance transaction processing over a wide area network (WAN) for about a decade. It evolved in the on-line transaction processing (OLTP) environment, due to processing requirements, technological constraints, and cost/benefit trade-offs.

The Typical Three-Tier Architecture

Examining the reasons for the three-tier architecture's success, it is possible to see that two of the three factors—technology, costs,

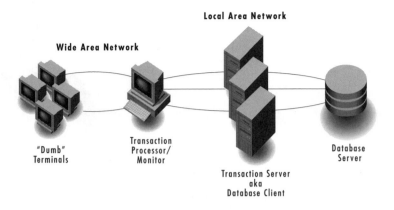

Figure 5–1 *The traditional three-tier architecture.*

and benefits—have evolved. In general, the three-tier architecture:

1. Handles transactions on a WAN;
2. Provides parallelism in the application; and
3. Offers load leveling.

The representation of the three-tier architecture, as illustrated in Fig. 5–1, exhibits four tiers, not three. Often, this diagram is drawn with the transaction processor off to the side. However, in actuality, there are four processes involved in handling each transaction.

Factors which contributed to this solution include the following:

1. Low speed and response time of the WAN;
2. Cost of large numbers of point-of-entry "dumb" terminal hardware; and
3. Demand for some parallelism in the processing of large volumes of transactions.

The three-tier architecture addresses these factors by:

1. Providing efficient custom message traffic over the WAN. Generic client/server communications, accomplished by placing database clients directly on point-of-entry systems over a

WAN, are many times the volume and round-trip communications of the custom protocol. The net result is slower performance. In practical terms, the difference means waiting seconds instead of minutes for a transaction to complete.

2. Minimizing the cost of point-of-entry hardware by reducing CPU or memory requirements.

3. Allowing parallel processing in the database application processes. From a database-centric point of view, these were database/client applications. From the application-centric point of view, these processes were themselves transaction "servers" which recorded the results in the database.

Benefits of the Transaction Processor/Monitor

The transaction processor/monitor provides a standard communications framework between the point-of-entry systems and the LAN. This frees the applications from the need for custom communications. The older database's client/server communications also free the application from communication headaches, but cannot provide the necessary performance for the WAN. Also, the transaction processor/monitor facilitates parallel processing by performing load-leveling between the transaction "servers," or database clients.

Transaction processors/monitors also generally have the capability to maintain distributed transactions with multiple databases via a two-phase commit protocol. However, typical applications do not make use of this additional capability.

Drawbacks

There are two "bottlenecks" in this architecture which effectively limit the amount of parallelism possible. These bottlenecks are the transaction processor/monitor, and the database server. The former has some overhead per message. The ratio of time to queue a message to the time for a transaction server to complete a transaction places practical limits on parallelism in the "under 10" range. The latter (database server) also performs a significant percentage of the processing. In the 1990's, this meant putting the database server on the fastest (and most expensive) hardware available.

A second performance limitation is the need for three processes to deal with each transaction on the LAN side. The overhead in the response per process is lower than in the WAN, but remains a contributing factor which limits both the response time and the throughput of the system.

Another drawback is cost. Both the high-end hardware and transaction processor/monitor software are typically in the million-dollar range. For large networks, this cost can be amortized to a reasonable cost per point-of-entry system. From the cost perspective, however, software that is capable of running a greater degree of parallelism on much cheaper hardware is a more ideal solution.

Factors Influencing the Three-Tier Architecture

Several factors have changed, none of which is sufficient to move to a new architecture. When taken as a whole, these factors point to the availability of new high-performance, lower-cost transaction processing systems which can be developed and brought to market much faster than any three-tier system.

One factor is that the cheapest point-of-entry system is now generic Windows PC hardware. It is neither starved for CPU or memory. In fact, it is now cheaper to buy high-performance generic computing equipment than to attempt to buy a custom, "low cost" point-of-entry hardware system.

Another factor is the increased bandwidth performance of both LANs and WANs. Of course, it is fairly safe to assume there will always be a relatively greater speed for LANs, and architectures that reduce the demand on the WANs remain important. However, the need to "hand-tune" message traffic to compress every last bit or round trip is no longer there, nor is it advisable nor cost effective to perform excessive message traffic tuning. At the beginning of the 90's, 2400-baud was considered fast. Now, 28.8 K is standard on normal phone lines, with 56 K appearing on the horizon as the next standard. WAN bandwidth is effectively ten times cheaper and faster today than a decade ago.

Instead of hand-tuned messages, an architecture which generally reduces WAN traffic, and retains the capability to rapidly evolve and adapt to changing market conditions will be more successful. Simply, there is no measurable performance difference if WAN messages are 2 K instead of 1 K. The important factor will be to retain the capability to tune or minimize the number of round-trip messages per transaction, not the size of the message itself. This can be accomplished by using a single message to run a "smart" application routine on the other end of the wire.

DataBlades—Key Enabling Technology for Lower Cost, Higher Performance Systems

The last and most important factor that enters the equation is the performance, functionality, and customizability of available database technology. Informix Dynamic Server with Universal Data Option is the leading example of this new technology. It has two capabilities which are key to providing higher performance and more cost-effective solutions: the server's parallel processing capability, and DataBlade capability. Other leading vendors are also making progress in providing similar functionality; however, conservatively, they remain many years behind Informix.

Putting all these new developments together, a new simpler architecture suggests itself. First, the "dumb terminal" can be replaced with a lower cost, smarter computing unit which is easily capable of hosting a sophisticated database client application. WAN performance can be effectively optimized by the use of custom DataBlade application software, resident in the database server process. Communications requirements can be reduced by Custom DataBlades in a manner similar to the use of stored pro-

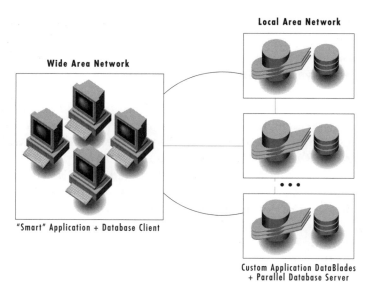

Local Area Network

Wide Area Network

"Smart" Application + Database Client

Custom Application DataBlades
+ Parallel Database Server

Figure 5–2 *Transaction processing for the next century.*

cedures. DataBlades go several steps further in performance by allowing the creation of application-specific datatypes, and because they can be implemented in standard compiled languages, such as C, instead of nonstandard, slower, interpreted stored procedure languages.

This architecture has no need of transaction processor/monitors. Load leveling is provided by the parallel database server architecture. The database's client/server communications framework replaces the redundant client/server framework of the transaction processor/monitor. The "customized" instruction set—implementable with custom DataBlades—effectively allows an application to be tuned to run on a WAN by moving the application intelligence directly into the database server as needed, note Fig. 5–2.

The most striking change here is the architectural simplicity. There are fewer components to design or debug, fewer interprocess communications, and fewer response times in a transaction's path. Some of the processing is moved to the many cheap, but powerful point-of-entry systems. Other processing is moved to parallel server processes, which are capable of load leveling and run on hardware that is selected for optimal cost/performance.

What About Lower Costs?

The expensive transaction processor/monitor component's functionality has been absorbed into the database and DataBlade system, thus eliminating its cost. The database system can be hosted on multiple hardware platforms. The sum of their performance is much higher than a single high-end processor or symmetric multiprocesssing SMP, while the sum of their costs is much lower. The WAN and point-of-entry costs are about the same as before. Development costs are much lower, both in terms of direct engineering costs, and time-to-market/lost opportunity costs, simply because the system design is simplified into a single client/server system, instead of two back-to-back systems. The components are all written in standard compiled languages, and this yields another development and maintenance cost savings.

Conclusion

In today's Internet-driven world, we are all much closer together. Unfortunately, that also means our competition is that much closer to us. A decade ago, five percent of the information processing budget may have seemed cheap. In tomorrow's world, it may be the difference between profitability and simply breaking even when your competitors' information processing budget is next to nothing. Profitable companies in the next decade will be those who keep ahead of the curve—to drive up performance and functionality, and drive down costs. Those that try to simply keep up are likely to find themselves left far behind.

Defining a Project Lifecycle for Informix Web DataBlade Development

by Matthew Eichler

Introduction

The architecture of the Web, and the development environment for Web sites that work with the database backend, present a dramatic break from previous methods of engineering information systems. However, in an effort to reduce costs, while delivering projects on time and achieving benefit goals, it is best to think about process at the onset of pilot Web DataBlade projects.

A popular misconception is to treat each project as if completely new and different solely because it uses new technology. We can build on our previous experiences, even when the new technology presents new challenges, or the tools change radically from those of the last project.

It is now characteristic of Web development that Information Systems (IS) groups are willing to experiment with new processes and tools in order to take advantage of the tremendous benefits of Web architecture on the Internet or within intranets. Whether for addressing a much larger audience or reducing administration costs by using the browser as a thin client, the Web holds much promise. However, this type of experimentation can lead to dead-ends and wasted resources. Rigorous project management techniques and process planning can help to avoid the pitfalls of this new paradigm.

This article proposes a Web database project lifecycle based on the time-tested waterfall model, which allows for the rapid prototyping made possible by Informix's Web tools. While the Informix Dynamic Server with Web Integration Option™ is used as the example development tool, this lifecycle can also be adapted for Informix Web Connect and Informix Web Kit applications development, as well as for tools from partners such as *Bluestone Software*, *HAHT Software*, *Symantec Corporation*, *Wallop Software*, and *Net Dynamics,* all of which leverage database technology for Web site development and management.

Overview

The Web database project lifecycle consists of six phases:

• Project definition;
• Analysis;
• Design and coding;
• Integration testing;
• Roll-out and launch; and
• Closure.

The concepts, deliverables, and tools for each phase will be examined in detail.

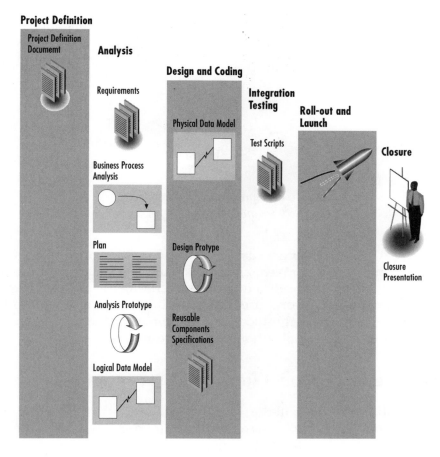

Figure 6–1 Web project lifecycle overview.

Keys to Success

Use HTML to Prototype

An HTML prototype provides end users with the initial "look-and-feel" of the site. Visualization facilitates end users' acceptance of system requirements.

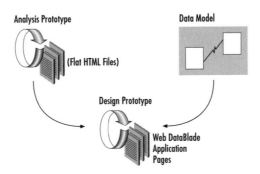

Figure 6–2 Separate the data model
from the user interface.

HTML pages are easy to code and make available to a wide
audience via a Web server. This makes HTML ideal for prototyping
a site and reviewing it with users in order to capture feedback
on page flow and user interface. It is best to analyze this feedback in the early stages of development before too much is
invested in application-page programming.

Separate the Data Model from the User Interface

Use flat HTML files to prototype the site, while separately modeling the data to ensure that the database will support the site. Do
not try to code application pages while building the database on
the fly, which can lead to confusion and dead-ends. Begin application-page programming only when the team is reasonably confident that the physical data model is complete.

Establish Measurable, Reasonable Success Factors

The team should have something concrete with which to measure the success of the project. There are many analysis tools that
parse the access logs of the Web server and indicate who is viewing the site. If the project has a wide audience, it may be difficult
to determine how many hits will make it a success, but make an
educated guess nonetheless. Customer and user surveys can
also be used to gain feedback and to measure success. If such
feedback mechanisms are used, make sure to allocate adequate

resources and tasks for their development, distribution, collection, and analysis.

Gather Metrics for Process Improvement

From the inception of the project, anticipate ways to measure system processes for continuous improvement or future Web site development.

To measure project management processes, consider the:

- Number of tasks completed ahead of schedule;
- Number of tasks completed behind schedule;
- Number of changes to the schedule after publishing the baseline; and the
- Difference between planned and actual cost totals for milestones, as well as costs for the entire project.

To measure project complexity, consider the:

- Number of defects;
- Cost to fix defects;
- Number of times each standard Web DataBlade tag was used;
- Number of user-defined tags and the number of times each was used;
- Number of application pages;
- Number of images and/or other multimedia objects;
- Number of tables and relationships; and the
- Number of stored procedures, triggers, and database functions.

Involve the Users in All Phases

Prototyping techniques on the Web can encourage close end-user involvement in all phases of the site's lifecycle, and the site will prove to be more useful and acceptable to end users in the long run. Obtain commitment from the end users who will be involved in the following:

- Review of project definition;
- Ownership and review of requirements;
- Review of business process analysis;

- Review of project plan;
- Review of analysis prototype;
- Review of logical data model;
- Review of design prototype;
- Execution of integration testing;
- Feedback for closure presentation; and
- Closure and signoff meeting.

Revisit the Plan

Schedule tasks to revisit the plan in the original baseline plan at important milestones.

Take Time to Look Back

Always take a breather between projects to examine the strengths and weaknesses of development processes. Obtain feedback from the end-user team regarding what worked and what didn't work. This can be accomplished during the closure and sign-off meeting.

Develop Document Templates

When creating project documentation, it is advisable to have templates. This can be accomplished easily by using documents from the first Web database project and modifying the documents based on the lesson learned.

Determine if it is possible to turn the documents from the first Web database project into templates for the next project. Hindsight when the project is complete will also help to improve these templates.

Create a Project Lifecycle Web Site

Begin to build a Web site to support the project lifecycle. This is an excellent communication tool for both IS and end-user teams in the standardization and documentation of development processes. The project lifecycle Web site can include:

Figure 6–3 *Project definition.*

- Project documents;
- Document templates;
- Lifecycle overview (including a business process analysis of the lifecycle itself);
- Detailed guides to executing development phases and processes;
- Recommended tools for each phase;
- High-level description of the project and all team members' roles; and
- Status reports.

Project Phases

Project Definition

Deliverables

Even if the gathering of requirements has already begun, take time to go back and create a project definition document. This will make it clear to the team the mission, objectives, and scope of the project, including some of the driving factors for measuring the success of the Web site. This document should contain all of the following sections:

- **Mission Statement**
One or two sentences stating the overall goal and scope of the project.
- **Objectives**
A more detailed listing of what the project is attempting to accomplish.
- **Scope**
A summary of which business processes and user group(s) the site will support, plus any notes about what the project will exclude, or any significant limitations. Where functionality will be delivered in phases, identify the scope by phase.
- **Project Sponsor**
Determine the business owner of the project who provides the funding and is ultimately responsible for the removal of road blocks. There may be situations where a sponsor is difficult to identify as the functionality crosses the organizational structure. In such cases, a committee of decision makers (or a steering committee) may be the best route.
- **Project Team**
Determine who are the key end users and IS developers to be involved in all phases of the project. Their roles regarding the project should be clearly delineated.
- **Return on Investment, Cost/Benefit Analysis, or Success Measures**
Whatever technique is used, the project should have realistic, measurable goals for determining its success. This is particularly difficult to achieve for Web sites; however, consider metrics, such as number of hits expected, the amount of time saved while searching for information, the reduction of system administration costs, the reduction of publication and distribution costs, or the reduction in user administration costs.
- **Risk Analysis**
All new technology projects present greater risks than a well established development environment, so ensure this is stated in quantifiable terms. Also, evaluate the risks of the project which is secondary to other IS projects. What is the level of commitment from the entire organization to the project's success?

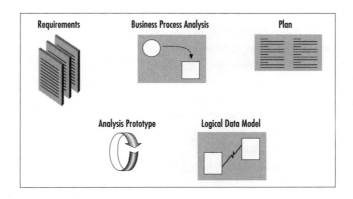

Figure 6–4 *Analysis.*

Tool

Project Definition Document Template

Tips

While this may be the most important document of the project, it is often overlooked when developers gather requirements. It is critical for the core team and sponsor to achieve a consensus on all sections. If there is ambiguity about any aspect of the project definition, it will greatly impact costs in later phases.

Analysis

Deliverables

- **User Requirements**
  A point-by-point detailed description of expected Web site functionality.
- **Business Process Analysis**
  A graphical representation of the processes supported by the Web site, external inputs/outputs, and the general areas where data is stored.

- **Plan**

  A resource-leveled baseline project plan which the team will work from in following phases.
- **Analysis Prototype**

  A flat HTML file representation of the basic site interface and the navigation from page to page. The team may start out with a **Storyboard** or **Site Map** which they will develop into a working flat site that is viewable from the browser.
- **Logical Data Model**

  A first pass at defining the structures of the data in the database. This version of the data model is used to communicate ideas about the data between the end-user team and the IS team. The IS developers should own the model, but the end-user team should review it.

Tools

- **User Requirements Document Template**

  A list of end-user defined requirements.
- **Business Process Modeling Tool**

  Products by Informix partners include LogicWorks *BPWin* and SILVERRUN *BPM*. If the IS team has never used this kind of tool before, and needs a quick start on the pilot, a basic computer graphics tool will suffice. Some of the advantages of using more advanced modeling tools include the ability to store models in a central repository, and integration with data modeling tools.
- **Data Modeling Tool**

  Products which support the Informix Dynamic Server with Universal Data Option include LogicWorks *Universal Modeling Architecture* and Silverrun *Universal Modeler*.
- **Project Planning Tool**

  Planning can be accomplished by hand; however, there are several excellent software packages which can help the team become more productive.
- **HTML Editing Tool**

  This tool is used to create the prototype.

Tips

- The end-user team should own the requirements document, but the entire team should work on it together and creatively brainstorm their ideas. It is important for end users to understand that the project cannot move forward without a thorough description of requirements.
- Prioritize requirements into three categories—"must have," "should have," and "nice to have." Some requirements which are "nice to have" can be assigned to future enhancements, depending on deadlines and resource allocation.
- While planning, use the requirements and business process model to identify the distinct components of the site. For a site supporting the publishing process, these might include the viewing pages, publishing pages, and site administration pages. For a site supporting business processes, components will roughly correspond to the processes they support. Milestones should be set for each component. Prototyping activities in the next phase will also follow the component structure.
- Planning should also include tasks for setting up the development, test, and production environments, including Web server configuration and the rollout of the database to each version of the site.
- With new technology projects, include tasks to "revisit the plan" in the plan. By doing so, it becomes possible to track the new tasks that may spring up as the team works in the untried environment.
- The storyboard or site map can be a one-page graphical overview of the Web page flow and interrelationships. If used, either of these representations can be included in the end-user requirements.
- Use the storyboard or site map as a basis to create a prototype site using the HTML editor and flat HTML files. If the end-user team is familiar with standard HTML publishing, they can own these pages; otherwise, the IS developers need to author them. In either case, publish these pages to a Web server and review them as a team.

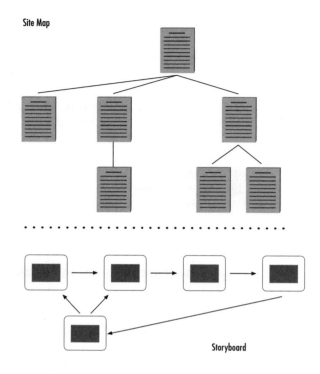

Figure 6–5 *Storyboard and site map tools.*

- The purpose of the prototype is to show the basic interface to the Web site and site navigation. Buttons and links that require database functionality behind them can be broken at this stage, but those required to move from page to page within the site should work. List boxes or tables which will be filled eventually with data from the database can be filled with sample data. Full graphics are not necessary; utilize existing graphics, if they are required, to show the site's "look-and-feel."
- Review the prototype from the browser and rework it as a team until all are satisfied with the user interface. The simple technique of creating a site model will prevent a lot of wasted coding.

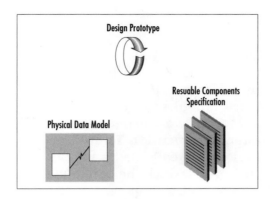

Figure 6–6 *Design and coding.*

- The purpose of the logical data model is to capture the basic data structures required to support the site. The end-user team should review the model for completeness, even if it means bringing the team up to speed on the symbols and formalism used. For the first version of the data model, it is not necessary to provide every detail to generate an actual database schema.

Design and Coding

Deliverables

- **Physical Data Model**
  This is the final version of the data model which can be used to generate the database schema and create a development database.
- **Design Prototype**
  The design prototype contains the working components of the site (built with application development tools) which can be reviewed by the end-user team.
- **Reusable Components Specification**
  This specification contains the design documentation on the shared components of the site.

Tools

- **Data Modeling Tool**
  The same tool used for the logical model should support the physical model. If a full-fledged modeling tool is not available, a basic graphics tool can be used. However, the SQL scripts used to create a schema must be created by hand.
- **Design Specification Template**
  Develop this template for use in documenting the reusable components which the development team will share.
- **Application Development Tool**
  For Informix Dynamic Server with Web Integration Option, the basic component of development is the application page. In addition, the developer will be coding using the Web DataBlade tags, as well as standard HTML tags.

Tips

- The physical data model will have all the data elements required to generate an actual schema. Most of the differences between the physical and logical models will be related to normalizing and/or de-normalizing database tables to render it a workable, maintainable schema. Users do not need to be involved in the review of this version of the model. Use the generated schema to build the development copy of the database. As application pages are developed, holes in the schema may be discovered and the physical model revisited.
- During planning, the site should be broken into distinct components. As each component is developed, review this "design prototype" with the end-user team (make sure they are informed on the missing pieces which will come later). They will provide valuable insight into the site design and will develop a strong vested interest in the project's success. If a particular page presents unusual problems with the user interface, produce two or three versions. Try each version out with the end-user team, soliciting their feedback regarding all versions.
- Much of the code from the analysis prototype will be thrown away; don't be surprised at this. The insights gained from coding the application pages will significantly alter the original prototype.

Test Scripts

Figure 6–7
*Integration
testing.*

- The reusable components specification is used when more than one developer codes application pages and several components. This document will specify the database's stored procedures and functions, as well as the user-defined tags which are needed across multiple components. Examples are tags that handle security, page headers and footers, and functions to create valid URLs which are based on content type. If the pilot Web project is small and there is only one developer, forgo this document.

Integration Testing

Deliverables

Test Scripts

Tools

Test Script Template

Tips

- The test scripts should be derived from the end-user requirements, and the collective experience with the prototyping phase. The complexity of the site and the processes it supports will determine how much effort and resources should be allocated. A document repository, knowledge base, and publishing processes will require less rigorous testing, while stricter business process support will require more testing.

- While IS developers are responsible for the testing of pages and components as the design prototype is built, end users should be responsible for the integrated testing of the entire site. Although developers believe they have tested the site adequately, end users' perceptions of the site will sometimes differ considerably from that of developers.

- The test scripts will indicate the specific navigation, inputs, and outputs of the site. The scripts should specify tests with invalid or illogical inputs, as well as valid, logical inputs.

- Text search tests should cover a wide range of search criteria, from single words to longer phrases. End users should be prompted to answer such questions as "Does the search return what I expect?" and "Are the results missing anything I expected to see?"

- Widen the audience for integration testing to a significant group of end users. The core end-user team can recommend who should be included in this testing phase. Make sure they understand the level of commitment required and plan to give them sufficient time to perform the testing, based realistically on their regular workload.

- Testing should have its own environment. It should not overlap the development or production environments. As defects are uncovered, fix them for the specific application pages in the development environment, and repeat the testing cycle.

- The site should not be deployed until the users have signed off on the integration testing results.

Roll-Out and Launch

Tips

First, configure a production Web server and roll out the production copy of the database. Then, the site will be ready for launch. Procedures for the backup and restoration of the

Figure 6–8 *Roll-out and launch.*

database, and the troubleshooting of servers (to keep them up and running), should be documented for system administrators.

Closure

Deliverable

Closure presentation (a.k.a., postmortem).

Tips

The closure presentation is a chance for the development team to share the positive and negative experiences of the project with other IS groups. This is an opportunity to talk about what can be improved and to better define the Web database site's development lifecycle. Consider the following questions:

• What are better tools to use?
• What are some techniques which were missed?
• How could the plan have been more accurate?

This is also a chance to educate the other IS groups on the differences between Web site development and traditional systems development.

The development processes should be in a constant state of improvement. Look for concrete measurements of successful project management. For instance, the number of tasks completed

Closure Presentation

Figure 6–9 Closure.

behind or ahead of schedule, and the number of defects uncovered during testing. The team should also present a list of enhancements for future versions of the site. These features may have been put off in the early phases due to time constraints, or only merely suggested during prototype reviews and integration testing.

It is also important to obtain closure from the end-user team and discuss the following:

- Improvements that can be used by future development teams and end-user teams.
- Does the site meet end-user requirements? If not, can defect fixes and enhancements proceed to the next phase, or can they be resolved during the site maintenance phase?

Conclusion

While it is tempting with Web database development to dive directly into coding application pages without a clear plan, a lifecycle approach to site development can help to guarantee a successful project. As with any new technology, the development processes will not always be predictable, but continually defining and improving the processes will yield significant cost benefits over time, as well as ensure the involvement and satisfaction of the end-user community.

Acknowledgments

Special thanks to Denise Taylor of Informix MIS, for her input to this article.

Chapter 7

Data Security Using the Prime Factors Descrypt DataBlade

by Eric Horschman

Introduction

Informix Dynamic Server with Universal Data Option supports familiar methods to protect access to sensitive data through the granting and revoking of access privileges. These methods work well within the boundaries of the database and applications that use it, but it is still possible for malicious outsiders or dishonest insiders to gain undesired access to data at the operating system level, or through the possession of database storage devices or backup media.

To adequately protect against threats from a disgruntled employee or disk-drive thief, critical data must be encrypted. Current encryption technology has been shown to resist all but the most extravagantly expensive attacks and is trusted daily where security matters most—in the electronic transfer of funds between banks.

The Prime Factors Descrypt DataBlade Module extends the Informix Dynamic Server with Universal Data Option to provide easy-to-use encryption of objects within the database. Developers can incorporate Data Encryption Standard (DES) based encryption into applications without concern for the complexity of the underlying algorithms. However, like any technology, effective encryption relies on proper management and administrative practices as much as the core mathematics of the encryption algorithm.

Database Security Concerns

GRANT and REVOKE

Informix Dynamic Server with Universal Data Option allows you to set privileges on database objects to protect data from unauthorized access by database users. Familiar SQL GRANT and REVOKE commands permit the fine-tuning of access privileges at the database, table, type, and routine levels. However, sensitive data is still vulnerable to users with operating system access to the database files or access to the physical media. A malicious user with operating system access to database files can extract data using external utilities, despite any limitations imposed within Informix Dynamic Server with Universal Data Option. Perhaps someone who manages to steal a disk drive or backup tape can access the data you worked so hard to protect from your database users.

For complete security, it is necessary to encrypt highly sensitive data within the boundaries of Informix Dynamic Server with Universal Data Option. Once encrypted, the data is protected even from those who can access database files from the operating system, or through the physical possession of disks or tapes. Without access to the keys used to encrypt the data, hostile parties have no way to decrypt and view sensitive information.

Compliance with Privacy Laws

Protecting sensitive records in your database is not just a good security practice—in many cases, it is required by law. Statutes

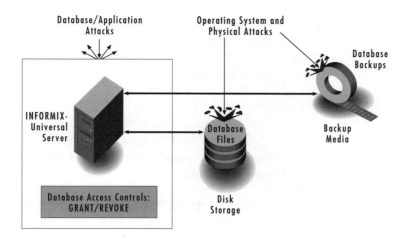

Figure 7–1 *Despite database access controls, database files and backups remain vulnerable.*

exist requiring government agencies and private organizations to protect the privacy of personal data records. Disclosures to unauthorized parties can result in civil and criminal penalties to those responsible. Reliance on one technical barrier, such as database access privileges, is unlikely to be viewed kindly by a court looking to assign blame for a damaging security breach.

By using the Prime Factors Descrypt DataBlade to store selected data in encrypted form, together with database access controls and physical protection of media, you can create multiple barriers to the misappropriation of data, protecting end users and the organization itself.

Encryption Basics

What is DES?

Encryption is a reversible process which renders data unintelligible. Of the many available encryption schemes, the Prime Factors Descrypt DataBlade uses a method called the Data Encryption Standard, or DES. DES was developed originally by

IBM Corporation and has been adopted as a Federal Information Processing Standard by the United States (US) government. DES is the most widely used encryption method and is the *de facto* standard in banking and financial services for the protection of electronic funds transfers.

DES is a private key cryptosystem that uses a single 56-bit key to encrypt and decrypt data. The key must be kept confidential, since any third party that comes into possession of the key can decrypt data. A private key system is ideal for protecting database records for two reasons:

- The DES algorithm is typically ten times faster than alternative public-key cryptosystems. When data is encrypted and decrypted in real-time as part of a database application, performance of the algorithm is critical.
- Protection of database records is usually a one-party operation—the same system that encrypts the data also performs the decryption. Therefore, no private keys need to be exchanged between parties, and the risk of compromised keys is avoided.

Encrypt Wisely

Encryption and decryption of database records unavoidably imposes a processing burden on any system. However, any performance impact can be minimized by wisely selecting to encrypt only essential data. For example, in a database table of human resource records, perhaps only the **salary** column requires protection by encryption.

The Prime Factors Descrypt DataBlade Module

DataBlade Benefits

The Prime Factors Descrypt DataBlade shares the key benefits of all Informix Dynamic Server with Universal Data Option DataBlades:

- It extends the capabilities of Informix Dynamic Server with Universal Data Option to include DES encryption. Applications developers require no knowledge of the intricacies of encryption and key generation.
- The encryption/decryption functions of the Prime Factors Descrypt DataBlade are fully integrated with Informix Dynamic Server with Universal Data Option. The DataBlade's encryption functions are available as simple SQL command language extensions.
- The execution of the encryption/decryption functions internally in the Informix Dynamic Server with Universal Data Option kernel provide optimal performance.
- Development is simplified, since there is no need to deal with concurrency, locking, logging, buffering, or recovery issues.

Using the Descrypt DataBlade

The Prime Factors Descrypt DataBlade Module supplies three functions to support encryption, decryption, and key generation. After the installation of the DataBlade, these functions are available as SQL commands which can be incorporated in any routines or stored procedures.

Key generation with pfnGenHexKey

The key value used by DES to encrypt data must be extremely resistant to guessing, and security is further enhanced when knowledge of the key is kept from the application developer. The function syntax is as follows:

```
pfnGenHexKey("seed")
```

The above syntax takes an eight-character seed argument value, combines it with several dynamically changing values, and processes the result with triple-DES encryption to generate a highly random 16-character hexadecimal (a 56-bit key value, plus an 8-bit checksum) return value. The pfnGenHexKey function will return different keys, even if the same seed is reused. This enables data to be secured even from users who are able to view the SQL commands used by the application.

Encryption with pfnEncrypt

The `pfnEncrypt` function applies DES encryption to convert cleartext of the type LVARCHAR into ciphertext of the same type. The function syntax is as follows:

```
pfnEncrypt("source", "hex_key")
```

The argument `hex_key` can be the return value of `pfnGenHexKey` or a literal 16-character hexadecimal value. If used in the following fashion, the encrypted data cannot be recovered by a dishonest insider with access to the SQL code:

```
update hr_data
      set salary = pfnEncrypt('65000'::lvarchar,
pfnGenHexKey("my_seed"))
where emp_name = "Smith"
```

The obvious drawback to the above example is that the encrypted salary cannot be decrypted, since `pfnGenHexKey` will never again generate the exact key used for encryption. A practical approach would be to insert the key values into a key table at the time of their generation, and then use those stored key values for encryption, as follows:

```
insert into KeyTable values ("Smith", pfnGenHexKey("my_seed"))

update hr_data
      set salary = pfnEncrypt('65000'::lvarchar,
      (select KeyValue from KeyTable where KeyName="Smith"))
where emp_name = "Smith"
```

Decryption with pfnDecrypt

The `pfnDecrypt` function applies DES encryption to convert ciphertext of the type LVARCHAR into cleartext of the same type. The function syntax is as follows:

```
pfnDecrypt("source", "hex_key")
```

The argument `hex_key` can be the result of a select statement to lookup the key value in a table or a literal 16-character

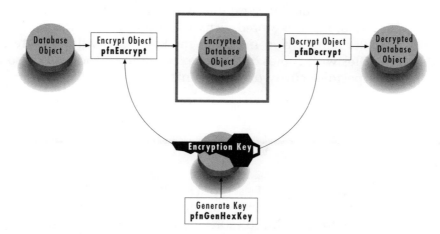

Figure 7–2 The same DES encryption key is used to encrypt and decrypt database objects.

hexadecimal value. Following the previous example, the employee's salary can be recovered in the following manner:

```
select hire_date, dept_num, pfnDecrypt(salary,
        (select KeyValue from KeyTable
        where KeyName="Smith"))::integer
from hr_data
where emp_name="Smith"
```

Safe Management of Keys

Of course, the data protected by the Prime Factors Descrypt DataBlade Module is only as secure as the encryption keys used; thus, special precautions should be taken to ensure the security of the keys.

- If keys are stored in a separate table, grant DBA access to as few persons as possible.
- Grant Select privilege to the key table to as few persons as possible.
- Locate the key table on physical media that can be disconnected or removed when not needed.

- Backup the database files with the key table to separate media that is stored securely or separately encrypted.
- Remember that indexing the key table will generate index files with copies of the indexed columns that may also require special security arrangements.

Summary

The Prime Factors Descrypt DataBlade provides access to proven and trusted DES encryption through three easy-to-use functions. The DataBlade handles key generation, encryption, and decryption without requiring any knowledge of the complex mathematics behind the DES algorithm. By storing critically sensitive database objects in encrypted form, protection is provided from attacks which originate outside the environment of Informix Dynamic Server with Universal Data Option.

Chapter 8

Name Recognition Using DataBlade Module Technology

by Terence A. Di Benigno

Introduction

Data itself has less intrinsic value than the information it provides. Name recognition is a method that allows an organization to extract valuable information from data, and to identify hierarchies and relationships among data. For example, a name recognition tool can identify "Bank of New York," treat it as a company name, and even recognize that it may be the same as BONY or BNY (but not bony); however, it will not confuse these names with "a bank in New York." It can do the same for millions of names of individuals, organizations, and other entities. It can suggest that "Bob Jones" may be the same person as "Robert Jones," and that "$1,000" is the same as "one-thousand dollars (U.S.)." Given this example, it is important to note that a name recognition tool can extract various artifacts from text besides names of people, organizations, and locations. It extracts the names of products, numerical expressions, or other named entities as well.

Until now, this technology has been used mainly in select government and corporate applications where competitive information is at a premium. Now, economies of scale, along with the widespread availability of improved, compatible, text-management software, make it possible to bring this solution to the desktop. Organizations that require fast, accurate data extraction, summarization, and indexing can benefit from name recognition tools.

NameTag: A Name Recognition DataBlade

IsoQuest's NameTag DataBlade Module is a user-installable extension to the Informix Dynamic Server with Universal Data Option. It provides advanced data extraction and indexing capability within the database engine.

The NameTag DataBlade Module extends Informix Dynamic Server with Universal Data Option by supporting document indexing and retrieval services through the NameTag application programming interface (API). Application developers gain the ability to use server-side DBMS features for storage and retrieval, while taking advantage of the NameTag DataBlade Module's ability to index proper names and other artifacts within documents.

The NameTag DataBlade Module allows application developers to store document types—either in SGML format or text format—in Informix Dynamic Server with Universal Data Option, and use the NameTag API to build an index of names found in the documents. The index that is produced can be manipulated from the client side, or stored within the server. To accomplish this task, the functionality within the NameTag API is exposed to the database server, as well as to any new datatypes defined to support the application domain.

The NameTag DataBlade Module:

• Introduces advanced text-search and indexing capabilities within the database engine;

- Offers full relational database management system (RDBMS) capabilities;
- Eases and accelerates application development;
- Provides high performance; and
- Leverages Informix Dynamic Server with Universal Data Option's infinite extensibility.

The Advantage of NameTag

The NameTag DataBlade Module is an automatic indexing system that finds and classifies key phrases in text, such as personal names, corporate names, place names (geographic locations), dates, and monetary numeric expressions. NameTag finds all mentions of a name and links names that refer to the same entity together by combining dynamic recognition with static lookup to achieve high accuracy and coverage at a very high speed. It consists primarily of sophisticated pattern matchers, lexical resource utilities, and a name recognition rule base that can recognize key phrases in the text and—through a set of function calls—perform operations on the matched text.

By identifying and interpreting proper names, NameTag allows users to find relevant content quickly, and eliminate unwanted or inappropriate material. For example, users who seek information about Mountain View, California, will receive information about the community, not about "mountain vistas." This capability is a significant feature in time-critical information searches.

NameTag creates a custom electronic index, much like the indexes provided in books. This index is a valuable component in applications such as document management, custom clipping, and text retrieval. NameTag is an extremely powerful tool for sorting through vast amounts of data to quickly locate specific information.

NameTag finds topics based on proper names by analyzing natural language text with a technique known as "finite state interpretation." This technique combines computational linguistics and pattern matching methods to determine the following information:

1. What is a name;
2. The variations of the name (for example, DEC, Digital, Digital Equipment Corporation); and
3. How to categorize the name (for example, person, location, company, etc.).

An Overview of NameTag

NameTag consists of a C-linkable library that developers can incorporate into their own applications. This API allows the developer to:

- Set parameters to ensure the best performance for a wide variety of text formats;
- Load documents into the system from files, C strings, or individual token units;
- Output an SGML-annotated version of the input document;
- Access extracted entity names, text offsets, and classification information; and
- Access an index of words for purposes of full-text indexing.

The system consists of two basic pieces: the text processing engine and an extensive set of patterns which the engine tries to match within the document. A document can be any ASCII file in SGML or non-SGML format. The API gives the developer the power to define not only how text is tagged and extracted, but the type and/or configuration of the documents to be tagged. A typical application is to recognize proper names in text and extract them for use in text retrieval or database systems.

The API is the programmatic interface used to develop Name-Tag applications. Pattern Data is provided as a part of the NameTag product and cannot be modified by the developer. The Custom Name List and Name Lexicon are user-created lists of names used to customize the performance of NameTag. The user simply creates files of names in a special format and reinitializes NameTag.

IsoQuest's NameTag is robust, fast, and accurate, and can serve as a piece of "companionware" to on-line text management and electronic filing products. The software adds value to these products by extending the underlying word recognition component to include names and other special artifacts.

IsoQuest's NameTag uses a fast language processor that recognizes words and phrases in context; thus, embedded knowledge about how names are used is just as important as knowledge about how names are written.

The software also comes with extensive (and extensible) lists of proper names, locations, titles, and corporate designators, and uses an innovative, proprietary search strategy to handle difficult and ambiguous cases. For example, NameTag provides the user with the ability to:

- Recognize that an ambiguous name such as "Monte Carlo" may be a simulation method, a city, a mountain, or a car.
- Recognize that many words (for example, "Apple" or "Bush") can either be common nouns or proper names.
- Resolve variations in company and individual names (for example, "Smith Motor Company" can be referred to as "Smith" and so can "Mr. Smith").
- Recognize that many proper names (for example, "Cruella de Ville") are not capitalized.

NameTag Processing Model

NameTag's primary focus is to process a document and return index information about that document. For each document, NameTag must receive the following information:

1. Document name and length; and
2. Document type (for example, SGML).

Given that information, NameTag will process and return the following information:

1. A list of names found in the document. The names are grouped by name type and subtype. Each name consists of the following data: name string; byte offset in the document; type (enumerated value); subtype (enumerated value); confidence (0-100); relevance (0-100); and a sublist of names that are aliases of this name (each of these alias names contains all of the above data, except that they do not contain a sublist of names).
2. A list of descriptions in the document. Descriptions are returned in no particular order. Each description consists of the following: reference to a returned name; context string; and byte offset of a context in the document.
3. A list of relationships in the document. Relationships are returned in no particular order. Each relationship consists of the following: reference to two returned names; relation type (enumerated value); and byte offset of relation in document.

NameTag DataBlade Product Architecture Outline

The NameTag DataBlade Module consists of the following components:

- A single datatype (NameTag), and server functions, that support the storage and retrieval of a NameTag datatype.
- Supporting functions that allow for NameTag indexing of various document types.
- An SQL interface for client application development. The SQL API allows third parties to develop database applications that incorporate NameTag indexing—without requiring that they know the internal representation and functionality.

As with other DataBlade Modules, the client and server processes may execute on different machines connected via a network, or on the same machine. The client and server machines need not have the same architecture.

Functionality and Features

Release 1.0 of the NameTag DataBlade Module provides the following functionality:

• Permits users to retrieve the documents stored in a database;
• Permits users to execute NameTag functions on the server;
• Permits users to create tables that contain the NameTag datatype; and
• Supports query-by-content on the NameTag datatype via an SQL interface.

Document Storage and Associated Datatypes

Users are allowed to store documents in a database as either a large object or large text type which are candidates for indexing via the NameTag engine. The NameTag DataBlade Module also supports document access via the native file system for those users who prefer that method. These documents are either in ASCII or SGML format.

Users can choose to store the resulting index as a NameTag datatype within Informix Dynamic Server with Universal Data Option. The DataBlade module features allow the user to create tables and columns based on the datatype.

Users of the DataBlade module can develop additional application features on the client side to manipulate the datatype, so that end-users can view the indexed material in a variety of interesting ways. End users can also select a document, or a set of documents, from the visible index for retrieval based on a document ID. The documents can be viewed using an ASCII editor or a popular Web-based browser such as Netscape Navigator.

NameTag Functions

Applications using the NameTag DataBlade module can index retrieved documents using NameTag functions on the server. The NameTag API is exposed as server functions on Informix Dynamic Server with Universal Data Option. The NameTag API can be implemented as SQL extensions, allowing the users access to a familiar and powerful data manipulation language.

General Extensibility

The functionality described previously is integrated and accessible to the DataBlade module via C functions.

Datatypes

NameTag

The NameTag datatype is used to store the information extracted from a given document type. The datatype is represented as a collection type using the SET constructor. Tag definitions and attributes are discussed in this section.

NameTag tags the names according to general purpose definitions. Each definition consists of a top-level category (TYPE) and a secondary classification (SUBTYPE). The top-level categories are used in the API to instruct the system as to which names to extract. The secondary classification—corresponding to the SUBTYPE attribute—provides additional information and another grouping level for the name.

The top-level categories (TYPES) are shown in Table 8-1.

The SUBTYPE attribute discussed above is only one of the attributes of a given tag that can be extracted and examined using NameTag. These attributes provide additional information about the name that NameTag has classified. Table 8-2 is the list of attributes which can be examined for any entity.

Table 8-1 Top-Level Categories (TYPES)

PERSON	Named person or family;
PLACE	Political or geographical place names;
ENTITY	Named corporate, governmental, or other organizational entity;
TIME	Dates, days of week, time of day;
NUMERIC	Percentages, monetary values, measures;
OTHER	Other named things;
MISC	Miscellaneous phrases, such as e-mail addresses; and
UNK	Capitalized phrase, not classified as a name by NameTag.

Table 8-2 Attributes

ID	The identification string of the tag.
SUBTYPE	The secondary classification of the type. The secondary classifications are dependent on the TYPE and are defined as follows:

PERSON:	None.
PLACE:	CONTINENT, COUNTRY, PROVINCE, COUNTY, CITY, REGION, DISTRICT, WATER, LANDFORM, ROADWAY, ASTRONOMICAL.
ENTITY:	ORGANIZATION, COMPANY, GOVERNMENT, UNION, MILITARY, EDUCATION, FACILITY, PUBLICATION, RELIGIOUS, POLITICAL, ENTERTAINMENT.
TIME:	DATE, TIMEOFDAY, AGE, TEMPORAL.
NUMERIC:	PERCENT, MONEY, PHONENUM, MEASURE, DOCPART.
OTHER:	PRODUCT, EQUIPMENT, OTHER.
MISC:	OTHER, ADDRESS.
UNK:	None.

Table 8-2 (continued)

PATTERN | The name of the pattern used to classify the name. Several patterns may apply to the name NameTag classified. This attribute provides the name of the pattern that was selected as the best determiner of the classification of the name.

RELEVANCE | The relevance value of the name. NameTag assigns a relevance value to each name and its alternative forms, such as acronyms, found in the document. The relevance value is a real number between 0.0 and 100.0, where 100.0 is the highest relevance, and is computed based on a weighted sum of factors, including the number of occurrences and the position of the occurrences (an occurrence at the beginning of the document, for instance, is assumed to be of greater relevance than one at the end).

This value provides information on how important, or relevant, the name is within the context of the whole document. You can use this value to determine if the article is about the name or if the name is merely mentioned in passing. Because names can be extracted in an application in their order of importance, it is possible to design applications to only extract those names that are more relevant to the information sought within each document, and "throw away" or skip the names with a low relevance.

CONFIDENCE | The confidence value of the tag. NameTag assigns a confidence value to each tag. The confidence value is stored as a CONFIDENCE attribute of the tag, which can be extracted through the standard API functions. The confidence value is a real number between 0.0 and 100.0, and is computed based on the weight of the maximum matching rule, the sum of the assigned tag's weight, the amount of conflict with other tags, and the tag assignment for the name across the entire document.

If the program is designed to collect context (descriptions) and relation (relationships) information, there are additional attributes to extract and use, as shown in Table 8–3.

Table 8–3   Additional Attributes

For Contexts:

HEAD	Returns a pointer to the name for which the context applies.

For Relations:

HEAD	Returns a pointer to the first entity associated with the relation.
TAIL	Returns a pointer to the second entity associated with the relation.

Provided Functions

This section describes the functions that are provided in order to implement and operate the NameTag DataBlade Module.

The NameTag DataBlade Module uses a high-level server function that is callable from SQL. The high-level function will, in turn, call the lower-level functions, defined as follows to implement document processing and extraction. The NameTag index that is extracted from documents will populate the NameTag collection datatype documented under the datatypes above.

An example of the SQL interface is as follows:

```
select doc_id, NAMETAG(doc_image)
from doctable
where doc_date >= (value)
```

This code will invoke the NAMETAG server function to process the documents (doc_image) stored in the Informix Dynamic Server with Universal Data Option table (doctable). The function populates and returns a collection-type data structure, as well as the document ID (doc_id). The NameTag DataBlade Module programmer can then evaluate the datatype and choose to store it in an Informix Dynamic Server with Universal Data Option table, or reject it if no names are found that are of interest to the application domain. A client application can then manipulate the table and present the browsable index to the user via the user interface (UI).

Server Functions

Table 8–4 shows definitions and descriptions of the server functions.

Table 8–4   Server Functions

NAMETAG(parms)

Definition	Server function callable from SQL to process documents and extract an index of names.
Description	The NAMETAG function calls the functions documented as follows to process text, extract names, and populate the NameTag datatype.

NTinit

Definition	Initializes NameTag.
Description	This function initializes the NameTag system. It must be called before any other NameTag API function is used. Calling this function initializes the document, phrase, preprocessing, and extraction objects used by the NameTag system.

NTshutdown

Definition	Shuts down NameTag.
Description	Shuts down the NameTag system and frees all memory associated with it. After calling NTshutdown, it is necessary to restart NameTag using NTinit before performing any further processing.

NTbatchConfigure

Definition	Configures NameTag parameters from a batch file.
Description	This function reads NameTag parameters from the file fname and calls the appropriate API functions. Users may edit the file to re-configure NameTag without re-compiling their application program. If echo is non-zero, this function displays each line in

Table 8–4   (continued)

the file as it attempts to configure NameTag, which is useful for debugging. Each line of the file must contain a parameter name and its value(s). The parameter and values are separated by whitespace, and multiple values are separated by commas.

NTlastError

Definition   Returns last error message.

Description   If an error has occurred in the system, this call returns a pointer to a null-terminated character string containing a description of the error. It returns an empty string if no error has occurred.

NTresetError

Definition   Resets error status.

Description   If an error has occurred in the system, this function resets the error status and clears the last error message. Use this function after retrieving an error with NTlastError() to reset the system for further processing.

NTloadFile

Definition   Prepares to operate on a file.

Description   This function opens the file with the given name and sets up the tokenizer to begin reading the file. Any previously open file is closed. Note that this function does not actually read the file into the system. Use NTloadDocument() to actually load information from the file.

NTloadDocument

Definition   Loads a document from the opened file or string.

Description   This function loads the next document in the file previously opened with NTloadFile() or NTopenString() into the document buffer. The document buffer is cleared before loading occurs. Note that this function will not necessarily read the entire file—it only reads one 'document' as defined by the Document configuration parameter (NTdocumentTag). However, if no SGML document

Table 8–4   (continued)

tags are present in the file and the document configuration parameter has been set inferred, using the pipe symbol, then this function will read the entire file as one document.

NTprocessDocument

Definition   Processes a document.

Description   This function begins processing a loaded document. Processing a document entails running the pattern matching engine over sections of the document to add markers in the document buffer where entities are found. Those entities can then be extracted. The user may optionally pass in the address of a function in cb, which will be called after each section of the document is processed, for example, to service an event loop if the NameTag engine is running in an event-driven GUI environment. The function should have no arguments and should return nothing. If no such callback function is needed, cb should be set to NULL (0). Prior to calling this function, it is necessary to have loaded a document into the document buffer using NTloadDocument().

NTextractEntities

Definition   Performs entity extraction.

Description   This function causes the system to collect all tagged entities in the document buffer whose types were registered with NTaddExtrTag() and organize them according to their ID attribute. For most entity types, this means that aliases of a particular entity (for example, variations of the same name, such as "John Smith", "Mr. Smith", "Mr. John Smith") will be grouped together so that they can be extracted as one unit, rather than as multiple entities. If "words" is non-zero, all instances of "words" will be collected in the document under the handle zero. If "words" is zero, no word collection will occur. Do not perform word collection unless it is necessary to make use of the extracted words, since collecting the words takes time and memory. After this function has been called, entities may be examined

Table 8–4 (continued)

using NTextractTag() and NTnextEntity().

NTextractTag

Definition   Prepares to iterate over entities for a given tag. Query information for a tag.

Description   Given a handle in tag that was returned by NTaddExtrTag(), this function returns the number of entities of that type which were extracted in the last call to NTextractEntities(). It also sets up an internal iterator so that subsequent calls to NTnextEntity() return information about each entity of the given type.

NTnextEntity

Definition   Retrieves information on an entity.

Description   After calling NTextractTag() with a desired entity type, use this function to obtain information on each entity of that type. This function may be called more than once and will return TRUE (1) as long as there are entities to extract. It will return FALSE (0) when no more entities of the given type are available. The parameter name will be set to a static area containing a null-terminated string representing the text of the entity. In cases where an entity has multiple aliases, the value returned in name will be that of the longest alias. The value returned in num is the number of times that this entity was found in the document. For each of those occurrences, there is one entry in the array occurrences which contains a pointer to the internal marker for that occurrence. Offsets and attributes for the occurrence can be retrieved using NTentityOffset() and NTentityAttr(), respectively.

NTentityString

Definition   Retrieves the character string of the specified entity.

Description   Given an entity returned by NTnextEntity(), this function returns the character string of the text of the entity. The return value points to a static area; thus, the result should be copied into a program-defined variable.

Table 8–4 *(continued)*

NTentityOffset

Definition   Retrieves character offsets within the document of the specified entity.

Description   Given an entity returned by NTnextEntity(), this function returns the starting and ending character offsets of the entity in the input text.

NTentityAttr

Definition   Retrieves attributes for an entity.

Description   Given an entity returned by NTnextEntity(), this function will lookup the attribute, given as a null-terminated string in attribute, and return the value of the attribute in the null-terminated string value. If the entity has more than one value for the given attribute, the values are separated in the result string by vertical bars (|).

Client Functions

This DataBlade module does not provide any client functions.

Access Methods

The NameTag DataBlade Module does not require special indexing methods, nor does it provide additional access methods above those provided by Informix Dynamic Server with Universal Data Option.

Installation

Release 1.0 of the NameTag DataBlade Module is constructed using the techniques described in the Informix DataBlade Module Developers Kit, and is compatible with the BladePack and the BladeManager.

Chapter

9

Online Optical Storage Management for Databases

by David Sharpe

Introduction

Fundamental to the success of a growing number of database applications is the storage and management of large data objects, such as images, multimedia, and scanned documents, along with standard text and character string datatypes. OptiLink from Consistency Point Technologies (CPT) is specifically designed to integrate database systems, including relational database management systems (RDBMSs) and object-relational database management systems (DBMSs), with optical storage subsystems and metadata to create a *unified information framework*. OptiLink provides object management, integrity, access performance, and information asset control. OptiLink is especially suited to any organization which must manage on-line documents, multimedia, images, and other information from a variety of data sources within a single information management framework.

The OptiLink DataBlade module provides database and optical subsystem integration through its modular plug-in intelligence. Upon the installation of the OptiLink DataBlade module with Informix Dynamic Server with Universal Data Option storage management functionality is extended into the database. In combination, Informix Dynamic Server with Universal Data Option and OptiLink DataBlade module can control:

- Data object descriptions, type, and storage locations;
- Data object transaction integrity;
- The removal of data objects—Data objects cannot be removed without the DBA's knowledge;
- Object storage locations—The database can control object storage locations to optimize performance;
- Database security mechanisms—Database security mechanisms are extended over the storage subsystem; and
- Business policies—Business policies can be controlled through the database.

OptiLink Capabilities

OptiLink features auto discovery, object integrity, optimized read performance, fail-safe architecture, broad support for RDBMs, optical media portability, and information asset protection.

Auto Discovery

OptiLink automatically recognizes a supported optical device by its response to a SCSI inquiry command, and configures itself to the attached device. Supported devices can be handled in any combination and there is no effective limit to the number of platters that can be tracked and managed.

Object Integrity

Maintaining the integrity of the data objects committed to the optical platter is of paramount importance. For this reason, OptiLink writes are accomplished using the *WRITE WITH VERIFY* command with blank-checking enabled. In addition, OptiLink enforces exclusive opens on a given optical device and the routine that commits objects to the platter, and does not return a "good" status until the object *and* its associated metadata information are successfully written to the platter. This allows a platter to be exported from one system and imported to another without requiring additional steps, such as performing a backup or flushing directories.

Optimized Read Performance

To achieve the best performance in reading objects back from the optical subsystem, the object is written sequentially onto the platter and an enhanced read mechanism is utilized to expedite the retrieval of objects.

Fail Safe Architecture

This facility ensures that if the database or its application is inoperable, the stored objects are still accessible through the OptiLink Administration interface.

Broad Support

OptiLink supports all major database systems and a broad range of Write Once Read Many (WORM) and MO optical media from ANSI/ISO 5.25-inch, up to 14-inch formats. Optical devices can be supported in either a standalone mode or a variety of jukebox configurations.

Optical Media Portability

Optical volumes are *self-describing*; thus, platters written on one platform can be "read *and* written" on any other. As client needs become more demanding, the optical drives can be migrated to higher performance server platforms.

Information Asset Protection

Due to the nature of the WORM optical media, all objects committed to storage are protected indefinitely. Additionally,

OptiLink provides for the archival of objects from platters to tape—while the platter remains online.

Architectural Overview

OptiLink is a suite of software components which coordinate on-line optical access requests for large data objects. These requests come from database users or application programs which run on UNIX and Windows NT servers. To provide these capabilities, OptiLink consists of:

- Database storage extender modules;
- Custom device drivers;
- An optical library server (*opmounter*);
- A C library application program interface (*Open/C API*); and
- Optical library administrative tools.

Figure 9–1 illustrates how these components fit together in a database server. Each component is discussed briefly in the following pages and in more detail in the section entitled "OptiLink Components."

The database storage extender modules expand the storage potential of a database by:

- Directly linking into the database server (Informix Dynamic Server/Optical DSA), supporting the storage and retrieval of binary large objects (BLOBs) or TEXT datatypes; and
- Adding a new OPTICAL datatype to object-oriented databases, such as Informix Dynamic Server with Universal Data Option.

These storage extender modules enable the SQL query language to retrieve and store large objects on optical media. The extender to Informix Dynamic Server with Universal Data Option is called a DataBlade module and the extender to IBM's DB2 is called an Extender. Figure 9–2 illustrates the plug-in capabilities of a DataBlade module and how it interfaces with other DataBlade modules that require optical storage.

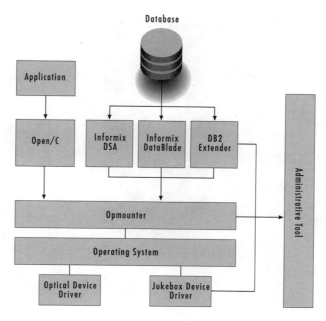

Figure 9–1 *OptiLink components.*

Device drivers provide complete control over optical media and subsystem devices. A complete list of supported devices and libraries is provided at the end of this paper. A single device driver is utilized to control any combination of optical drives. Similarly, a single device driver can control any combination of optical jukeboxes. Drivers support the swapping of an optical device in favor of a different manufacturer's subsystem without a corresponding change to the controlling device driver.

The optical library server, *opmounter*, automatically coordinates the activities of optical libraries and standalone optical drives. It keeps track of the following items:

- Queued optical I/O requests;
- Pieces of optical media currently mounted in an optical drive;
- The location of platters in an optical library;
- The available space on each platter's surface; and
- The status of optical drives.

Opmounter also optimizes media I/O requests and minimizes optical library robotic arm movements. Communication between *opmounter* and database storage extender databases,

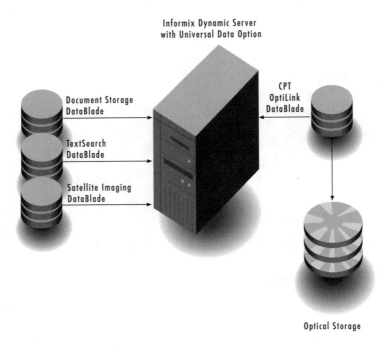

Informix Dynamic Server
with Universal Data Option

Document Storage
DataBlade

TextSearch
DataBlade

Satellite Imaging
DataBlade

CPT
OptiLink
DataBlade

Optical Storage

Figure 9–2 *OptiLink DataBlade module.*

C applications, or administrative tools is achieved through message queues—a UNIX interprocess communication mechanism. As a result, this mechanism enables simultaneous access to optical resources from database storage extender databases, server applications, or tools.

The Open/C module is a library of C callable functions that provides application programs the same media access functionality found in database storage extenders, OptiLink DataBlade module, or DB2 Extender. Applications can be written to store and retrieve large objects, and to control the optical library to import or export optical media. These applications can work in combination with a database storage extender.

A concept fundamental to OptiLink is the identification of optical media—how to tell one piece of media from another. Individual pieces of optical media are uniquely identified by combining a family name, and volume number. The *family name* is an alphanumeric character string grouping one or more pieces of media into a set. The *volume number* identifies

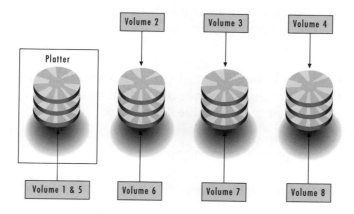

Figure 9–3 Optical platter organization

the members of a family. Depending on how the optical media surface is addressed, either each surface on a piece of optical media receives a volume number or the entire piece of optical media receives just one volume number. Some optical drives have dual read/write heads and both surfaces are treated as one addressable region. Volume numbers are integer values and are sequentially assigned when media is labeled. Figure 9–3 illustrates the Family, Volume concept for an 8-volume family on four (4) optical media or platters.

OptiLink Components

The OptiLink components consist of administrative commands, optical device driver, jukebox device driver, optical file system, OptiLink DSA, OptiLink DataBlade module, and Open/C.

Administration Commands

The administrative commands provided with OptiLink afford the system administrator with complete control over optical libraries and standalone optical drives. Administrators can create named platters, list the file content of a platter, add or remove optical jukeboxes, and import or export platters in an optical jukebox. All commands are available from the UNIX command line and can be incorporated into shell scripts to customize the maintenance of an environment. Following is a complete list of the available commands.

Media Management Commands

Media management commands control optical media.

Table 9–1 *OptiLink media management commands.*

Command	Description
oparchive	On-line archive of optical media. Supports archive levels and allows I/O during the archive.
opcheck	Synchronizes the volume information recorded on optical media with OptiLink media management tables.
opexport	Removes a platter from an optical library or drive.
opimport	Inserts a platter into an optical library or standalone drive.
opinfo	Displays volume information for a mounted platter.
opinventory	Lists the volumes in a jukebox.
oplable	Initializes a platter with a family name and volume number.
opls	Lists the files found on a volume.
opmove	Moves the platter from slot to slot within an optical library.
oprestore	Restores the archived volume using the output from oparchive.
opsamount	Mounts a volume in standalone optical drive.
opsaunmount	Dismounts a volume in a standalone optical drive.
opsize	Displays the free space remaining on an optical volume.
opspindown	Spindowns a platter and enables dismounting.

Mounter Commands

The mounter commands start and stop the OptiLink media manager, opmounter.

Table 9–2 *Mounter commands.*

Command	Description
opmounter	Daemon managing the optical environment.
opqrm, opstop	Halts the mounter daemon, *opmounter*.

Diagnostic Commands

The diagnostic commands diagnose SCSI connections.

Table 9–3 *SCSI diagnostic commands.*

Command	Description
jbmodes	Displays jukebox SCSI mode sense information.
jbset	Sets the jukebox driver diagnostic messaging level.
jbutil	Displays the jukebox element status.
odmodes	Displays the optical drive SCSI mode sense information.
odscan	Scans the optical media that returns written or blank sector locations.
odset	Sets the optical driver diagnostic message level.
odutil	Controls the low-level drive access utility.

Optical Platter Device Driver

The optical platter device driver is a raw character device driver that transparently supports most of the optical platter devices on the market today. This optical device driver can control any of the supported optical drives found in the section entitled "Supported Optical Drives." It is also possible to use this driver to control optical drives from different manufacturers which are connected to the same server at the same time.

Note the following characteristics of the optical platter device driver:

- The device driver recognizes a supported device by its response to the SCSI INQUIRY command and it configures itself to the attached device.

- If the system supports it, the SCSI bus can be reconfigured "on the fly" and the device driver can handle new, supported drives correctly.
- Supported devices can be attached in any combination.
- The Opmounter interface to the drive is the same regardless of the server platform.
- Rather than set drive modes to a (probably undesirable) default, the drive modes are sensed on open() and a copy is stored, so that they can be restored if necessary.
- The optical platter device driver automatically handles most non-fatal check conditions within the device driver; for example, note the following conditions:

  - On a MEDIUM CHANGED, the device driver determines the medium type (rewritable or WORM), the medium capacity, and the current volume label.
  - If the drive is NOT READY and a platter is present, the driver issues a spin-up command and retries the medium access command.

- Drivers support optical volumes up to two (2) terabytes of addressable storage. This is more than enough to handle any optical platter which is likely to be introduced in the near future.

Utilities are provided with the device driver to sense and set drive modes (odmodes), exercise the drive (odutil), scan WORM platters (odscan), determine drive performance (perf), and set the debug and error reporting levels within the device driver (odset).

Jukebox Device Driver

A single jukebox device driver transparently operates with all jukeboxes listed in the section entitled "Supported Jukebox Devices." The jukebox device drive can concurrently manage multiple jukebox subsystems from the same or different manufacturers.

Note the following characteristics of the jukebox device driver:

- Supported devices are recognized by their response to the SCSI INQUIRY command, and the device driver automatically configures itself to the attached devices.
- If the system supports dynamic reconfiguration, the driver can recognize newly configured devices, assuming that they are supported.
- Supported optical subsystems can be connected in any combination.
- The device driver provides a device-independent method of determining certain operations whose implementations vary widely among the supported jukeboxes (for example, extending and retracting the mailbox). There is no need to "hard-wire" jukebox parameters in an application program, nor is it necessary for the applications programmer to understand the jukebox's SCSI implementation detail.
- The device driver automatically handles most non-fatal check conditions within the device driver. No intervention is required by the application program.

Utilities are provided with the device driver to sense jukebox modes (jbmodes), exercise the jukebox (jbutil), and set the debug and error reporting levels within the device driver (jbset).

Optical File System

The optical file system (OFS) describes the format of information on optical media: the volume label, object file format, and directory structure. The structure of this information is similar to the ANSI tape label format, however, it has been modified to allow random access. In the industry, this is commonly referred to as a "Log Based File System." The format of each optical volume is as follows:

- The first sector of each volume contains information that describes the family to which the platter belongs and its volume number within that family;
- Following the first sector are one or more optical objects, each preceded by a one sector descriptor of that object; and
- At the end of the media is the directory structure which grows from the center of the media outward. Each directory entry

contains a one-sector description of an object found on that volume and its location.

Key OFS advantages include the following:

- **Data Integrity**
  - Objects and their metadata are written using WRITE WITH VERIFY. Metadata are written before a commit returns success.
  - The optical volumes are self-describing, that is, all information necessary to access all objects on the platter can be retrieved from the platter.

- **Performance**
  - Objects are written to consecutive sectors so that they can be accessed with a single seek.
  - All outstanding requests for a given volume are satisfied before the volume is removed from the drive.

- **Flexibility**
  - Platters written on any supported platform can be read and written on any other supported platform.
  - Supported jukeboxes and standalone drives can be used in any combination.
  - Volume sizes up to two (2) terabytes are supported. There is no limit on the number of volumes that can be tracked.

OptiLink DSA

OptiLink DSA provides optical storage and retrieval for Informix OnLine/Optical Dynamic Server. OptiLink DSA interfaces with Informix's Optical Application Programming Interface (API), extending the storage capabilities of Informix's BYTE and TEXT datatypes from magnetic storage to optical subsystem storage (OptiLink). The application can continue to store and retrieve BLOBs without any code changes or knowledge that the BLOB data is stored on optical media. OptiLink handles all platter movement and faulting of volumes for reading and writing, thereby providing the user with transparent access to the optical media.

OptiLink DataBlade Module

The OptiLink DataBlade module provides optical storage and retrieval for the Informix Dynamic Server with Universal Data Option. The OptiLink DataBlade module extends the available datatypes by adding a new OPTICAL datatype. This datatype, and the OptiLink DataBlade module functions which support it, are all available at the SQL layer from either a client workstation or the server running Informix Dynamic Server with Universal Data Option. The OptiLink DataBlade module can work in conjunction with other Informix DataBlade modules, thus providing them with on-line optical media access.

The OptiLink DataBlade module provides:

- Storage functions to place large data objects onto optical media;
- Retrieval functions to recall large objects from optical media;
- Administrative functions that enable the explicit control of optical devices;
- Access to optical subsystem content;
- Unified system view for applications; and
- Full access to OptiLink metadata through DataBlade module functions.

Storing and Retrieving Optical Data with the OptiLink DataBlade Module

Using the OptiLink DataBlade module, users can copy data from non-optical storage formats to optical storage, and vice versa, from within an SQL query. The following storage and retrieval functions are used to access and move data objects:

- *Optical* creates an optical object by copying data from a BLOB, or a file, to optical storage. It can also copy an optical object from one location to another location in the optical subsystem.
- *OptToFile* retrieves data from optical storage and copies it to a local server or workstation file.
- *OptToBlob* retrieves data from optical storage and copies it to a BLOB in the database.

Administering Optical Media with the OptiLink DataBlade Module

The OptiLink DataBlade module provides administrative functions that enable the control of the optical environment and which can be used to monitor optical resources. Administrative functions enable the user to perform the following operations:

- *OptLabel* labels platters with optical families and volumes;
- *OptImport* brings a volume into an optical library, making it known to the optical system;
- *OptInfo* obtains information about a volume, such as the family name, available space, and the number of objects stored;
- *OptInventory* obtains information about an entire optical inventory;
- *OptFamily* obtains the family name of a specified optical object;
- *OptVolume* obtains the volume number of a specified optical object;
- *OptSize* obtains the available space remaining on a specified volume; and
- *OptExport* removes a volume from an optical library, and places it on the shelf.

Open/C

Open/C provides applications with a C interface to the OptiLink Storage Server Software. It allows applications to be constructed that store and retrieve objects on optical media. It offers the same level of flexibility as the OptiLink DataBlade module. It supports the Family, Volume concept introduced in the OptiLink DSA and OptiLink DataBlade module products. Objects written in those environments are accessible through Open/C, and the applications written using Open/C can work simultaneously with OptiLink DSA and OptiLink DataBlade module.

Through Open/C, the hierarchical storage management (HSM) or work flow application developer can connect to the OptiLink Server and perform optical I/O. The following list of functions are available for that purpose.

- *cpt_clearVolume* clears the volume number specified by a previous call to *cpt_setVolume*.
- *cpt_close* terminates optical I/O and reduces the media access count.
- *cpt_connect* creates and initializes an OptiLink connection structure.
- *cpt_disconnect* terminates a connection with the OptiLink server.
- *cpt_getFamily* returns the Family name given to a family identifier.
- *cpt_getOpticalOid* returns the current large object's optical object identifier.
- *cpt_getSize* returns the size of a large object in bytes.
- *cpt_optiLinkStatus* determines if the OptiLink daemon opmounter is running.
- *cpt_read* reads an object from optical media.
- *cpt_setFamily* associates a family name with future calls to *cpt_read* or *cpt_write*.
- *cpt_setTimeOut* sets the time limit, in seconds, in which an application is willing to wait for a volume to be mounted in an optical drive.
- *cpt_setVolume* identifies a specific volume within a family of volumes.
- *cpt_write* writes an object onto optical media.

Open/C provides administrative functions that enable the control of the optical environment and which can be used to monitor optical resources. Administrative functions enable the application program to perform the following operations:

- *cpt_export* exports the named volume from an optical library or standalone optical drive.
- *cpt_import* imports the named volume into an optical library or standalone optical drive.
- *cpt_info* returns information about a volume known to OptiLink.
- *cpt_inventory* returns a list of all known pieces of optical media, their family name, volume number, and location.
- *cpt_label* labels an optical platter with a family name and volume number.
- *cpt_ls* lists all of the available objects on an optical volume.

- *cpt_mount* requests opmounter to load a volume into an available optical drive.
- *cpt_unmount* requests opmounter to unload a volume from an optical drive.

Supported Optical Drives

Following are the supported optical drives.

Table 9–4 Supported optical drives.

Manufacturer	Model	Capacity	Size	Media Type
ATG	GD6000	6.5GB	12"	WORM
	GD9000	9.0GB	12"	WORM
	GD9001/s	9.0GB	12"	WORM
Hitachi	OD-152	2.0GB	5.25"	MO/CCW
HP	Corsair1	650MB	5.25"	MO/CCW
	Corsair2	1.3GB	5.25"	MO/CCW
	C1113F/H	2.6GB	5.25"	MO/CCW
IBM	0632 C1x	650MB	5.25"	MO/CCW
	0632 C2x	1.3GB	5.25"	MO/CCW
	0632 CBx	1.3GB	5.25"	MO/CCW/WORM
	0632 CHx	1.3GB	5.25"	MO/CCW/WORM
	0632 C4x	2.6GB	5.25"	MO/CCW
Kodak	6800	10.4GB	14"	WORM
	2000	14.8GB	14"	WORM
LMSI	LD510	650MB	5.25"	WORM
	LD4100	5.4GB	12"	WORM
	LD6100	12GB	12"	WORM
	LF4500	27GB (5 @ 5.4GB)	12"	WORM
	LF6600	72GB (6 @ 12GB)	12"	WORM
MaxOptix	Tahiti I	650MB	5.25"	MO
	Tahiti II	1.0GB	5.25"	MO
	Tahiti IIM	1.0GB	5.25"	MO/CCW
	T3-1300	1.3GB	5.25"	MO/CCW
Nikon	DD-121	8GB	12"	MO
Optimem	600	650MB	5.25"	WORM
	1200M	2.4GB	12"	WORM
	2400	2.4GB	12"	WORM
	4400	3.9GB	12"	WORM
Pioneer	DD-C5001	650MB	5.25"	WORM
Pinnacle	Sierra	1.3GB	5.25"	MO/CCW
	Apex	4.6GB	5.25"	MO/CCW
Sharp	JY-800	1.3GB	5.25"	MO/CCW
Sony	SMO-E501	650MB	5.25"	MO
	SMO-E511	650MB	5.25"	MO/CCW
	SMO-F521	1.3GB	5.25"	MO/CCW
	SMO-541	2.6GB	5.25"	MO/CCW
	WDD-3000	3.25GB	12"	WORM
	WDD-600	6.5GB	12"	WORM
	WDD-931	6.5GB	12"	WORM

Note

CCW is an implementation in which an otherwise rewritable medium is treated as WORM, with the cooperation of the drive firmware. The previous table distinguishes between drives that implement WORM as true ablative WORM (that is, the WORM characteristic is inherent to the medium) and CCW (that is, the WORM characteristic is imposed upon the medium with the cooperation of the drive firmware).

Supported Optical Libraries (Jukebox)

Table 9–5
Supported optical libraries.

Manufacturer	Model	Media	Supported Drives
Cygnet	5250	25 5.25"	1 or 2 LMSI LD510
	ASM-series	22 12"	1 or 2 ATG GD900x. LMSI LD4100, or Nikon DD-121
	1602 (SCSI)	29 12"	1 or 2 LMSI LD4100, ATG GD6000/GD900x, Sony WDD-3000, WDD-600, WDD-931, Nikon DD-121 (MO), or Optimem 2400/4400 drives
	180x (SCSI)	22-141 12"	1-5 LMSI LD4100, ATG GD6000/GD900x, Sony WDD-3000, WDD-600, WDD-931, Nikon DD-121 (MO), or Optimem 2400/4400 drives
DISC	all	47-1054 5.25"	up to 32 drives
DSM	T5500	40 12"	1 or 2 drives
HP	C/T-series	16-144 5.25"	2 or 4 HP Corsair 1 or Corsair 2 drives
	ST-series	32-238 5.25"	up to 6 HP Corsair 2 drives
	FX-series	16-238 5.25"	up to 12 HP C1113F/H drives
IBM	3995	32-144 5.25"	2 or 4 IBM 0632 drives
	3995 c-series	20-258 5.25"	1-4 IBM 0632 C4x drives
Kodak	560E	up to 60 5.25"	1-5 MaxOptix Tahiti II/IIM, Sony SMO-E501, SMO-E511, or IBM 0632 drives
	2000	up to 150 14"	up to 2 Kodak drives
NKK	N-520	20 5.25"	1 or 2 IBM 0632, MaxOptix Tahiti II/IIM, Sony SMO-E501 or SMO-E511 drives
	N-556	56 5.25"	2 MaxOptix Tahiti II/IIM, Sony SMO-E501, or SMO-E511 drives
	N-5160	up to 161 5.25"	2 or 4 MaxOptix Tahiti II/IIM, Sony SMO-E501 or SMO-E511 drives
Plasmon/IDE	7x00	10-20 5.25"	1 drive
	9000	20 5.25"	2 drives
	Multi	20-258 5.25"	1-6 IBM 0632 or Sharp JY-800 drives
	M-series	20-258 5.25"	1-6 Sony SMO-F541 drives
Sony	OSL-2000	20 5.25"	1 or 2 Sony SMO-F521 drives
	WDA-E930	up to 77 12"	1-4 WDD-931 drives

Supported Server Computer Operating Systems

Following are the supported server computer operating systems.

Table 9–6 Supported operating systems.

Hardware	Operating System
Hewlett-Packard	HPUX 9.0.3/9.0.4/9.0.5
	HPUX 10.x
IBM RISC/System 6000	AIX 3.2.x
	AIX 4.1.x
Intel 80386 or 80486 & Pentium	SCO UNIX (3.2.4)
	Solaris 2.x
Windows NT	3.5.1, 4.0 (available 1st quarter 1997)
Sun4c/4m (SCSA)	Solaris 2.x

Acknowledgments

Special thanks to Robert Albertson for his contribution to this article.

Chapter 10

Database Extensibility and Industrial Applications

by Paul Brown

Much of the media attention surrounding Object-Relational Database Management Systems (ORDBMSs) has emphasized the fact that this exciting technology enables systems that manage rich media, such as digital imagery, video, audio, and so on. However, the inspiration for the ORDBMS originated from the need to deal with mainstream commercial data management problems that relational database systems handled poorly. This paper focuses on this idea, and explains why ORDBMS technology is relevant to commercial customers looking to build industrial information systems today. The article explores several examples that demonstrate how Informix Dynamic Server with Universal Data Option, the most scalable and highly functional ORDBMS available on the market, provides new solutions to old data management problems.

Please note that references to other works are indicated by brackets "[...]". For more information about each reference notation, refer to the section at the end of this paper entitled "References."

Introduction

Object-relational, or extensible, database technology clearly represents the next great wave of database innovation. All of the major database vendors are either shipping or have announced products that support the central concepts of ORDBMS technology [STON96]. While the quality of these efforts varies greatly [STON96], the message from customers, analysts, and vendors is clear: ORDBMSs are now here.

The rapid and multi-market interest in this new technology is due to several factors:

- First, the modern enterprise is awash with digital data. Rich content, in the form of documents, digital imagery, video, and audio, is available to everyone with a personal computer. Significant economic advantages accrue to organizations which are able to manage these new media types efficiently [SEY96], [FEGU93].
- Second, it is likely that phenomenon like the World Wide Web (Web) and the Network Computer will drive the demand for the kinds of light client/heavy server configurations which are well suited for ORDBMSs. The defining characteristic of the light client computer is the way in which it can neither store nor process large volumes of data, making it necessary to push complex business logic and processing into the server software. An ORDBMS is an open server that provides developers with a framework to integrate and organize the code that implements application logic.
- Third, object-oriented languages and methodologies have achieved mainstream acceptance in MIS departments. However, OO and RDBMSs do not work together particularly well, so MIS is looking for DBMS technology that is more closely aligned to their client language technology.

The hype surrounding many new "universal" database systems, however, has ignored many potential consumers. Few MIS shops envisage creating multimedia editing applications or video repositories any time soon. Customers who need document management or geographic information systems have probably already invested in technology to meet their immediate needs.

While ORDBMSs are ideally suited to applications like intranet Web sites, these systems do not yet represent the mainstream of MIS applications. For many organizations, there does not seem to be, based on the initial marketing messages, an obvious fit for this technology in applications that make up the mainstream of industrial information management.

In this paper, we provide evidence for the immediate importance of ORDBMS technology to mainstream MIS by illustrating how ORDBMS approaches provide superior solutions to several common DBMS problems. The practical relevance of ORDBMS technology becomes clear when you consider its origins, a story that takes us back to the mid 1980's. At this time, the SQL standards committee mandated that all of the vendor's database languages include support for temporal datatypes; that is, *date* and *time* datatypes and operations which behave like any digital watch and calendar. Unfortunately, the standards committee's efforts were not well received in all quarters. It turns out that many database users have more specialized requirements.

On Wall Street, for example, bonds are traded in twelve blocks of thirty days, making the SQL datetype useless for calculating dividends and yields. Regions of the world where daylight savings time is used, or nations with multiple time zones, found that using the new time datatypes was difficult, at best. Even upon the arrival of SQL-92, these problems persisted. When using the SQL-92 versions of date, time, and both interval types, for example, it is impossible to ask how many days certain conditions have existed—intervals between dates more than 999 days apart cannot be expressed in days—or what the average stay at a hospital is—the datatype returned from (datetime - datetime). Thus, operations vary according to the interval type [DATE94].

The difficulties in managing date and time data are symptoms of deeper problems relating to the way relational database systems (RDBMS) are designed. Early relational database systems were built to compete against the data processing tools that used third-generation languages like COBOL. Even as RDBMS technology began to dominate, facilitating fourth-generation languages, RDBMS vendors had no motivation to consider handling type systems more sophisticated than that required by mainstream business applications. Today, this situation is changing rapidly. The variety and complexity of datatypes found in modern enterprise information systems is exploding. This is partly due to the growing use of rich media datatypes in the modern enterprise mentioned earlier, but it is also due to the mainstream acceptance of object-oriented analysis and design techniques.

Some database vendors have reacted by extending their engines with even more proprietary features. Clearly, this approach cannot be used to solve every customer problem: database companies have neither enough staff nor the necessary in-house expertise to write everyone's applications for them. The most common practice—forced on applications developers because of the inflexibility inherent in monolithic DBMS software—is to write code which runs either in the application's user interfaces or in a separate **third tier** of middleware ("distant-ware" might be a proper term). The database retains its role as repository, but all processing of data occurs in an external process. This "band-aid" approach can lead to higher implementation costs, and causes performance, functional consistency, and administrative difficulties—problems we will now take a moment to explore.

The initial difficulty with implementing external extensions to the database is that this approach requires developers to write a great deal more code. Consider the example which will be examined in more detail in a later section of this paper, entitled "Part Numbers." Part numbers tend to be complex data objects, possessing a multi-part structure which encodes information about the parts they also identify. Further, part number lists often have a natural sort order which conveys intuitive information about relationships between the parts. Often, the sort sequence is quite complex, and frequently includes special cases, if the sorting is to appear natural. Traditionally, application developers have managed part numbers by de-composing the format of the code into several components. Whenever the part number was required in the schema, as a primary or foreign key, this nested sequence of components was repeated. Queries over the part number, even if they were conceptually quite simple, were required to explicitly (and hierarchically) list every one of these components.

For example, the part code may have a component made up of a string where, for sorting, the letters are treated numerically, instead of handled as a single word. For instance, the string 'A' will sort before 'B', but 'AA' will sort after 'Z'. The user's request may be for a sorted list of all part codes between '101-BR' and

'101-ACF'. Solving this problem using traditional relational technology requires developers to write code that runs in middleware, or the client program to perform the desired filtering and sorting. This resembles situations common before relational databases became popular, when developers implemented entire sorting and searching libraries themselves. Sorting and searching routines are subtle, specialist algorithms, so this code tends to be both complex and error prone.

In addition to system quality and programmer productivity considerations, this approach results in poor operational response times and drastically increased network loads. The query which the client sends to the server—in standard SQL—cannot express the range predicate very precisely; thus, more data than is necessary is returned to the client, and often significantly more. Once on the client this data must be filtered, discarding much of the data brought across the wire, and sorted, without the benefit of server parallelism or indexing facilities.

A far better solution is to let users describe to the database the data they want to use, and let the database deal with the details. The database engine provides a framework for storing data and managing queries, including generalized indexing and sorting routines which application developers can hopefully tailor to their needs. For example, sorting algorithms like quicksort [KNU73] require a single comparison operator, LessThan. (The term "less than" alone, can mean many different things—depending on the datatype being processed at the moment.) Most programming languages include this operator for built-in types, and the database engine can legitimately "special case" these for performance. For the types that users define themselves, the same sorting algorithm is used, but at the point of decision, whenever two elements of the list being sorted are compared, a routine supplied by the datatype's definer is called.

This seemingly simple idea has profound consequences. First, it demands that database vendors re-write their engines to make them "open" to user extensions. Second, it can drastically reduce development costs and risk by allowing a production site to write code only once and use it everywhere—code re-use. Third, it is leading to a thriving market in third-party plug-ins to the database server, allowing it to include specialist (domain expert) functionality, directly integrated into the heart of the database server. Finally, it coincides nicely with the advent of the explosive growth of rich media datatypes.

All of these innovations are folded into the "object-relational" database technology, which was pioneered by start-ups like Illustra Technologies early in the 1990s.

This paper uses several practical examples to illustrate how ORDBMS technology overcomes an amazingly large set of common (and always painful) database design problems that have defied any possibility of elegant RDBMS solutions. Along the way, it will be possible to see why the approach of Informix Dynamic Server with Universal Data Option to extensibility is the only one which can reasonably deliver the kinds of solution described in this article.

The examples in this article are all taken from real customer applications and prototypes which use ORDBMS technology. It is important to emphasize at the outset that these are early examples. Once the creative project manager and programmer understand how to use the database's extensibility in this way, they will rapidly realize the potential of ORDBMS technology. The key idea is that an object-relational database system, like Informix Dynamic Server with Universal Data Option, represents the best of both object and relational approaches. The combination of the two within a single system amounts to objects *to the power of relations* (or vice versa).

This paper consists of six examples that show how extensibility is used to solve an otherwise difficult design problem in an industrial application. Each problem is presented in a separate, self-contained section. Within each part, the problem is described, and the current solutions illustrated. Then, the extensible alternative is designed and implemented, before several examples of its use are shown. Where possible, code is included to illustrate the examples.

Fuzzy Searching in Extensible Databases

One of the most common requirements in industrial applications is the ability to perform approximate, or "fuzzy" searches. Often, an application's user has only partial or approximate information to use. In most tele-sales systems for example, a user interacts with customers over the telephone, and must find customer details as quickly as possible.

Customers in this situation rarely have their account code handy, and asking them to spell their names is awkward. All the user has to go on is how the customer pronounced their name. In another example, naïve applications allow users to inconsistently mix-and-match capitalization and punctuation in character fields, but expect them to enter it consistently when retrieving data. Similarly, users may want fast searches where "near enough is good enough." Building systems to meet these requirements has always been a challenge with relational databases.

The most common solution is to write a routine in either the user-interface application or in the middleware that transforms what is typed by the application user into some kind of canonical form. In situations where users have the sound of the name but not the name itself, Soundex() algorithms are popular, and this is the example which this section focuses on. Soundex() algorithms substitute symbols for similar vowel sounds and transform consonants to phonetic families. Thus, 'John', 'Juan', and 'Joan' are all transformed into 'J05', 'Paul' becomes 'P04' and 'Saul' becomes 'S04'. An example of one such algorithm—represented as follows in the 'C' programming language—is shown in Figure 10–1.

Figure 10–1 Soundex Algorithm in 'C'.

```
/*
 *      File: soundex.c
 *
 *      Found at: http://
*/
#include <ctype.h>
#include <stdio.h>
#include <string.h>
#include <stddef.h>
#include <mi.h>

mi_lvarchar *
soundex(intext)
mi_lvarchar * intext;
{                          /* ABCDEFGHIJKLMNOPQRSTUVWXYZ */
    static mi_char *table = "01230120022455012623010202";
```

Figure 10–1 (cont.): Soundex Algorithm in 'C'.

```
    mi_integer count = 0;

    mi_lvarchar * outtext;
    mi_char      * instr,
                 * outstro,
                 * outstr;

    instr = mi_lvarchar_to_string(intext);
    outstro = (mi_char *)mi_alloc(6); /*
      Always returns 6          characters */
    outstr = outstro;
    while(!isalpha(instr[0]) && instr[0])
          ++instr;

    if(!instr[0])      /* Hey!  Where'd the string go? */
            return(NULL);
    if(toupper(instr[0]) ==
      'P' && toupper(instr[1]) == 'H')
    {        instr[0] = 'F';
             instr[1] = 'A';
    }
    *outstr++ = (char)toupper(*instr++);
    while(*instr && count < 5)
    {
  if(isalpha(*instr) && *instr != *(instr-1))
  {
            *outstr = table[toupper(instr[0]) - 'A'];
        if(*outstr != '0')
        {
            ++outstr;
            ++count;
        }

    }
    ++instr;
 }
 *outstr = '\0';
 return(mi_string_to_lvarchar(outstro));
}
```

Several RDBMS vendors have augmented their systems by adding Soundex() functionality to their database query languages, although it is not required by any language standard. This is a small comfort to international customers, who must contend with sounds which are associated with letters that do not reflect American English usage. In any case, the Soundex() example explored in this article is merely one of many similar situations.

Where the vendor's database does not include a function that performs precisely what the customer needs—the vendors' version of Soundex() is inappropriate or the desired function is any of the other multitude not supported by the query language—the following general solution is common. First, the table containing the name being searched is extended by a column where the Soundex() version, or another transformation, is stored. The code shown previously is implemented in each user interface application, for example, in Visual Basic, in 'C' for occasional bulk-loading, and PERL for Web applications. The queries issued by the application use the transformed version of the name against the extra column, and an index may then be built over this extra column to speed up these queries. This situation is illustrated in Figure 10–2.

Figure 10–2: Conventional solution to storing Soundex.

```
CREATE TABLE Customer
( Customer_Id    integer      NOT NULL     PRIMARY KEY,
  Surname               varchar(60) NOT NULL,
  FirstName             varchar(48) NOT NULL,
  Initials      varchar(4)   NOT NULL,
  Area_Code             varchar(6)   NOT NULL,
  Phone_Number  varchar(12) NOT NULL,
  Soundex_Name  varchar(10) NOT NULL
);
SELECT *
  FROM Customer C
  WHERE C.Surname = 'Stuger'
  AND C.FirstName = 'Lary';
 SELECT *
  FROM Customer C
  WHERE C.Soundex_Name = 'L5678';
```

There are several problems with this approach. First, it requires considerable effort to retrofit this facility to an existing system, and the pattern must be repeated for every table where a Soundex() query is necessary. Second, once the solution outlined above is in place, maintaining identical algorithms in several different languages is a burden. Changing the Soundex() algorithm often requires re-writing it in several languages. Third, the extra columns add to the tuple's width, which negatively impacts scan times and overall performance. Collectively, these difficulties mean that a fuzzy search makes sense if it is not part of the application's functionality; thus, the cost of implementing and maintaining can exceed the benefits.

A better solution can be to allow developers to define the Soundex() function once in the database, and reuse it thereafter.

In an ORDBMS, like Informix Dynamic Server with Universal Data Option, an algorithm may be added to the database as a user defined routine (UDR). The code shown in Figure 10–1 can be compiled into a special kind of file called *a shared binary*. Then, the function is declared to the database using syntax such as that shown in Figure 10–3(a). Once this is accomplished, the function can be used in queries similar to the one shown in Figure 10–3(b). Note that the result of the Soundex(String) function need not be another String. In an OR database, it could well be its own special datatype, which obeys its own version of Equals and has its own indexing; this is an idea explored in greater detail in a later section of this paper.

When a third-party software vendor, a specialist in Soundex() processing, implements their own datatype and functions to facilitate the solution described above, the vendor may market it as a DataBlade™. This simply means that the Soundex() function is written once and can be re-used by other developers who purchase the DataBlade.

Suppose we are running a query which returns the Soundex() versions of every name in the table. If the extra column adds 10 percent to the width of the tuple, then it adds 10 percent to the table's scan time. If there are 1,000,000 records in the table, and there are 25 records per page, then there are 40,000 pages in the table. At ten milliseconds per page for I/O and processing, this means that a complete sequential scan will take about 400 seconds. Adding 10 percent to the column width, the scan time becomes 440 seconds. On the other hand, the Soundex() function itself will probably take about five microseconds per record to run. Adding an extra processing time of 25×5 microseconds per page adds 0.125 milliseconds to the page's I/O and processing, which makes the time taken to scan the table and process each tuple 405 seconds. Clearly, this result will vary, depending on the computational cost of the UDR and the extra columns addition to the tuple's width. The point is that disk reads are usually measured in milliseconds, while the execution time of a 'C' routine is typically in the microseconds. This means that it is frequently more efficient to calculate results than to store them redundantly.

Figure 10–3: a) Function creation and b) Function usage in a query over the schema in Figure 10–2.

```
—
— DDL to create the Function
—
CREATE FUNCTION Soundex(lvarchar)
RETURNS lvarchar
EXTERNAL NAME
  '$INFORMIXDIR/extend/Soundex/src/soundex.bld(soundex)'
LANGUAGE C;
—
GRANT EXECUTE ON FUNCTION Soundex(lvarchar) TO PUBLIC;
—
—  Schema creation.
—
CREATE ROW TYPE Name_Type
(        Surname   lvarchar,
         FirstName lvarchar
);
—
CREATE TABLE Names
OF TYPE Name_Type;
—
INSERT INTO Names
VALUEs
('Brown','Paul');
```

```
—
SELECT  Soundex(Surname)
  FROM Names;
—
SELECT  *
  FROM Names
  WHERE Soundex(Surname)  =  Soundex("Brown");
—
```

Typically, the extra record width is justified on the grounds that it allows database administrators to create an index over the column. This means that the database does not need to scan the entire table queries, which include lines in the WHERE clause that mention the extra column, as the last query in Figure 10–2. Instead, the ORDBMS can look up matching records using the index.

With Informix's ORDBMS, developers can have the best of both worlds. They can create what is called a *functional index* over the table. This means that the results of a function like Soundex() is used to construct an index—hash or B-tree—which the optimizer could use when the function is mentioned in the WHERE clause of a query, as in the last query in Figure 10–3. Figure 10–4 illustrates how to create this kind of index. As new records are added to the table, or as name values are updated, the index is maintained as any other index would be. The query in Figure 10–3(b) then becomes an index look-up, greatly improving the query response time and reducing the total resources required. The functional index is unique to the Informix's ORDBMS. It is a powerful feature, essential for the efficient processing of queries in an object-relational database.

```
CREATE INDEX Names_Ndx ON Names(Soundex(Surname)) ;
SELECT N.FirstName, N.Surname
  FROM Names N
  WHERE Soundex(N.Surname) = Soundex('Brown');
```

Simply upgrading an existing RDBMS, such as Informix Dynamic Server, to Informix Dynamic Server with Universal Data Option, makes these facilities available to developers. Other situations where this kind of technique can be applied include functions to make capitalization and punctuation consistent (although a better approach here would be to handle this as a special datatype and implement these consistency checks in the type's creation method), functions to capitalize a string or make it all lower case, functions to format objects like names into formal, semiformal, informal, and so on. Adding this functionality to the engine simplifies the overall system, improves performance by reducing both the amount of data which must be stored on disk, and the amount of data which must be moved across the network, and developer productivity.

The architecture of the Universal Data Option gives it several technical advantages over the solutions other vendors are beginning to propose. Because the Universal Data Option integrates the new function *into* the server, the overhead associated with calling the new Soundex() function is minimized. Other ORDBMSs must call the new routine through an Inter-Process Communication (IPC) mechanism, like Remote Procedure Calls (RPCs), which adds several orders of magnitude to the call overhead [GRRE95]. Further, using specialist external facilities and accessing them through Common Object Request Broker Architecture (CORBA) presents severe difficulties to enforcing transactions, and physical and logical schema consistency. Finally, these alternative, middleware approaches cannot provide the same levels of functional integration that can be achieved through the more difficult core server extensibility approach.

A Soundex() function can be used just like any of the SQL built-in functions: in SELECT or WHERE clauses, in sub-queries and UNIONs, or as a join predicate between two tables. For MIS managers and developers who have grappled with this problem, extensible database technology like Informix's Universal Data Option provides new and compelling technical solutions to this difficult business problem.

Parts Number Management

Many computer systems automate the management of data which is integral to the efficient operation of some real world system. For example, location codes and part numbers are important to inventory control or in the managing of a manufacturing process. A large warehouse may contain millions of items and tens of thousands of distinct classes of items. These items are distributed throughout the warehouse so as to make the tasks of accepting shipments for storage and generating shipments from inventory as efficient as possible. To do this, special strings in the inventory system are designed to encode the physical location of parts within the warehouse. In manufacturing, parts used to construct larger and more complex pieces of equipment are identified using strings which encode information about each part's manufacture, its place in the overall design, or even a description of the part. Code designers sometimes create rules distinguishing legal codes from data entry errors. Credit card numbers, for example, have an internal structure which allows a complex algorithm to detect and reject illegal numbers before they are added to the database.

The sort order of a list of these codes can represent relationships between the things that the codes identify. Meeting an order from the warehouse requires generating a "pick list" which is an ordered list of location codes. The sequence of these codes is significant to the warehouse worker because it describes the route to be taken in loading the truck. In manufacturing applications, this sequence can show what parts are similar or give some idea of the manufacturing process. Because of the complex internal structure of these data objects, sorting them into the correct order requires more than simply ordering the strings based on their character representation. For example, using upper case letters as a base 26 numbering system—i.e., a system where 'A' < 'Z' < 'AA'—is impossible using conventional string sorting. Further, the process of allocating a new code is complicated by the way the algorithm needs information about what the code identifies or describes.

Developers trying to solve this fairly common data management problem with conventional RDBMS technology have faced a number of performance and functionality challenges. Users often need to retrieve all items within some range of part codes and display them in sorted order. Also, because these codes identify entities in the schema, they are often used in the queries used to join tables, which record facts about the entities.

Common RDBMS solutions to this data modeling problem include laboriously decomposing the string into its components and writing SQL to enforce the schema constraints and get the queries correct. Alternatively, all the data can be moved from the database to the client side or into a middleware layer for sorting, searching, and further processing. As we have seen, this approach leads to additional complexity and development cost, renders maintaining the schema an economic burden, and limits the overall performance of the information system. Object-relational technology offers another solution which resolves all of these difficulties.

In an ORDBMS like Informix's, developers can extend the set of datatypes used to define a table's columns in a schema. This is best accomplished with a fast, powerful 3GL like 'C' or Java. The database engine's core extensibility allows developers to express complex behavior in low-level languages and encapsulate this complexity behind an interface which is surfaced as part of the ad-hoc query language. One of the key insights of object-oriented approaches to software engineering is that by hiding the complex structure and behavior of data objects behind this kind of high-level interface leads to higher productivity and improves software quality.

In this way, user-defined abstract datatypes improve the performance and quality of the information system. Firstly, by placing code that implements object behavior closer to the data, Informix Dynamic Server with Universal Data Option avoids the Inter-Process Communication (IPC) and data transfer overhead necessary in middleware or client-side execution of data management code.

Second, using an object abstraction to deal with user defined datatypes means that database developers are able to present a more intuitive view of the problem domain to application developers; the SQL in user interface programs is simplified and the productivity of application development engineers thereby improved. User defined datatypes and functions are central to the object-relational database approach of Informix Dynamic Server with Universal Data Option. Sets of related user defined datatypes and functions can be bundled together into a DataBlade. This bundling mechanism is how third-party domain experts can re-sell their expertise to a broad range of application developers.

To explore these ideas, we will develop a solution to the part codes problem faced by a hypothetical car manufacturer. A big part of this organization's business is bound up in manufacturing and stocking car parts, both for assembling new vehicles, and to supply mechanics who repair vehicles owned by consumers. In managing its manufacturing processes, the company tries to minimize the number of distinct kinds of parts it needs to build, and the total number of parts it produces. It does this first by re-using parts in the assembly of several different vehicles and second, by trying to estimate how many of each part to produce. The challenge faced by the manufacturer is to arrive at an efficient information systems approach to the managing of parts data.

The manufacturer's planners define a part code that mimics certain features of its manufacturing process. This part code must be readable. A knowledgeable user, who is familiar with the way information is encoded in the string, can compare two part code instances and make sense of an ordered list of part codes. Figure 10–5 presents the definition of the part code.

Figure 10–5: Part numbers.

```
number := 0|1|2|3|4|5|6|7|8|9;
part_segment := [number number number];
letter := A|B|C|D|E|F|G|H|I|G|J|L|M|N|O|P|Q|R|S|T|U|V|W|X|Y|Z;
part_supplement := letter[{letter}];
part_number := part_segment ' ' part_segment ' ' part_segment
[ ' ' part_supplement ];
Examples;
   '151 831 155'
   '151 832 156 A'
   '151 832 156 B'
   '151 832 156 AA'
   '161 832 157 NM'
   '162 832 157 NM'
```

The left three numbers indicate the make and model of the vehicle for which the part is initially intended. Later models may re-use entire assemblies from previous vehicles. The middle three numbers indicate the primary sub-assembly (body, engine core, electrical system), and the last three digits indicate what sub-part of the sub-assembly we are dealing with (panel, inch screws, battery). The final optional characters indicate manufacturing runs of a part; if a manufacturing process changed but a part's design and role does not, this is shown by the addition of the final letters. What is most interesting is that the part numbers in Figure 10–5 are presented in sorted order as they appear in a parts list. According to the manufacturing view, the middle three parts of the part number are the most significant, then the final three, and then the suffix string, if it exists. The first three numbers are the least significant. The part_supplement component in the part code is an example of the "base 26" representation introduced earlier in this article.

In Informix Dynamic Server with Universal Data Option, this part code is handled by creating a User Defined Type (UDT). Defining behavior for this type requires specifying several User

Defined Routines (UDRs). These functions can be surfaced as an SQL interface, or are used by internal DBMS facilities like generic sorting, indexing, and aggregation. This integration of UDTs and UDRs into the server's relational framework is one way that the object-oriented approaches to software engineering have influenced object-relational database systems. You can think of the UDT/UDR additions as a new *class of objects* which the server stores and performs queries over. For the remainder of this section, we will explore how this is accomplished in the case of the part code described previously. First, we will briefly discuss the tools a user would employ. Then, we will illustrate the example with several important code segments. Finally, we will show the SQL which an application developer would write to use the datatype in a small sample schema and in queries over that schema.

Creating a new datatype for Informix Dynamic Server with Universal Data Option involves some effort. The more information about the new datatype and its behaviors that the developer can give the server, the better the job that the engine can do to efficiently manage queries. Informix ships a DataBlade Developers Kit (DBDK), which takes the tedium out of the process. In the case of the part code defined in Figure 10–5, the DBDK wizard can be used to create the function stubs required by the DBMS in 'C'. The most difficult aspect of integrating user defined routines is getting the function headers, the arguments, order, and the handling of return values right. So DBDK automates as much of this as possible. DBDK also creates the platform-specific makefiles, and SQL scripts to create the new extensions in the database. Developers supply code which runs in the function stubs.

Prototyping the new datatype and functions in SQL/SPL is generally a good idea. A UDT and the functions declaring its behavior can be written using a mix of SQL-3 DDL to create the type, and Informix's Stored Procedure Language (SPL) to create the functions. Informix SPL is a small procedural language, historically used to create database procedures, but is reused in Informix Dynamic Server with Universal Data Option as a quick way to develop user defined routines. SPL affords all of the well known benefits of rapid application prototyping; iterative feedback, parallel development, clarification of objectives, and so forth. Once the type's implementation in SQL/SPL is finalized, it can be used to generate testing scripts and detailed functional specifications for developers who will work in 'C'. The code in Figure 10–6 is an example of what the Part Number datatype would look like in SQL/SPL.

Figure 10–6: SQL/SPL implementation of the VW part number datatype.

```
—
— User Defined Row type for the Part Code described in
— Figure 3.1
—
CREATE ROW TYPE Part_Code
( Vehicle_Code        integer      NOT NULL,
  Major_Assembly      integer      NOT NULL,
  Minor_Assembly      integer      NOT NULL,
  Process                    char(10)
 );
```

It is possible that the SQL/SPL implementation of the datatype is entirely adequate to solve the business problem—if the new datatype does not have particularly complex behavior which requires a 3GL like 'C' and the datatype fits comfortably onto a data page, for example. On the other hand, the cost of calling and running an SPL routine is quite high, relative to the cost of calling and running a 'C' routine. Further, in applications where there may be millions of parts, indexing this user defined type is clearly necessary. Implementing the new type in a 3GL like 'C' resolves these problems. 'C' routines can be called with very little overhead, making them more efficient than SPL routines.

DBDK can be used to generate the C stubs for the 3GL implementation of the Part Number type. The bodies of these functions must be filled in by the developer. For others, the developer may accept the defaults, or DBDK understands enough to know it can implement several functions by having them call a single routine and using that routine's return result to determine what they should return. For example, the ordinal operator functions—LessThan(), LessThanorEqual(), Equal(), GreaterThan(), GreaterThanorEqual(), NotEqual()—can be implemented by simply calling a single function: Compare(). Compare() returns -1 where its first argument is 'LessThan' is second, 0 when they are Equal, and 1 otherwise. The Compare() function is used in B-tree indexing, while LessThan() is used in sorting and operations which merge-join tables together. All these functions can also be called explicitly from SQL.

For many functions, like those handling client/server communications, database backup and data export, developers can usually use the functions DBDK generates by default. In unusual cases, the developer needs to overwrite these defaults for efficiency reasons, or because they have used unusual data structures which encode information at the bit level.

In Figure 10–7, we show the header for the data structure, the 'C' code used to implement the PartNumberOut() function, and the Compare() function. This code is compiled, and used to create a shared object. In Figure 10–8, we illustrate the DDL used to define this new type to the database.

Figure 10–7: Structure for part number, 'C'' code for PartNumberOut() and Cmp().

```
/*
 *   File: PartCode.h
 *
 */
typedef struct _PartCode
{
  vehicle int,
  major   int,
  minor   int,
  process char[11]
} PartCode;

/*
 *   PartCodeOut
 *
 * Part of the definition of a new user defined opaque
```

```
* type is the creation of a routine to format the
* 'on-disk' data into a publicly readable format.
*
*/
mi_lvarchar *
PartCodeOut( pPartCode )
PartCode * pPartCode;
{
  char    pChar[128];

  sprintf(pChar,"%d-%d-%d",
          pPartCode->vehicle,
          pPartCode->major,
          pPartCode->minor);
  if (pPartCode->process)
  {
    sprintf(pChar,"%s-%d",
                  pChar, pPartCode->process);
  }

  return (mi_string_to_lvarchar(pChar));
}
/*
* PartCmp
*
*   In order to use the generalized b-tree indexing that
*   the Informix Dynamic Server with Universal
*   Data Option provides for user defined
*   datatypes, the developer needs to define a function
*   similar to strcmp().


*
*   TypeCmp(A,B) returns -1 iff. A < B, 0 iff. A = B and
*   1 iff. A > B. This function, in a sense, defines the
*   ordering of the datatype.
*/
```

Figure 10–7 (cont.): Structure for part number, 'C" code for PartNumberOut() and Cmp().

```
mi_integer
PartCodeCmp( pPCa, pPCb )
PartCode * pPCa;
Partcode * pPCb;
{

}
```

The code shown in Figure 10–7 is compiled into a shared object, which is linked to the database kernel the first time when an implemented function is used in this code.

Figure 10–8: DDL to declare the new type and functions to the server.

```
–
– The DDL to create the functions used by the SQL
– language interface.
–
– The first function is the TypeOut() function. This takes
– an instance of the type's internal representation, and
– returns a string for public consumption; to appear in a
– column as the result of a query, for example.
–
CREATE FUNCTION PartNumberOut(PartNumber)
RETURNS lvarchar
EXTERNAL NAME '$INFORMIXDIR/extend/PartCode/bin/\
PartCode.bld(PartNumberOut)'
LANGUAGE C;

–
– This is the Compare() function, which is used by the
– engine to create a b-tree index over the new type.
–
CREATE FUNCTION Compare(PartNumber, PartNumber)
```

Figure 10–8 (cont.): DDL to declare the new type and functions to the server.

```
RETURNS integer
EXTERNAL NAME '$INFORMIXDIR/extend/PartCode/bin/\
PartCode.bld(PartNumberCmp)'
LANGUAGE C;
—
```

Once the new type and the functions which operate over it are defined, they can be used in a schema. These new types are equivalent in every respect to the built-in datatypes that ship with the core engine in terms of their use. In the Informix Dynamic Server with Universal Data Option, operators like 'Equal()' are mapped by the SQL parser to their corresponding symbol ("="). The engine's generic sorting algorithm is able to make use of the LessThan() function to sort a list of values into the desired order. If the type has a Hash() method defined for it, then the engine can use the advanced join and GROUP BY techniques which employ hashing. Figure 10–9 illustrates how this type can be used with a small schema and queries.

Figure 10–9: Schema and queries using part number.

```
—
— This schema is an example of how the Part Number
— defined above may be used in a database schema.
—
CREATE TABLE Parts
( Id      PartNumber  NOT NULL    PRIMARY KEY,
  Name          lvarchar    NOT NULL,
  Cost          US_Dollars  NOT NULL
);
—
— 'Show me a sorted list of all parts worth less than
—  $100.'
```

Figure 10–9 (cont.): Schema and queries using part number.

```
—
SELECT Id
 FROM Parts P
 WHERE P.Cost < '$US100'
 ORDER BY Id;
—
— The functions which users can add to operate over the
— new type may include facilities to get and set
— elements of the complex data structure. This query shows
— how a function like GetAssembly(PartNumber) might work.
—
— 'Show me all the parts with cost that go into making
— the engine, order by Id'
—
SELECT P1.Id, P1.Cost
   FROM Parts P1, Parts P2
   WHERE P2.Name = 'Engine'
   AND GetAssembly(P2.Id) = GetAssembly(P1.Id)
   ORDER BY P1.Id;
—
```

The example shown here is only an indication of what is possible with the type and function extensibility of Informix Dynamic Server with Universal Data Option. Other sections of this article will indicate how this basic technique can be applied to many other kinds of situations. When adding user defined types and routines, there are many other factors the developer needs to consider. These factors include:

1 Function cost. Not all functions are created equal. So-called "expensive" functions which perform operations over large data objects, or which consume considerable amounts of CPU time, need special handling by the optimizer to ensure that they are executed as few times as possible in any query execution plan.

2. An extensible database provides new solutions to the problem of missing data, which is handled within SQL-92 by the NULL

value and three-value logic. Information may be missing for many reasons. It may be either unknown, not yet available, or simply not entered due to user error. The design of the datatype may take this into consideration and provide for data states that reflect each of these. Operations which compare instances of datatypes must be extended to deal with missing information.

3. Allowing the engine to use an index over the new datatype is important, but it is almost as important to allow the engine to know when *not* to use the index. This involves supplying the statistics gathering and selectivity estimation functions associated with the UDT that the optimizer uses to create query execution plans.

4. The size of the new datatype affects its implementation. Small data objects which fit entirely on a data page should be implemented that way for greater efficiency. However, larger objects which are accessed less frequently may be stored off the tuple.

It is interesting to note that the relational model as defined by Ted Codd [CODD71] does not explore what it means by the concept of a *domain*. As originally envisioned, columns of tables in a relational database were not typed to numbers or strings, but were associated with a domain of values. Because it allows implementers to use complex datatypes as column types, the object-relational data model is considered by some [DATE96] to be simply a more complete implementation of the model described by Codd. However, subsequent writings about Codd's relational model focused on issues like correct schema design; keys, constraints, normal forms, and so on. The original relational model contains nothing to assist the analysis and design of domains, a task which is ideally suited for object-oriented analysis and design.

Temporal Queries

In this section, we will explore how an object-relational database system can be used to speed up a common but difficult problem—temporal queries. Information systems which auto-mate reservation systems—hotel and motel room booking systems, for example—typically need to record the time or date interval of the reservation. A reservation record in a hotel reservation system records the room number, a check-in date, and a check-out date. The data in this system is used in OLTP queries like "Find rooms which are empty between two dates" and decision-support queries, like "How many rooms were reserved for such-and-such a date?" Other industrial applications that exhibit this kind of problem include airline reservation systems, workflow or process scheduling, and systems which track periods of activity or intervals where contracts apply.

There are two principle difficulties encountered when dealing with this kind of data. If the problem domain being addressed by the database system includes temporal problems, creating the schema and writing queries, such as those introduced previously, can become awkward. In the conventional solution to this problem, the database stores both the start and end dates in separate columns of a table. These two attributes are really impossible to separate: the one is meaningless without the other, constraints exist over values in the two columns, and if one attribute is used in a query, then the other is always used too. An example of the conventional solution to this problem can be seen in Figure 10–10.

Figure 10–10: Conventional solution. a) Schema. b) Several Queries. c) Join Query.

```
—
—   Reservations table
—
CREATE TABLE Reservations
(   Room_Id                 integer     NOT NULL,
    Start_Date      date        NOT NULL,
    End_Date        date        NOT NULL
    CHECK ( Start_Date <= End_Date )
);
—
—   Rooms Reserved 'now'
—
```

```
SELECT Room_Id
 FROM Reservations
 WHERE 'now' BETWEEN Start_Date AND End_Date;
 —
 — Rooms reserved between date_1 and date_2.
 —
SELECT R.Room_Id
 FROM Reservations R
 WHERE R.Start_Date BETWEEN 'date_1' AND 'date_2'
 AND R.End_Date    BETWEEN 'date_1' AND 'date_2';
 —
 — Join example. Find all reservations which overlap
 — the reservation for Room 5.
 —
SELECT R1.Room_Id
 FROM Reservations R1, Reservations R2
 WHERE R2.Room_Id = 5
 AND NOT (( R2.End_Date < R1.Start_Date)
    OR  ( R2.Start_Date > R1.End_Date  ));
```

When writing a complex query, this approach is cumbersome and complex. The CHECK constraint must be repeated each time that the date range columns are used in the schema, and enforcing this constraint in a declarative database engine is clearly less efficient than enforcing it in an encapsulated object. Additional constraints make creating a table even more cumbersome—consider a table containing two of these date ranges which not overlap. The queries in Figure 10-10 are either verbose or subtle in their details. For example, the join query requires that the developer understand several logical laws in order to write the query into the form presented here. While the intuitive specification of the query is clear, the limited type system of SQL makes it difficult to translate the intuition into clear code.

But the second, more profound problem with queries of this kind is related to performance, and is best illustrated by exploring how the queries in Figure 10–10(a) must be evaluated. A database optimizer may scan the entire table and evaluate the BETWEEN predicate over each record, although this is probably impractical for large tables. If a B-tree index exists over either the START_DATE or END_DATE, then the optimizer can use the index to reduce the number of tuples which it needs to check. In this situation, however, the optimizer is obliged to evaluate half the tuples in the index (on average), which means that the optimizer will almost always choose to scan the table anyway.[1] Although it is possible to create a single composite index containing both attributes, realizing that this index can be used to evaluate the entire predicate requires additional complexity and, therefore, pathlength in the optimizer. In addition, the Overlaps() query introduced in Figure 10–10, because it contains an OR, cannot use any indexing scheme very effectively.

For a more thorough examination of the issues relating to query processing with non-ordinal predicates, refer to [DATE94a].

Extensible or object-relational databases provide solutions to both the problem of language complexity and performance. Creating a datatype which encapsulates the interval data and operations reduces the complexity of both the DDL and SQL, which uses the type to make the schema and queries more intuitive. Further, because extensible database systems, like Informix Dynamic Server with Universal Data Option, support a feature called object-indexing, appropriate kinds of index can be constructed over this data, so that queries which include the datatype can be accelerated. Informix Dynamic Server with Universal Data Option is open to other access methods to support specialist indexing of very unusual datatypes.

The remainder of this section will illustrate how to create this datatype—including the routines necessary for indexing—and show its use.

Figure 10–11 specifies the datatype, and several operators over it. These operations are surfaced as SQL functions, which can be used as SQL statements. In the Informix Dynamic Server with Universal Data Option, function names can be overloaded, with

---

[1] If half of the tuples in the index satisfy the predicate, and there are more than four tuples per page, it follows that the executor will probably have to read every data page. Under these circumstances, the optimizer will probably elect to scan, to gain the advantages of chunked I/O and scan parallelism.

the resulting ambiguity resolved by examining the parameter types.

Figure 10–11: Specification of the DateInterval datatype and several operations.

```
DateInterval  :=   (StartDate  Date, EndDate Date);

Contains (A DateInterval, B DateInterval)
RETURN    ((B.StartDate > A.StartDate)  AND (B.EndDate <
      A.EndDate));

Overlaps (A DateInterval, B DateInterval)
RETURNS NOT ((B.EndDate < A.StartDate) OR (B.StartDate >
      A.EndDate));
```

The details regarding how this type should be implemented using 'C' are beyond the scope of this article. Several alternatives exist. Because this type is limited to days, simply store the two dates as integer days. Appropriate methods could be written which would take the integer and return the string corresponding to the date. Alternatively, you could store the start date and an integer reflecting the number of days for the duration of the interval. A third possibility would be simply to re-use a third-party code library which implements date arithmetic.

Constraints over the new datatype can be enforced in the code which creates instances of the type. Part of creating a new type involves writing a function to take the type's public format—a string like '02-12-97 to 02-15-97'—and turning it into the type's internal storage format. Constraints like the one enforced by the CHECK syntax in Figure 10–10(a) can be checked in this function. Constraint violations can be handled by generating an exception which causes the database server to report an error message to the client and optionally rolls back the transaction. Operations like Contains() and Overlaps() can be used in SQL queries, instead of expressions that combine more primitive operators and directly address multiple columns. Once created, this type can be re-used in several tables, reducing the overall code required. If a specialized kind of interval must be created, one where both the START_DATE and END_DATE need to be within a certain range, then a DISTINCT version of the interval type can be created which has some kind of declarative constraint.

Creating this type would replace the code in Figure 10–10 with the code in Figure 10–12.

```
—
— Schema and queries identical to what is shown in Figure
— 4.1, only using the new DateInterval datatype and the
— functions defined over it.
—
CREATE TABLE Reservations
( Room_Id        integer          NOT NULL,
  DurationDateIntervalNOT NULL
);
—
SELECT Room_Id
  FROM Reservations
  WHERE Contains('now'::DateInterval, Duration);
—
SELECT R1.Room_Id
  FROM Reservations R1, Reservations R2
  WHERE R2.Room_Id = 5
  AND Overlaps(R1.Duration, R2.Duration);
—
```

Note that in Figure 10–12, the second query *casts* the date datatype to the DataInterval datatype. In Informix Dynamic Server with Universal Data Option, datatypes can be cast from one to the other by running them through a user defined routine. In this example, a function must be written which takes a date datatype and returns a DateInterval. Through the CREATE CAST syntax, users notify the database that it can use this function whenever necessary to cast between the datatypes. Casting between datatypes is an important facility in a strongly typed object-relational system. Features like user defined datatypes, functions, and casts simplify queries, and bring query language expressions closer to the intuitive intention of the query.

The second way in which Informix Dynamic Server with Universal Data Option helps to solve this problem is in the indexing options built into the server. Indexing this kind of user defined datatype requires that the database support object-indexing. Several access methods are supported by Informix Dynamic Server with Universal Data Option: hash, b-tree and r-tree. Any of these index structures can be used if the definer of the new datatype provides a set of functions—called an *operator class*—which the database can apply in generic indexing routines. This article indicated how the Compare() function could be used to build a b-tree routine. In the case of the DateInterval datatype, we can apply the r-tree access method. Instances of DateInterval datatypes can be thought of as line segments, or collapsed rectangles. The r-tree access method is most generally applied to index spatial data in two and three dimensions but the operations it can accelerate, Contains(), Within(), and Overlaps(), apply here.

The server requires seven functions to use r-trees to index a user defined datatype. Exactly how these seven functions are used is beyond the scope of this article. Readers should consult [GUTT84]. These functions are as follows:

```
Overlap(Type, Type) RETURNS boolean ;
```

This function returns true if the arguments Overlap. This function is defined in Figure 10–11.

```
Equal(Type, Type) RETURNS boolean;
```

This function returns true if the arguments have equal value. It may be defined for the DateInterval type as follows:

```
Equal   (A DateInterval, B DateInterval)
RETURN  ((A.StartDate = B.StartDate) AND (A.EndDate =
        B.EndDate));
```

The Contains function is defined in Figure 10–11.

```
Contains(Type, Type) RETURNS boolean;
```

The Within() function is the commutator of the Contains()
function.

```
Within(Type, Type) RETURNS boolean;

Within  (A DateInterval, B DateInterval)
RETURN  ((B.StartDate >= A.StartDate) AND
          (B.EndDate <= A.EndDate));
```

These four functions are those which the database optimizer
knows it can use in an R-tree index. There are other functions
like Outside() and Disjoint() which can be re-written as NOT
Within() and NOT Overlaps(), respectively. Knowledge about
what functions can be re-written as negations of others must be
provided by the type's developer. Thus, when the database parser
sees a predicate like Outside(), it generates a query plan in terms
of the operations it can perform indexing over. For reasons of efficiency, these functions are best implemented in a low-level language like 'C' or 'C++', to reduce execution time and calling
overhead.

In addition to these functions, the database engine requires
four support functions to manage operations within the R-tree.
These functions include the following:

```
Union(Type,Type,Type) RETURNS Type;
Size(Type) RETURNS double precision;
Inter(Type,Type,Type) RETURNS Type;
Hilbert(Type) RETURNS integer;
```

These functions are used for operations within the r-tree, split-
ting nodes, merging nodes, and so on. The Hilbert() function is
used by the engine to build r-tree indices more efficiently,
through a 'bottom-up' approach, than what is possible using an
iterative insert strategy.[2] All support functions should also be
written in 'C'. When a user specifies that an r-tree index is to be
built over a column of this datatype, the database finds the

---

[2] The Hilbert() function is not used at this time and parallel, bottom-up builds of R-
tree structures are not part of the Informix Dynamic Server with Universal Data
Option's core functionality.

functions it needs in the system catalogs. Then, it uses these functions in the generic r-tree (built into the engine) to construct the index.

Indexing user-defined datatypes to accelerate queries is an important feature for an object-relational database to support. While the majority of new types will be able to use the kinds of b-tree indexing illustrated earlier in this article, there will be some datatypes which require more sophisticated access methods. Some of these datatypes will need to employ indexing structures which the engine does not supply. In [HNA95], the authors describe GiST, a generic interface which allows for the specification of user-defined access methods. An object-relational database must be open so that users can build their own specialist access methods, or buy them from third-party vendors. Many searching structures have been described: quad-trees, kdb-trees, etc. [SAMET94]. Informix Dynamic Server with Universal Data Option is unique among object-relational databases in that it supports object indexing and access method extensibility.

This paper has demonstrated how datatype extensibility works to solve the specific problem of temporal datatypes and queries over them. Datatype extensibility simplifies the schema creation scripts and SQL queries which implementers need to write. Using a technique called object indexing, the performance problems associated with this kind of query are also solved. Support for temporal queries is one application of object indexing, but there are many others. Many objects are fundamentally multidimensional; geo-spatial objects, voice prints, and so on. Unstructured data, like document datatypes, require specialized data structures to speed up queries over their content, thus an object-relational database must be open to users, to extend the list of access methods it can use.

Handling Aggregation Values

A common problem in database systems revolves around the need to manage either data from different sources or data which has several alternative representations. Consider an international airline which manages information about fuel consumption. Such data may have many uses. Comparing information about fuel purchases with information about aircraft refueling may aid fraud detection. Consumption totals for different kinds of aircraft for the same route may assist in capacity planning decisions. Examining long-term trends in consumption may help in planning purchasing contracts. However, a difficulty arises when you consider where this data comes from.

Different countries, standardized on different systems of weights and measures, will report information differently. The raw data—an integer—is meaningless without some information about its unit: liters, gallons, or barrels. 6,000 gallons is much more than 6,000 liters. Furthermore, rates of consumption, which are arrived at by aggregating information from various time periods, are only meaningful if you know the time interval. A consumption rate of 6,000 liters per day is vastly greater than 6,000 liters per week. Storing these values as simple integers does not provide sufficient information for comparison, or for the calculation of new values.

The difficulty becomes clear when you consider the kinds of queries which run over this kind of data. A Boeing 747 refuels at the JFK airport, taking on 11,500 gallons of aviation fuel. Then, eighteen hours later, it takes on 7,500 liters at the Heathrow airport in England. If the Boeing specification says that the capacity of that aircraft is 250,000 cubic inches, how much fuel was consumed on the flight? If we record the number of gallons per week at the JFK airport and liters per day at the Heathrow airport, which airport consumes more fuel? What is the average consumption rate, in gallons per week, for the airports to which we fly? These questions all require complex libraries of mathematical operations to convert between units and intervals.

Conventionally, solving this problem requires that the database design include grouping two or three attributes together. For quantity information, store the value and unit together, and storing consumption involves storing the interval too. In this case, all queries over this kind of data are resolved by pulling all the data to the client side and performing the appropriate conversions there. Alternatively, the schema may employ a single integer value in the table, and all of the data must be converted to and from localized representations in the client and a standard representation on the server. Of course, information about the original values, units, and intervals is lost via this approach. If more than one application runs against this database, the conversion code must be written several times. When more than one client language is used, this code must be written in multiple languages.

In an extensible database, developers can create a datatype which encapsulates all the required information about the type's data and write functions, which allow users to compare, combine, and index instances of this type. Part of this new datatype's specification includes mathematical functions to add, find differences, and aggregate sets of data values. The example in this article explores how to implement both the fuel consumption and the consumption rate types described previously. Then, the use of these new datatypes and operators is shown in a schema. Finally, we move on to show how to implement an aggregate function to convert a set of the consumption datatypes into a single rate datatype.

The external view of the Fuel_Quantity and Fuel_Consumption datatypes are shown in Figure 10–13. The Fuel_Quantity type encapsulates both the value and the unit. Several implementation alternatives are possible. Firstly, the internal representation of the type may consist of just the relevant features parsed out of the public format; value as a floating point number and unit as a CHAR array. In this case, all of the functions which perform mathematical or comparison operations over the type need to convert this internal format to some canonical format at runtime. Transformation operations like this can be quite CPU intensive, so an alternative implementation suggests itself. The datatype's input function may perform the transformation at the time that the type's public format is parsed. The comparison and mathematical operators can therefore simply compare these precalculated internal formats, considerably reducing the required CPU resources at the expense of a little more IO overhead. A third alternative is to store only the canonical format, although this does not achieve the objective of retaining the original format. The same considerations apply to the implementation of the Fuel_Consumption datatype.

To support queries which compare values in different units, the new type requires functions which convert values among the various units. This is a fairly common design pattern. For example, a temperature datatype must contend with Celsius,

Fahrenheit, and Kelvin temperature. More sophisticated data-types where the conversion rates were not fixed, like foreign currency values or financial instruments dependent on variable interest rates, must perform some kind of look-up in the conversion routines.[3]

```
Value:= float;
   Unit:= 'gallons' | 'liters' | 'barrels';
   Fuel_Quantity:= Value Unit;
   Interval:= 'second' | 'minute' | 'hour' | 'day';
   Fuel_Comsumption = Fuel_Quantity ['per' | 'a' ] Interval;

   Examples;
       '10.5 gallons per second'
       '100 liters per minute'
       '15.5 barrels per day'
       '15 liters a day'
       '1000 barrels hour'
```

Implementers can make the public format of the datatype very flexible. For example, in many parts of the world, the idiomatic expression is "gallons a second," rather than "gallons per second." The "a" or "per" component of the public format is entirely superfluous, and can be eliminated from the format optionally. There are typically well known abbreviations for various units, all of which can be understood by the type. This flexibility helps to build a more intuitive database schema.

An important feature of query languages in extensible databases is that these languages are strongly typed. For example, fuel consumption may be considered in terms of unit distance rather than unit time—gallons per mile rather than gallons per minute—but given the way that these datatypes are defined, it is impossible to confuse instances of the two.

---

[3] Datatypes which require table look-ups in their conversion functions cannot use datatype indexing. The database is unable to change the index over Table A, due to changes in certain values in Table B.

Any operation which compares or operates over instances of these different datatypes requires that implementers explicitly create a function that takes a pair of arguments of the appropriate type. This inability to combine data which has different types is a strength of the object-relational data model. Syntactically correct queries posed against an object-relational database are also semantically correct.

Figure 10–14 introduces a small schema to illustrate what must be performed in more detail. This schema could be useful for the airline capacity planning system introduced earlier in this article. The main table in this schema logs the refueling schedule of one of the airline's international aircraft. The queries reflect a mix of what OLTP and DSS applications would be interested in. It is worth noting that there are few SQL-92 datatypes in this schema, in keeping with the direction in which extensible technology appears to be headed.

Figure 10–14: Small schema and queries using the fuel consumption datatype.

```
—
— This schema implements a section of a database which
— services a capacity planning system for an international
— airline.
—
CREATE TABLE AirPorts
( Id              AirPort_CodeNOT NULL    PRIMARY KEY,
  LocationPoint       NOT NULL,
  Name              Airport_NameNOT NULL
);
—
CREATE TABLE AirCraft
( Id              AirCraft_Id NOT NULL    PRIMARY KEY,
  Make              AirCraft_Make       NOT NULL,
  CapacityFuel_Quantity     NOT NULL,
  Lease           DateIntervalNOT NULL
);
—
CREATE TABLE FuelLogs
```

```
( AirCraft       AirCraft_Id      NOT NULL,
  AirPort             AirPort_Code      NOT NULL,
  FuelDate       date             NOT NULL,
  Qty                 Fuel_Quantity      NOT NULL
);
— The following queries are run over these tables.
—
— Q1. How many times did we get to below 10% of fuel in the
— last month?
—
— Q2. What was the average fuel consumption rate for all
— aircraft leased between '01-jan-1985' and
— '01-jan-1995'?
```

Queries can be handled by providing functions which implement the necessary mathematical operations. In Informix Dynamic Server with Universal Data Option, functions of the appropriate names are bound to symbols which can be used in queries. For example, the mathematical "+" operator is bound to the Plus() function. New functions may be bound to new operators through the CREATE OPERATOR command. The query in Figure 10–15 requires a function which can multiply the datatype's value by a floating point number. In the query, the results of this function are compared with another instance of the Fuel_Quantity datatype. Figure 10–15 first illustrates the creation of the function which performs the multiplication, and the query which shows the function's use in SQL.

An important function of a database system is the way it acts as a venue for analysis, as well as a store for state. The second query in Figure 10–14 illustrates this. Extensible database software must be open to user defined aggregates, which are really just another form of object behavior. Creating a user-defined aggregate is a little more complex than creating a function. This is because aggregation behavior must deal with a set of datatypes, rather than a single function which can be considered

Figure 10-15: Creating the Multiply() function and using it in a query.

```
—
— Creating the Multiply function.
—
CREATE FUNCTION Multiply(Fuel_Capacity, float)
RETURNS Fuel_Capacity
EXTERNAL NAME
'$INFORMIXDIR/extend/Fuel_Capacity/bin/FC.bld(FCTimesFloat)'
LANGUAGE C;
—
— Query 1, given the schema in Figure 5.2
—
SELECT COUNT(*)
  FROM AirCraft AC, FuelLogs FL
  WHERE FL.Qty              > (0.9 * AC.Capacity)
  AND FL.AirCraft_Id = AC.Id
  AND FL.FuelDate       > 'now' - '1 month';
```

in isolation. An additional complication with user-defined aggregate functions concerns the underlying data management. Big aggregation queries can only be made to perform quickly by employing intra-query parallelism. If the aggregation function must look at a million records, then the query's response time can be improved by an order of magnitude simply by looking at ten records at a time.

To create a user-defined aggregate in an extensible database that supports intra-query parallelism, implementers must supply six functions. This is due to the way that aggregation must be implemented in general and the mechanisms necessary to support parallelism. In order to support parallelism, the database engine must run localized aggregation for each of several subsets of the main set of records. The results of these local aggregations are combined in a second set of three functions, which return the result. Both of these sets of three functions consist of an initiator function that is run once, an iteration function which is run once for each record or result of a sub-aggregation, and a finalize function.

Alternatively, implementers could simply write cast functions between the new datatype and the built-in floating point datatype. This would allow implementers to use the facilities which are already present in the engine to perform aggregations queries. However, this limits the kinds of aggregation which can be performed. Many potentially interesting aggregation functions are not included in SQL: correlation, standard deviation, and so on. A group of extensions which make up a statistical DataBlade module would supply these functions. This is an example of how DataBlade modules may be combined within an extensible database.

Conclusion

The examples contained in this article provide an introduction to the use of Informix Dynamic Server with Universal Data Option for industrial applications. What these examples represent, over and above being solutions to specific problems, is a new way of thinking about the role that the database plays in an information system. Extensible technology opens up the database engine to user code and creativity.

In all of the examples provided in this article, the conventional relational solution can be adapted to work in Informix Dynamic Server with Universal Data Option, demonstrating that the SQL-92 datatypes and functions are just simple examples of what is possible.

References

[CHEL94]   Chelko, Joe. *SQL for Smarties*. San Francisco: Morgan Kaufmann, 1994.

[DATE94]   Date, C. J., and Darwen, Hugh. *A Guide to the SQL Standard: Third Edition*. Menlo Park, CA: Addison-Wesley, 1994.

[DATE94a]   Date, C. J., and Darwen, Hugh. "An Optimization Problem" in *Relational Writings, 1989–1991*. Menlo Park, CA: Addison-Wesley, 1994.

[FEGU93]   Fetterman, L. Roger, and Satish, Gupta K. *Mainstream Multimedia: Applying Multimedia in Business*, New York: VNR Computer Library, Van Nostrand Reinhold, 1993.

[GUTT84]   Guttman, A. "R-Trees: A Dynamic Index Structure For Spatial Searching," in *Proc. ACM-SIGMOD International Conference on Management of Data*, Boston, June 1984.

[JAGA90]   Jagadish, H.V. "Linear Clustering of Objects with Multiple Attributes," in *Proc. ACM-SIGMOD International Conference on Management of Data*, 1990.

[KNU73]   Knuth, Don. *The Art of Computer Programming: Volume III. Sorting and Searching*. Reading, MA: Addison-Wesley, 1973.

[SAMET94]   Samet, Hanan, *Spatial Indexing*. San Francisco: Morgan Kaufmann, 1994.

[SEY96]   Seybold Group, *Seybold Reports on Internet Publishing, MultiMedia*, 1996. http://www.media.sbexpos.com/

[STON96]   Stonebraker, Michael. *Object-Relational DBMSs: The Next Great Wave*, San Francisco: Morgan Kaufmann, 1996.

Chapter 11

Designing High-Performance Web Applications

by Jim Panttaja and Craig O'Connor

Introduction

This paper demonstrates a number of techniques which will improve the performance of Informix Dynamic Server with Universal Data Option Web applications developed using the Web Integration Option™. This paper is written for Informix Dynamic Server with Universal Data Option; however, most of the information is applicable to the Illustra Server. This paper originated as a presentation by Craig O'Connor at the 1997 Informix Worldwide User Conference and Exhibition held in San Francisco, California.

This article discusses a methodology for tuning performance, including the areas that should be considered, and how to monitor various resources. It then discusses the basics of database management as it applies to maintaining Web applications, and finally, focuses on the architecture and tuning of Informix Dynamic Server with Web Integration Option.

Performance Tuning Methodology

The first thing to remember in performance tuning is that tuning is never general in focus—always tune for a specific situation. In particular, know where you are starting from in order to verify any resulting improvements.

Therefore, start with a problem. Perhaps you are trying to address user complaints of too many timeouts on a particular page. Identify how often this happens. If possible, isolate the problem so it can be duplicated, and simplify the process of tracking improvements. However, this isn't always possible. Sometimes the problem only exists in a complicated environment. For example, a performance problem can occur only during one week per month, and only when a number of activities converge.

Once the problem is identified and isolated, establish a goal, or goals. One initial goal may be that a user never waits longer than ten seconds for a page.

Next, evaluate the performance, change one thing, and then try it again. Pinpoint what changes are productive, and which aren't.

For each test, analyze the work that occurs during the test. Depending on your goal, you may be interested in throughput (overall system performance transactions per second), response time (how fast is the page served), or resource utilization for some specific resource (CPU, memory, disk, or network).

One of the complications of the Web environment—especially a Web environment utilizing Informix Dynamic Server with Universal Data Option and the Web Integration Option—is that there are a large number of components.

In a Web server environment that includes a database, there are four key components:

- **Web Browser**
  Examples of Web browsers are Netscape Navigator, Internet Explorer, but also consider more advanced browser support including Java, JavaScript, or Active-X.

- **Web Server**

  Examples of Web servers include Netscape Enterprise Server, Microsoft Internet Information Server, and the Apache Server.

- **Database Server**

  This discussion focuses on Informix Dynamic Server with Universal Data Option. This product, and the Web Integration Option, will be used to store the data in the database, as well as HTML, images, and other data required for the creation and delivery of our Web pages.

- **Network Environment**

  Is this an intranet (delivering Web pages within a company), an extranet (delivering Web pages to partner companies, possibly over the Internet), or the Internet?

Regarding performance, it is important to focus your work on activities that will yield the best results for the least amount of effort. Table 11–1 presents the experience of a number of performance tuning experts using Informix Dynamic Server with Universal Data Option-based Web applications.

Table 11–1 Performance tuning areas.

Area	Tuning Improvement Yields %	Implementation Effort	Application Impact
Operating System	5%	Low	None
Network	5%	Medium	None
Web Server	5%	Low	None
Database Server			
• Configuration	10%	Low	None
• Disk Utilization	10%	Medium	None
• Schema	25%	High	High
• Indexes	25%	Medium	None
Web DataBlade			
• Configuration	20%	Low	None
• Page-embedded SQL	15%	Medium	Low
• Page Construction	10%	Medium	Low

There are a variety of ways to address specific issues. If the problem is related to network performance, it is possible to increase network bandwidth, or decrease the information that is transmitted. Ensure that you use the latest version of all components.

One useful way to look at Table 11–1 is to sort it by application impact (how much do I have to change my Web pages), implementation effort (how much do I have to do overall to improve it). Clearly, one approach is to focus on the items that take the least effort to implement, as Table 11–2 indicates.

Table 11–2 *Performance tuning areas by application impact.*

Area	Tuning Improvement Yields %	Implementation Effort	Application Impact
Web DataBlade			
• Configuration	20%	Low	None
Database Server			
• Configuration	10%	Low	None
Operating System	5%	Low	None
Web Server	5%	Low	None
Database Server			
• Indexes	25%	Medium	None
• Disk Utilization	10%	Medium	None
Network	5%	Medium	None
Web DataBlade			
• Page-embedded SQL	15%	Medium	Low
* Page Construction	10%	Medium	Low
Database Server			
• Schema	25%	High	High

This analysis suggests that Web configuration is a great place to start. Next, look at the database server configuration, and then the operating system environment. Notice that database schema changes are at the bottom of the list. This doesn't mean that this area will not require changes, just that it probably isn't the first area to visit. Note that our experience is in database design. That may skew our conclusions, because we tend to get the database design almost right to start with.

You will need some tools to monitor performance. Table 11–3 indicates some of the symptoms to watch for, and the tools which can be used to collect the information.

Table 11–3 *Monitoring performance by symptoms.*

	Symptom	OS Utilities	Informix Monitoring Utilities
CPU	CPU approaching 100% on one or more processors. Load unbalanced.	vmstat, sar, ps	onstat -g act, ath, glo, ntd, ntt, ntu, qst, rea, sch, ses, sle, spi, sql, sts, tpf, wai, wst
Memory	Page outs, page scanning, swapping.	vmstat, sar, top, ps, ipcs	onstat-g ffr, dic, iob, mem, mgm, nsc, nsd, nss, seg, ufr
I/O Activity	I/O approaching 100% on one or more disks. Load unbalanced.	iostat	onstat-g iof, iog, ioq, iov
Network	Collisions, retransmissions, time-outs, excessive traffic.	ping, netstat -a, -n, -s	onstat -g nsd, ntd, ntt, ntu

One important point to note is that it is crucial to concentrate on improving things that cause problems. If you look at CPU utilization and it is high (for example, 98 percent), then adding additional processors may be helpful. However, if your CPU utilization is low (for example, 20 percent), adding a CPU will not help.

Memory utilization is especially important. Make sure that there is adequate memory for your environment, and that your database server is appropriately configured to take advantage of the memory that is there. As you make adjustments, monitor page swapping.

The value for "page outs" indicates how often a page that is part of your working set is moved from real memory to disk. With a database management system (DBMS), this is usually catastrophic. The goal is to let the DBMS perform its own management. If you see excessive page outs, reduce the amount of memory utilized by Informix Dynamic Server with Universal Data Option (or the Illustra Server).

Monitoring Resources on Windows NT

For Windows NT, there are a number of utilities and tools, including: Performance Monitor, which monitors all system resources and provides views of IIS and FTP statistics; the Task Manager, which monitors processes, and their CPU and memory requirements; and command-line tools in the Windows NT Resource kit, which might look familiar to a UNIX administrator (pstat, pmon, etc.).

Many of these tools allow you to monitor performance graphically.

Database Management Basics

When using the Web DataBlade to develop Web pages, the DBMS performs double duty. It holds all operational data for an application, but it also holds the Web page source code (usually HTML), and other objects (images, audios, video, etc.) that might be incorporated within an application. This places extra demands on the ability to tune the DBMS.

A few simple rules are as follows:

- **Memory**
  Allocate additional memory as long as the operating system isn't paging.
- **Separation**
  Spread data among the available devices.
- **Fragmentation**
  Take advantage of Informix Dynamic Server with Universal Data Option's ability to have one table spread across multiple devices.
- **Indexes**
  Make sure you have the right indexes, and that they are used.
- **Index Maintenance**
  Due to INSERT, UPDATE, and DELETE operations, your indexes may become less efficient over time. It may pay to drop

and recreate them. (This is especially true with the Illustra Server.)

- **Index Statistics**
  The index statistics provide information to the server on how to best optimize a given query. Updating the statistics can improve the query plans that are generated.[1]

The typical Web environment is heavy on reads, and light on writes. It's similar to OLTP without the writes, and with lots of short, fast requests. Memory tuning tends to be similar to what is performed for an OLTP environment.

Rules of Thumb

A few tips on implementing your database design include the following:

- **Keep Table Keys Narrow**
  Doing so reduces the size of the foreign key to be placed in any referencing table, and reduces the size of your indexes.
- **Use Appropriate Datatypes**
  Use the SERIAL datatype to generate surrogate keys. Use the appropriate size integer for your task (not so small as to fail to cover all possible values, and not so large as to waste space).
- **Use Nulls Only When Appropriate**
  The use of NULL is often misunderstood. Know why you are using it in a given table, and make sure that you know what it means in that table.
- **Add Indexes**
  Make sure that crucial queries have an appropriate index available to them. Adding indexes slows INSERT, UPDATE, and DELETE operations, which are not typically an issue for Web environments, fast SELECTs are generally more important.
- **Do Not Use Too Many Indexes (no more than three to five on a given table)**
  The problem with too many indexes is that they probably won't all be used. In addition, they require effort every time

---

[1] For the Illustra Server, the statement is: VACUUM FROM table_name WITH (STATIS-TICS). There is also an option to vacuum all tables with a single vacuum statement. Note that with the Illustra Server, this statement also deletes unused rows from the table. These old rows will waste space, and impact performance.

there is an INSERT, UPDATE or DELETE. Remember that Informix Dynamic Server with Universal Data Option adds indexes for referential integrity declarations.

- **Don't Perform Maintenance in the Middle of the Day**
Many maintenance tasks can be performed "off hours." Don't attempt a VACUUM ... WITH (STATISTICS) operation for the Illustra Server, or UPDATE STATISTICS operation for Informix Dynamic Server with Universal Data Option at 2:00 PM.

- **Selectivity Relax Referential and Other Constraints**
Typically, this is not suggested, because these constraints guarantee that your date is consistent. However, sometimes, the performance impact is too high, and the application does not allow us to violate the constraint. In one application, we couldn't afford the constraint during the day, but we had plenty of time to identify indiscretions overnight.

- **Selectively Denormalize**
Sometimes it pays to maintain duplicate data in a collection of tables. It may improve performance by reducing the number of joins required. There are a number of possibilities: you can either pre-compute some values (duplicating data in tables with summary data), or perform horizontal or vertical splits of tables.

Web DataBlade Architecture

Figure 11–1 shows the Informix Dynamic Server with Web Integration Option, version 2.2, architecture for the Illustra Server. In this version of the Web DataBlade, the webdriver is integrated with the Web Server, but there is a separate Webdaemon and Miserver process for each concurrent access. The Webdaemons hold a fixed number of open connections and are selected with a simple round-robin approach:

Figure 11–2 shows the enhancements provided under version 3.3 of the Informix Web DataBlade. The Webdaemon/Miserver processes have been replaced by a set of flexible TCP/IP threads, maintained so that the webdriver can communicate with the database. The number of threads can grow and shrink, based on activity, to a configurable value.

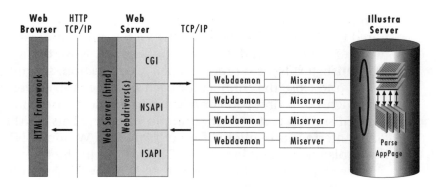

Figure 11–1 *Informix Dynamic Server with Web Integration Option, version 2.2, architecture.*

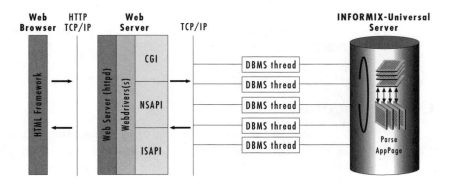

Figure 11–2 *Enhancements provided under version 3.3 of the Informix Web DataBlade.*

Web DataBlade Tuning

Using NSAPI or ISAPI

Using NSAPI or ISAPI yields a 25-percent improvement in the delivery of pages on UNIX, and over 40 percent on Windows NT, versus using the CGI-based interface. Using CGI is less efficient with Informix Dynamic Server with Universal Data Option, compared to Illustra Server because the Webdaemon process is gone (which held an open databased connection). Now, the webdriver CGI must startup as a process, open a connection, submit a query, and close the connect for each hit. The Web server API approach holds an open connection to the database and avoids the CGI startup cost by remaining in memory. This NSAPI or ISAPI interface is available for both Sun and Windows NT today. It will also be available on the SGI platform in the future.

To configure the ISAPI interface on Windows NT with the Microsoft IIS, it is necessary to:

• Create a virtual mapping to a directory on the Web server with execute privileges;
• Place driverISAPI.dll in the corresponding physical directory; and
• Set the application default in the WEB.CNF file as follows: WEB_HOME /web/driverISAPI.dll?

Large Object Caching

Performance can be improved by caching large objects and pages. The following values are set in the web.cnf file (in previous releases of the Web DataBlade, the values were set in web.conf):

Table 11–4 *Large object caching.*

MI_WEBCACHEMAXLO	/web/l_o cache	Specifies the directory for the Web cache.
MI_WEBCACHEMAXLO	1024000	Sets the maximum size in bytes for the large objects to be cached. The default is 64 K. This example sets it to 1 MB.
MI_WEBCACHELIFE	2d	Determines how long large objects should remain in cache. This example sets the value to 2 days.
MI_WEBCACHECRON	2h	Determines how often cache cleanup should be executed. This example sets the value to every 2 hours.
MI_WEBCACHEPAGE	on	Turns on the caching of Web pages.

When enabling the caching of Web pages, both static and dynamic pages are cached (if caching is enabled for that specific page with the cache_enable option of webdriver). However, AppPages retrieved with the POST method, or which contain HTTPHEADER functions, will not be cached.

To enable caching for a specific page, use the following command (from an operating system prompt):

```
webdriver cache_enable pagename
```

To subsequently disable caching for that page, use the following command:

```
webdriver cache_disable pagename
```

To clear a page from cache, use the following command:

```
webdriver cache_purge pagename
```

For static pages, it is best to cache them. Cache for dynamic pages only if there are a small number of variations in the arguments passed to them. If the arguments are different almost every time, the page is requested and caching will not be productive.

The cached copies of the pages and large objects will be located in the specified directory with the MI_WEBCACHEDIR variable in the web.cnf file. There will be a separate directory for each database containing cached objects.

Isolation Levels

The default isolation level in the Illustra Server is serializable. The default in Informix Dynamic Server with Universal Data Option, when used with the Web DataBlade, is committed read. Serializable means that read locks are held as pages are read. For many purposes, this is too restrictive. Consider using an isolation level of DIRTY READ or COMMITTED READ. For most application purposes, DIRTY READ is too generous. But when reading Web pages, it is probably reasonable to perform a DIRTY READ. For most database access, COMMITTED READ is a reasonable choice.

DIRTY READ allows you to read through locks. This gives you the maximum concurrency, but rows may appear in your result which never existed (an application tentatively made the change, but then rolled it back).

COMMITTED READ is more restrictive. It guarantees that the rows that appear reflect changes that were committed. However, if I immediately read the same data again, some other user may have changed it, since this setting doesn't acquire any locks on my behalf.

Note that with the SERIALIZABLE option, locks are held as one page, and any additional MiSQL tags for that page are formatted for the user.

Set the isolation level for the queries on a given page by using the MiSQL Tag:[2]

```
<?MiSQL SQL="SET ISOLATION LEVEL READ COMMITTED;">
```

After this is set (and until you set it to some other value on this page), all subsequent MiSQL tags use this new isolation level.

Note that changing the isolation level within a page only affects the life of the transaction as the dynamic page is constructed. With the Web server API, the isolation level will always revert back to the default mode for a new request, even reusing the same thread.

Minimize Network Traffic

Limit the amount of data that moves to the client over the network. Perform filtering on the server. For the second set of 25 rows that match a query, use the MiSQL WINSTART and WINSIZE (formerly MAXROWS) options:

```
<?MiSQL WINSTART=26 WINSIZE=25
    SQL+"SELECT column FROM table;">$1
    <?/MiSQL>
```

---

[2] For the Illustra Server, make these settings on an individual SELECT basis. The syntax is SELECT ... FROM tablename USING (isolation level "read committed") WHERE ...; On some releases, the double quotes in the example are not necessary. You can substitute 'read uncommitted' for 'read committed.' Read uncommitted corresponds to dirty read in the description above.

Development Tips

Developing small pages (or small pieces of pages that are Web-Exploded together) improves page concurrency. Create pages in sections, preferably using Dynamic Tags combined at Web-Explode time. Tags have far less overhead than all of the Web-Exploding webPage sections combined.

User-defined tags are an inexpensive way to reuse common page code. Look for opportunities to use tags. The last 10 to 20 tags are internally cached by WebExplode.

There is extra overhead on Informix Dynamic Server with Universal Data Option if a Web page exceeds 7,500 bytes. This isn't a huge impact, but there is an additional read to obtain the contents of the page.

Use stored procedures for complicated logic. This is often a more efficient way to execute the required SQL; use temporary tables if needed, as they allow for more sophisticated error handling, and simplify the Web pages.[3]

Tracing and Reviewing Query Plans

Capture all of the applications' SQL statements as they are sent to the server by setting the following two values in the WEB.CNF file:

Table 11–5 Values for capturing applications' SQL statements.

MI_WEBEXPLEVEL	32	Logs the SQL statements being executed.
MI_WEBEXPLOG	/web/sql.log	Location for the trace log.

The value for the MI_WEBEXPLEVEL setting is determined by adding together the values specified below:

You can also write your own information to the trace log (specified by the MI_WEBEXPLOG value, or a file in the /tmp directory if MI_WEBEXPLOG is not set). You can write records with the following MiVAR tags:

```
<?MiVAR>($TRACEMSG, Error: $MI_TRACEMSG<?/MiVAR>
```

---

[3] The Illustra Server allows the use of functions.

Also look at which indexes the server will use to satisfy a query. In most cases, there isn't time to perform this for all queries, but it is worthwhile to do so for key queries.

In DBACCESS:

```
SET EXPLAIN ON:

SELECT column
FROM table
WHERE key = 1;

SET EXPLAIN OFF;
```

Conclusions

Tuning your application that is based on Informix Dynamic Server with Web Integration Option is not that different from other tuning activities. Because the use of Informix Dynamic Server with Web Integration Option includes a browser, a Web server, a database server, and a network, it is often difficult to decide where to start. This article has provided some advice on how to pick a path, and described a number of useful tools. It is possible to deliver high-performance applications with Informix Dynamic Server with Web Integration Option, as a number of Web sites testify.

Acknowledgments

The authors would like to thank members of the Web DataBlade development group, and the Customer Services organization at Informix Software. In particular, we would like to thank Mark Mears, John Gaffney, Martin Siegenthaler, Willow Williams, and Susan Cline, who shared their experiences with us.

Web Client/Server Applications

by Jacques Roy

Introduction

There are compelling reasons for using the World Wide Web (Web) as the platform of choice for client/server applications. Some of these reasons include the fact that virtually everybody uses a Web browser. The Web browser serves as an homogeneous application platform and simplifies application access, distribution, and update processes.

The original architecture of the Web is inadequate for most client/server type applications. New developments in Web functionality, however, provide interesting possibilities that will make the Web architecture and the Web browser a more attractive platform for client/server applications.

This article covers some interesting possibilities that increase the range of implementation capabilities.

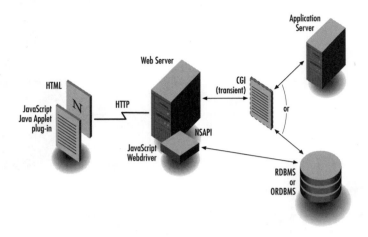

Figure 12–1 Web architecture.

Web Architecture

The Web was created with the idea of providing universal document readership through an easy to use hypertext interface. It is based on two main protocols, HyperText Transport Protocol (HTTP) and HyperText Markup Language (HTML). HTTP is used as the communication layer between the Web browser and the Web server, and HTML is used by the browser to format information received from the Web server or a local file, and to perform simple processing.

HTTP is a stateless protocol. A request must be self contained. All information leading to the request must be included. This characteristic of the HTTP protocol impacts all facilities which have been implemented since the birth of the Web.

The Common Gateway Interface (CGI) has long been the main facility to implement Web applications. It is still the most popular application interface today. A CGI program can be a shell script, a PERL script, a TCL script, a compiled program, etc. It is best suited for small programs that require few resources. CGI follows the lead of the HTTP protocol. It only lives for the duration of the query and then terminates. Because of that, it cannot maintain information for future queries. This can have a significant performance impact, particularly if database access is required. In this case, simple tests have shown CPU utilization 50 to 120 times higher than that of a program which maintains a persistent database connection.

To work around the performance issue, a CGI program could instead send its requests to an application server that will maintain the database connection. The application server could also keep state information for the requester and return an identifier that can be used to reconnect to the proper context. The application server must address the possibility that the user will not submit another query. It is usually performed with a time-out value. A value which is too small may cause the application to terminate inappropriately, and a value which is too long may cause undue resource consumption on the server.

The application server implementation needs to consider the multi-user aspect of the environment. If the application will be used by several dozens or hundreds of users, a one-to-one relationship between a user and an application server may not be acceptable. At this point, the implementer must face the same issues which database vendors have struggled with. The solution adopted by database vendors is a multithreaded server. However, an in-house implementation may raise the complexity to unacceptable levels.

An alternative to a CGI implementation is the use of a Web server Application Programming Interface (API). You can view this interface as a device driver for the Web server. The server-side JavaScript language is an example of an implementation using the Web server API.

An implementation which uses the Web server API is part of the Web server. It provides additional performance and, because it is part of the server, it can keep information between requests. You can also use this interface to communicate with an application server, or to interface with a database server directly.

Furthermore, any application code that is implemented using the Web server API becomes part of the Web server. It is dependent on the way that the server works. If the Web server provides scalability by starting several copies of itself, determine the impact that it has on your environment. If a client does not reconnect to the same physical server, the client context may not be accessible. If the Web server simulates multithreading, any blocking operation will block the Web server. In this context, there can be only one active database connection and a long query can stop all users.

The Web Browser

The Web browser provides several pieces of a solution for Web applications development. The plug-in was the first piece to appear. It can be as complex as needed. The plug-in is an application that runs in the browser. It provides little benefit over a standard client application, since it needs to be installed and must use platform-specific calls if it provides a user interface.

Through the Netscape LiveConnect environment, a plug-in could be used for background processing only, while the user interface is handled through a Java Script or HTML using JavaScript. However, this implementation does not resolve the installation issue but, hopefully, reduces the frequency of updates.

Client-side JavaScript provides the capability of generating actions based on an event. If a button is pushed, JavaScript can take over and perform some tasks. Its main purpose is to enhance HTML by providing some client interaction.

Finally, a Web browser can execute a Java applet which is downloaded from the Web server. This is particularly attractive, since it provides application flexibility. Furthermore, modifications to the application require updating only one location. In our context, the only issue left is to access the database without losing the benefits of a downloaded applet.

Informix Java Application Programming Interface

The Informix Java Application Programming Interface (Java API), sometimes referred to as the Java Object Interface (JOI), presents an interface to database server services and data for use in client- or server-side Java environments. The API is explicitly modeled on the existing C++ API and is also intended to present a superset of the JDBC API. Applications or applets developed using the Java API must use the Java Development Kit (JDK), version 1.1.1 or later.

The Java API provides two methods of connections: direct or remote. The direct connection method allows application or applets to communicate with a database server directly. The client environment must be set up so the Java API classes can be found and so that some shared libraries are part of the search path. By default, the Java API is installed in $INFORMIXDIR/lib/java, where $INFORMIXDIR refers to the Informix product installation directory. In this case, the following UNIX Solaris environment variables should be set as follows:

```
CLASSPATH=$CLASSPATH:$INFORMIXDIR/lib/java/lib/classes

LD_LIBRARY_PATH=$LD_LIBRARY_PATH:$INFORMIXDIR/lib/java/classes/
    sparc:$INFORMIXDIR/lib/esql:$INFORMIXDIR/lib/dmi
```

In the Windows NT environment, the libraries' directory paths must be included in the PATH environment variable. One example of the PATH environment variable is as follows:

```
PATH=%PATH%;%INFORMIXJAPI%\lib\pc;%INFORMIXDIR%\lib\
    esql;%INFORMIXDIR%\lib\dmi
```

The Java Remote Method Invocation (RMI) server provides remote connectivity to client applications. The RMI server is started as a service (default port 1099). Java applications or applets use the JOI to take advantage of this feature. No software needs to be installed on the client machine for database connectivity. This preserves one main feature of Web applications' architecture: virtually no software maintenance on the client side.

The Informix Java Object Interface

The Informix JOI provides a simple interface that minimizes the differences between direct and remote connections. Both methods can be present within a single applet or application.

A Java application or applet first interacts with an object that implements the Credentials interface. This object takes enough information from the application to open a connection to the DBMS. Once created, this parameter information must not change. The "provider" model of object extraction is used throughout the interface. In general, Java API objects are not created through the "new" operator, but are provided instead by extraction methods from other Java API objects. A Credentials object is the root of this tree.

To use the direct connection interface, an application should import as follows:

```
import informix.api.*;
import informix.api.direct.*;
```

In the case of RMI connections, the following should be part of the Java application:

```
import informix.api.*;
import informix.api.remote.rmi.*;
```

The direct connection credential provides two constructors. The first constructor does not take any parameters. The values required to connect to the server are taken from environment variables. The second constructor is as follows:

```
public DirectCredentials(String db, String user, String sys,
   String passwd) throws DBClientException
```

Where db is the database name, user the user name, sys is the database server name, and passwd the user password. The constructor would be used as follows:

```
Credentials cred;

try {
cred = new DirectCredentials((db, user, sys, passwd);
} ...
```

When using a remote connection, the DirectCredentials call should be replaced with a RMICredentials call. This call has the following format:

```
public RMICredentials(String appServer, String db, String
    user, String sys, String passwd) throws DBException,
    MalformedURLException, UnknownHostException
```

This call has an additional parameter, compared to the DirectCredentials call. This parameter, appServer, is the location of the RMI server. The format of this String parameter is as follows:

```
rmi://hostname<:port>/
```

The hostname is the name of the machine where the RMI server is located. The port number is the service port used by the RMI server. This parameter is optional if the default port number, 1099, is used.

Once an application has a credential, the database objects are the same for direct and remote connections. The general order of events is to obtain a database connection and then a query object from the connection:

```
Connection conn;
Query    query;
conn = cred.Connection();
query = conn.query();
...

conn.open();
```

At this point, a query can be passed to the query object and the result is then collected by the application.

Java Applet

A client/server application can be implemented through the Web using a Java applet. The first step consists of asking the Web server for a Web page. The Web server can use one of the Informix products through its API—either the Netscape Server

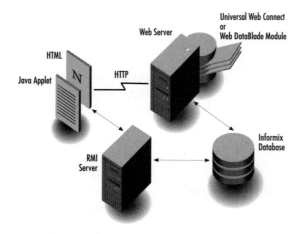

Figure 12–2 *Client/server Java applet.*

API (NSAPI), or Information Server API (ISAPI)—to access the Informix database where the page resides.

This database access usage through the Web server is consistent with the general structure of the Web, because it consists of a simple page request without additional expected interactions.

What is returned is a simple page that identifies the applet. The main section of the Web page is similar to the following:

```
<APPLET CODE="myapplet.class"
NAME="myapplet" WIDTH=500 HEIGHT=500 ></APPLET>
```

At this point, the applet takes over the browser's display and the application is started. The applet is allowed to communicate with the host. It can connect to the RMI server and begin accessing the database. It has control over the user interaction and the database access. It is, therefore, a client/server application.

Taking Advantage of Web Standards

The previous solution satisfies the requirements of a Web application. No additional software is required on the client machine and the application code is platform independent. It still has a few disadvantages.

One disadvantage is that all user interaction occurs through the Java applet. This means that the applet writer must use the Java Abstract Windowing Toolkit (AWT) to implement the user interface. As for any windowing programming environment, a significant learning curve may be involved. If Java is a strategic language in an organization, however, the effort is easily justifiable. In other cases, it could be questionable. Luckily, some products are available to simplify the creation of the user interface.

If a complete application requires a large Java applet, the download time can become an issue. In the case of the Java applet, this solution may be better suited for intranet environments.

Finally, the use of an applet may be overwhelming when it comes to small applications with simple user interactions. In these situations, it is probably better to use the Informix Dynamic Server™ with Web Integration Option™ to solve the problem.

We can take advantage of standard features and increase our choices of solutions. Following is an examination of some of these features:

- **JavaScript**
  The JavaScript language was introduced by Netscape a few years ago and has become available in competing browsers. The client-side JavaScript is the language that runs in the browser. The event-processing capabilities of JavaScript provide a way for a local application to take control of the browser after a button is pushed. A client-side JavaScript can also call *methods,* or functions, in a Java applet.
- **Frames**
  When a page is loaded, the entire content of the previous page is lost. You can divide the screen into a number of frames where each frame can be loaded separately. This allows you to preserve the content part of the browser.

With these two features, it is possible to take advantage of the present and future features of the Web browser. JavaScript can reference objects in different frames. This gives us the basis for a new implementation.

The basic idea is to divide the browser into two frames. The main frame will be used for the application, and the second will contain the Java applet. Because the applet has no interaction with the user, the second frame should be of minimum size. It could also be used to contain status messages.

This goal is accomplished by loading an HTML page that contains two frames. Each frame refers to other HTML pages as follows:

```
<HTML>
<HEAD>
<TITLE>SQL Demo</TITLE>
</HEAD>

<BODY>
<frameset ROWS ="*, 20" >
<frame border = 0 name="body" src="sqlframe1.html"
  scrolling="auto" >
<frame border = 0 name="message" src="sqlframe2.html"
  scrolling="no" >
</frameset>

<NOFRAME>
Frame needed!
</NOFRAME>

</BODY>
</HTML>
```

This HTML page defined two frames as part of a frame set. Both frames are named and indicate the location of their content. The second frame, named message, is very simple. It identifies the applet that will be loaded in the frame. An example of such a frame is as follows:

```
<HTML>
<HEAD>
<TITLE>DB interface</TITLE>
</HEAD>

<BODY>
<APPLET CODE="sqlapplet.class" NAME="dbi" WIDTH=10 HEIGHT=10>
</APPLET>
```

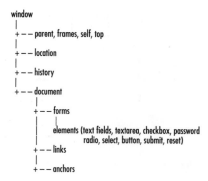

```
window
   |
   + − − parent, frames, self, top
   |
   + − − location
   |
   + − − history
   |
   + − − document
   |        |
   |        + − − forms
   |        |       |
   |        |      elements (text fields, textarea, checkbox, password
   |        |                 radio, select, button, submit, reset)
   |        + − − links
   |        |
   |        + − − anchors
```

Figure 12–3 *General object hierarchy.*

```
</BODY>
</HTML>
```

As mentioned earlier, we can add a message area to this page—it is the choice of the application designer. One simple improvement to this code is to add a JavaScript function that is activated when the page is unloaded (OnUnLoad). This provides for an orderly shutdown of the database connection.

What is left is to design an HTML page that will use JavaScript for local processing and communication with the database server. To better understand how the processing is accomplished, it is necessary to know about the browser object hierarchy. For a detailed discussion of this topic, refer to the following Internet location:

```
http://www.netscape.com/eng/mozilla/2.0/handbook/
   javascript/index.html.
```

The Web browser uses a hierarchy of objects that begins with a window. A window page will always contain a number of objects: location, history, and document. Each of these objects have properties. For example, a document has a title. The content of a document depends on the structure of the page. A general hierarchy of a window is as follows:

This hierarchy does not imply that it is only possible to work with a single window. You can create additional windows and

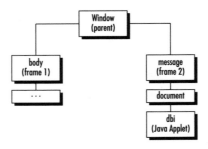

Figure 12–4 *Object hierarchy.*

provide for communication between the windows. Objects within the hierarchy can refer to their parent window as "parent."

In the case of the sample application, the hierarchy is depicted in Figure 12–4. As can be seen from the general object hierarchy, the frames are directly under the window. All objects can be referenced by name, when applicable. In the case of the main sample HTML page, the page defines two frames which are named "body" and "message." To find further definition of the hierarchy, look at the pages that constitute each frame. The content of the "message" frame was previously defined as an applet named "dbi."

The "body" frame can access the Java applet by referring to `parent.message.document.dbi`. The "document" level is implicit in the HTML page of the message frame. The applet methods are accessed as properties of the applet object. Assuming that the applet has a method called `getstatus()`, the method can be called by using `parent.message.document.dbi.getstatus()`.

The content of the "body" page is mainly HTML with some calls to local JavaScripts functions. Assume that a login HTML page is used as the first content of the body frame. This page could have a form containing the appropriate input fields. The action can come from pressing an OK button with the following definition:

```
<INPUT TYPE="button" VALUE="OK" ONCLICK="upd(this.form)" >
```

When the button receives the event ONCLICK, it executes the upd JavaScript function with, as argument, the entire form.

This allows the function to extract the parameters required for logging in. The function should conditionally change the content of the "body" frame, depending on the success or failure to connect to the database. The upd function can be as follows:

```
<SCRIPT LANGUAGE="JavaScript">

function upd(form) {
 parent.message.document.dbi.doConnect(form.dbname.value,
      form.username.value, form.servname.value,
      form.password.value);

if (0 == parent.message.document.dbi.getStatus() )
   form.errninfo.value =
      "Connection to the database server failed";
else
   parent.body.location.href="sqlframe1b.html";
}

</SCRIPT>
```

This function assumes that the form that is passed as an argument includes the following fields: dbname, username, servname, password, and errninfo. The function first calls the Java applet to establish the connection to the server. Depending on the success or failure of the login, the following events occur:

- **Failure**
  The content of the errninfo field is changed to display an error message; or
- **Success**
  The "body" frame source reference is changed to a different page. This changes the content of the frame to a different page. The new page then interacts with the applet to communicate with the database server.

By carefully designing the Java applet, the applet becomes a database API to the JavaScript language. In this way, all user interaction is kept within the Web environment and takes advantage of the new functionality provided by more recent HTML standards.

Conclusion

There is no single solution for Web applications. In some cases, the Universal Web Architecture provides an easy environment in which to develop applications. In other cases, more complex solutions must be developed. It is probably a good rule to start with a solution that provides the most flexibility. In this article, we have detailed a way to take advantage of the current Web standards without restricting ourselves. The interaction between HTML, JavaScript, and Java provides a powerful way to implement client/server applications, while conserving the advantages of the Web.

The Web is in constant evolution. Additional solutions will certainly appear in the future. It is important to keep apprised of Web developments that lead to new standards. By exploring how these new features fit within the current set of standards, easier or better solutions may be designed and implemented.

References

The following reference materials may provide additional information:

- *Informix Java API Programmer's Guide,* Version 1.04, published by Informix Press/Prentice Hall PTR.
- *The JavaScript Authoring Guide,* provided by Netscape Communications Corporation at the following Web location: http://www.netscape.com/eng/mozilla/2.0/handbook/javascript/index.html

Building a Document Management System using Informix Dynamic Server with Web Integration Option

by Matthew Eichler

Introduction

The scope of typical Information Systems (IS) development has been widening beyond traditional on-line transcript processing (OLTP) applications to include Document Management Systems. The development of these systems presents a new set of problems—as well as a new set of evaluation criteria for the best tools and servers to do the job. For many reasons, Informix Dynamic Server with Web Integration Option is an excellent choice for the development environment.

Qualities of a Usable Document Management System

When exploring software tools, packages, and user requirements, the following qualities contribute to the building of a successful Document Management system:

- The ability to easily publish to a wide audience—documents can be published in multiple formats and/or users can access the system from more than one platform;
- The ability to route documents and provide electronic sign-off capabilities—work flow and digital signature features;
- A friendly, graphical interface to maintain large numbers of documents;
- A flexible, easy-to-use search engine—documents can be searched by keywords or concepts;
- Documents can be activated or set for expiration and removal at a future date;
- Version control of documents;
- Documents are secure—with clear ownership and protection from accidental or intentional damage;
- Administration is manageable, even as the system scales up—a high-priority criteria in the evaluation are administration impact and costs.

Concepts

Given the desired qualities of a Document Management System development environment, consider the Web and Informix Dynamic Server with Web Integration Option.

The Web as a Publishing Environment

The Web is an excellent medium that organizations can use to publish information for a wide audience using simple open tools and servers. Many businesses now operate internal Intranets and/or Web sites on the Internet. If the objective is to publish information for customers outside the company, placing documents on the Internet makes them available to literally millions of users worldwide. In addition, internal Web sites—the Intranet—are widely popular as a direct and simple way to make documents available to all employees at once.

The Web solves the cross-platform problem. Web browsers are commonly available for popular graphical workstation operating systems.

The Challenges of Managing Static Files as Web Sites Scale Up

A major complaint about the Web as a publishing medium is the difficulty of managing huge numbers of documents in the file system as Web sites grow. Traditional file systems are not well-suited for the reuse of documents in different areas of a Web site. Members of a team of publishers easily insert references (*Hyperlinks*) to other documents. For instance, if a document is referenced by several documents, the links are broken when one publisher moves a file to another directory without notifying the other publishers. With very large Web sites, the task of keeping Hyperlinks up-to-date is formidable.

Web sites must be highly dynamic in order to invite revisiting users. Static file systems complicate the task of keeping the Web site dynamic. For example, if new documents are added, it is often necessary to update Hyperlinks in several areas of the Web site.

Other Issues

While the Web provides a simple, open architecture for serving up documents, some of the more advanced Document Management features must be built by the developer, such as metadata about documents—expiration and activation times, ownership, and versions. A standard Web server does not usually include text search capabilities—although there are quite a few popular engines available as freeware on the Internet, with varying feature sets. Routing and sign-off features are often provided by the developer, if required.

Security is an important issue for the Web. The issue of security must be carefully evaluated and planned—especially if a Web site is outside of a company's firewall. By design, the Web server accesses all documents with a single account. Therefore, by default, there is no built-in support for ownership and access privileges to protect documents.

The ORDBMS Server as a Document Repository

Informix's ORDBMS server, Informix Dynamic Server with Universal Data Option, applies database technology to document management. Documents, regardless of published formats, can be stored in the database. Metadata can be modeled around the documents for implementing security, routing, versioning, and automatic activation/deactivation features.

Informix Dynamic Server Integrates the Two Servers

Informix Dynamic Server with Universal Data Option and Web Integration Option provides a framework for integrating the functionality of the Web server and the ORDBMS server. Included in the Informix Dynamic Server with Web Integration Option extension are the following components:

- A CGI "stub" program that passes requests from the Web browser client to Informix Dynamic Server with Universal Data Option for interpretation;
- A *WebExplode()* server function[1] that interprets HTML pages and Web Integration Option tags and passes the results back through CGI. Five special Web Integration Option HTML tags allow the Web site developer to execute Illustra SQL, format query results, and execute conditional logic, as follows:

---

[1] Server functions "live" in the Illustra ORDBMS server. They have the powerful ability to off-load functionality from the client to the server.

- <?MISQL> to execute SQL statements;
- <?MIVAR> to store data in variables and perform some conditional logic;
- <?MIBLOCK> to execute blocks of HTML based on a condition;
- <?MIERROR> to handle exceptions; and
- <?MIEXEC> to evoke a program on the server machine.

- A basic database schema to store the Web site page and image components.
- An *Application Page Builder* (APB) application—a collection of Informix Dynamic Server with Web Integration Option pages—which gives the developer a jump-start on building the Web site. The APB contains some simple HTML forms to step the developer through building a Web site completely from the browser.

The APB gives the developer an introduction to Informix Dynamic Server with Web Integration Option development and is useful in building a basic prototype. It is not recommended, however, for building the final version of the Web site—since the developer needs tighter controls on versioning and the release of the Informix Dynamic Server with Web Integration Option pages.

Text Search Capabilities

Informix Dynamic Server with Universal Data Option provides choices for extending the database server to include text-search capabilities. Deciding which Text Search DataBlade module to use depends on the specific features and the publishing formats required.

Combining a Text Search DataBlade module with the Informix Dynamic Server with Web Integration Option requires careful study to determine their mutual compatibilities. Some custom conversion utilities or server functions may be required—depending on the document formats used.

The Example

The example examines the "Project Lifecycle" application, a repository-oriented Document Management System. The project managers and developers wanted a repository in which to publish the documents and status information of each project for easy access to the entire company. User requirements for the system include the following:

- A "one-page" summary and status information on each project;
- A means to publish all project documents in multiple formats—both native and open;
- A user-friendly navigation system to query information;
- A means for the user community to easily download project documents; and
- Several formats for reporting project information on a global, regional, and local basis. It should be easy to add new views into the documents after the initially released version.

The company already deployed many Intranet Web sites, so the user community was already familiar with the browsers on different platforms. The Web seemed like a natural, low-cost environment in which to develop a Document Management System.

The Illustra ORDBMS server and Informix Dynamic Server with Web Integration Option were selected so content would be dynamic, easily manageable, and scalable in size. The project was not mission critical—it was not expected to directly affect the business—and was small enough in scope to make it an ideal pilot application. This pilot would serve as a baseline for similar applications in the future.

Design

The Project Lifecycle Web site consists of two basic areas—the "view" area and the "project information management" area.

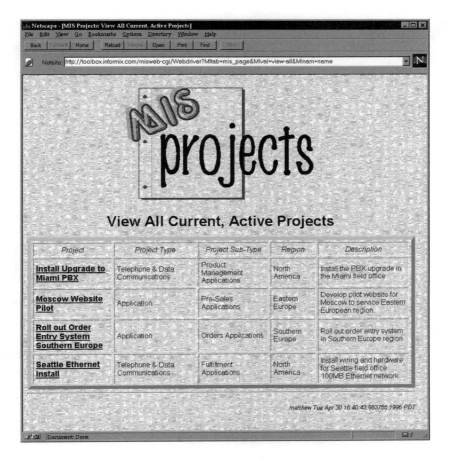

Figure 13–1 *The top-level view of all projects.*

The view pages are open to the public, and therefore are not secured. The objective of Project Lifecycle is to store all its associated Informix Dynamic Server with Web Integration Option pages in the database.

Figure 13–1 is a top-level view that lists all projects from the Netscape browser.

When the user clicks on the project title, the project detail view page is loaded, as shown in Figure 13–2.

Scrolling down to the project status and document sections on the project detail view provides additional information, as shown in Figure 13–3.

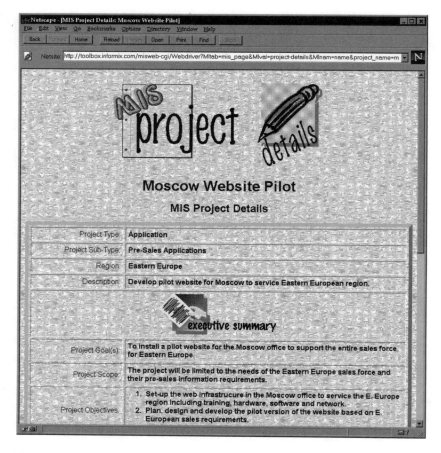

Figure 13–2 *The project detail view page.*

When the user clicks on the document title in the document section, the Document Published Formats page is loaded. This page illustrates how each document may be published in multiple formats, as shown in Figure 13–4.

The project managers and developers maintain project data in a different "area" of the Web site. The idea of separate areas is conceptual—since all Web objects are stored in a single

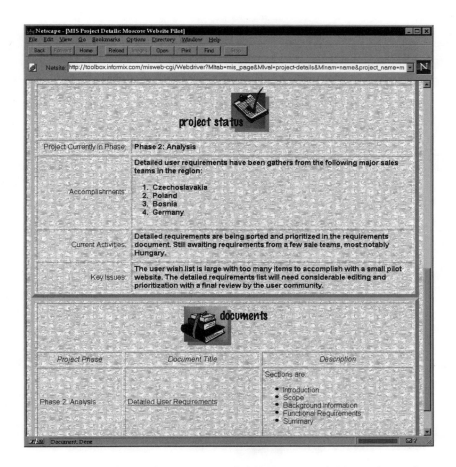

project status

Project Currently In Phase:	Phase 2: Analysis
Accomplishments:	Detailed user requirements have been gathers from the following major sales teams in the region: 1. Czechoslavakia 2. Poland 3. Bosnia 4. Germany
Current Activities:	Detailed requirements are being sorted and prioritized in the requirements document. Still awaiting requirements from a few sale teams, most notably Hungary.
Key Issues:	The user wish list is large with too many items to accomplish with a small pilot website. The detailed requirements list will need considerable editing and prioritization with a final review by the user community.

documents

Project Phase	Document Title	Description
Phase 2: Analysis	Detailed User Requirements	Sections are: • Introduction • Scope • Background Information • Functional Requirements • Summary

Figure 13–3 *The project status and document sections on the project detail view.*

ORDBMS server. The project information management area is secured so that projects have ownership and are protected from accidental change.

The menu for project information management appears in the browser as shown in Figure 13–5.

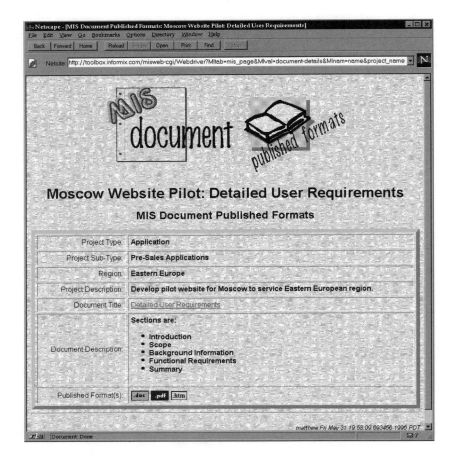

Figure 13–4 *Detailed user requirements.*

Data Modeling with the Illustra ORDBMS Server

Inheritance

The Object-Oriented (OO) inheritance technique can be used with the Illustra ORDBMS server to create consistency throughout the data model and to build maintainable structures (see Figure 13–6).

This model translates to the following Illustra Data Definition Language (DDL):

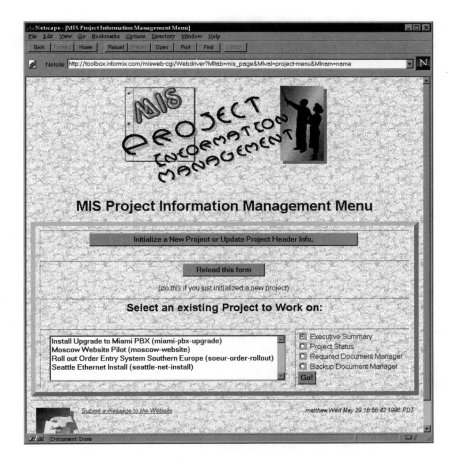

Figure 13–5 *Project information management menu.*

```
CREATE TABLE mis_obj OF NEW TYPE mis_obj_t
(
     name text NOT NULL,
     title text,
     description text,
     update_by text DEFAULT USER NOT NULL,
     update_time abstime DEFAULT 'now' NOT NULL,
     activate_time abstime DEFAULT 'now' NOT NULL,
     expire_time abstime
);
```

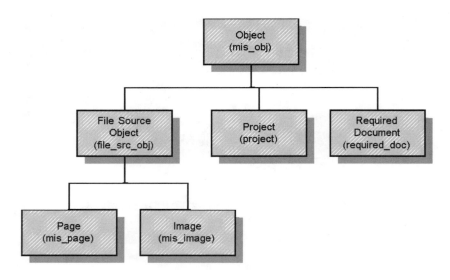

Figure 13–6 *The hierarchical structure.*

```
CREATE TABLE file_src_obj OF NEW TYPE file_src_obj_t
(
    source_path text
) UNDER mis_obj;


CREATE TABLE mis_image OF NEW TYPE mis_image_t
(
    image_type_ref ref(image_type_t) NOT NULL,
    image_type_name text virtual,
    image_type_title text virtual,
    mime_type_ref ref(mime_type_t) NOT NULL,
    mime_type text virtual,
    image large_object,
    UNIQUE(name)
) UNDER file_src_obj;

CREATE TABLE mis_page OF NEW TYPE mis_page_t
(
    page_type_ref ref(page_type_t) NOT NULL,
    page_type_name text virtual,
```

```
    page_type_title text virtual,
    mime_type_ref ref(mime_type_t) NOT NULL,
    mime_type text virtual,
    hyperlink setof( ref(url_t) ),
    page large_text,
    UNIQUE(name)
) UNDER file_src_obj;
```

Project Lifecycle used a basic single-object hierarchy. Almost every table in the schema inherits from an "abstract" object to include basic fields. This ensures that each table consistently contains the name, title, and description information. Also, every table will include date/time stamps that indicate when the row was last updated and the activation/expiration date/times.

Type Definition

Every table definition includes a corresponding type definition. These types are used later to define parameters and to return values from server functions.

For example, the following implements the automatic look-up of page type indicators for their corresponding name and title virtual columns:

```
CREATE FUNCTION page_type_name(mis_page_t)
    RETURNS text
    WITH ( late )
    AS
    RETURN deref($1.page_type_ref).name;

CREATE FUNCTION page_type_title(mis_page_t)
    RETURNS text
    WITH ( late )
    AS
    RETURN deref($1.page_type_ref).title;
```

Using the Built-In Key: oids, ref(), deref()

The Illustra ORDBMS server—as with other OO servers—automatically maintains a unique object identifier for every database object: the implicit oid column. Rather than explicitly declaring primary keys, the designer used this feature to relate tables to one another.

For example, the project table contains references to corresponding executive summary and project status rows that belong to a specific project:

```
CREATE TABLE exec_summary OF NEW TYPE exec_summary_t
(
    sections setof(html_section_t),
    UNIQUE(name)
) UNDER mis_obj;

CREATE TABLE proj_status OF NEW TYPE proj_status_t
(
    current_phase_ref ref(proj_phase_t),
    current_phase_name text virtual,
    current_phase_title text virtual,
    sections setof(html_section_t),
    UNIQUE(name)
) UNDER mis_obj;

CREATE TABLE project OF NEW TYPE project_t
(
    proj_type_ref ref(proj_type_t),
    proj_type_name text virtual,
    proj_type_title text virtual,
    proj_subtype_ref ref(proj_subtype_t),
    proj_subtype_name text virtual,
    proj_subtype_title text virtual,
    region_ref ref(region_t),
    region_name text virtual,
    region_title text virtual,
    required_docs setof(required_doc_t),
    backup_docs setof(backup_doc_t),
    exec_summary ref(exec_summary_t),
```

```
    proj_status ref(proj_status_t),
    UNIQUE(name)
) UNDER mis_obj;
```

If traditional table associations are designed using *PRIMARY KEY/FOREIGN KEY* constructs, referential integrity is built by the engine behind the scenes—as is expected of an ANSI compliant RDBMS. If the OO style associations are designed using *ref()/deref()*, referential integrity—if required—must be explicitly built by the designer using *rules*.

Aggregation: setof()

The OO concept of aggregation[2] can be implemented with ORDBMS SQL using the *setof()* construct—instead of using referential constraints and associative tables. Aggregation provides an alternative way for the designer to represent complex nested structures besides using traditional referential constraints.

For the example, the users required the publishing of each document in one or more formats. For instance, a project developer may provide a "Test Plan" document in Microsoft Word, Adobe Acrobat, and HTML formats—providing flexibility to the end users who will download documents.

The two types of documents in the system—required and backup—are an aggregation of published formats:

```
CREATE TYPE published_fmt_t
(
    mime_type_ref ref(mime_type_t),
    mime_type text virtual,
    source_path text,
    doc large_object
);
```

---

[2] Aggregation as an OO concept represents a group of components which together form a single entity. Actions on the aggregate whole may propagate to the individual components. A car, for instance, is an aggregation of the component parts—each of which is an object itself.

```
CREATE TYPE required_doc_t
(
    doc_type_ref ref(doc_type_t),
    doc_type_name text virtual,
    doc_type_title text virtual,
    published_fmts setof(published_fmt_t)
) UNDER mis_obj_t;

CREATE TYPE backup_doc_t
(
    published_fmts setof(published_fmt_t)
) UNDER mis_obj_t;
```

MIME-Type in the Data Model: Virtual Columns

The Web browser requires the MIME[3]-type to process the objects it downloads. Depending on the MIME-type, the browser may display the object itself or invoke a helper application.

To avoid hard-coding the MIME-types into the application, a table was designed to support the types dynamically. The other tables that require a MIME-type use *ref()* to point to the correct type. To simplify the look-up, a *text* virtual column and a corresponding function is written for each table:

```
CREATE TABLE type_ind OF NEW TYPE type_ind_t
    UNDER mis_obj;

CREATE TABLE mime_type OF NEW TYPE mime_type_t
(
    file_ext text NOT NULL,
    mime_type text NOT NULL,
    UNIQUE(name)
) UNDER type_ind;

CREATE TABLE mis_image OF NEW TYPE mis_image_t
(
```

---

[3] *Multi-Purpose Internet Mail Extensions.*

```
    image_type_ref ref(image_type_t) NOT NULL,
    image_type_name text virtual,
    image_type_title text virtual,
    mime_type_ref ref(mime_type_t) NOT NULL,
    mime_type text virtual,
    image large_object,
    UNIQUE(name)
) UNDER file_src_obj;
```

The image table above contains the actual reference to the
MIME-type in the *mime_type_ref* column. The *mime_type* virtual
text column provides the actual MIME-type data needed for the
browser once the following function is implemented:

```
CREATE FUNCTION mime_type(mis_image_t)
    RETURNS text
    WITH ( late )
    AS
    RETURN deref($1.mime_type_ref).mime_type;
```

Now, each time the *mime_type* column is selected from the
image table, this function will perform the appropriate look-up.
The alternative to this approach is to provide a *VIEW* which
defines the join between the two tables, and selects from the
VIEW to locate the MIME-type data.

Coding

After an initial pass at building the ORDBMS server's data
model, the developer can begin coding Informix Dynamic Server
with Web Integration Option HTML pages. The pages can be
coded and managed with the APB—or coded outside the browser
with the developer's favorite HTML editor—and subsequently
stored in a table using a standard *UPDATE* or *INSERT* statement.

How the Webdriver Works

First, *Webdriver—Webdriver* on UNIX, or *webdriver.exe* on Microsoft Windows for NT—is called by the appropriate URL from the browser. Then, several parameters are set correctly before the URL connects to the server as the correct account and finds the specific page in a particular table to pass to the *WebExplode* server function.

Many of the values that do not change from page to page can be stored in a configuration file, *Web.conf*, which resides in the CGI directory with *Webdriver*. The contents are typically similar to the following:

```
## Web.conf
MI_DATABASE        misweb
MI_SERVER              default
MI_SYSPARAMS       /isdev2/illustra/MiParams
MInam?                 ID
MIcol?                 page
MItab?                 web_pages
MIval?                 apb
RAW_PASSWD      1
MI_USER                http
MI_PASSWD          Sam+Trans?
WEB_HOME           /cgi-bin/Webdriver
MIdisplay_exception  on
```

Four of these variables specify the row, column, and table in which to find the page:

1. **MItab** specifies the table;
2. **MIcol** specifies the column which contains the actual page;
3. **MInam** specifies the column which contains the key value for the row; and
4. **MIval** specifies the key value for the row.

Variable names followed by the question mark (?) can be over-ridden by specifying their values in the URL. This allows the application to have a default page—if no parameters are passed to *Webdriver*.

The following URL overrides the default row, column, and table values to access the desired page:

```
http://literbox/cgibin/webdriver.exe?MItab=mis_page&MInam=name&MIcol=page&MIval=pmen
```

Variables

The contents of variables can be referenced with the dollar sign ($). Variables come from three sources:

1. The CGI environment—for example, SERVER_NAME, USER_AGENT, REMOTE_USER;
2. Informix Dynamic Server with Web Integration Option configuration file—*Web.conf* is located in the same CGI directory as the *Webdriver* executable. This configuration provides Informix Dynamic Server with Web Integration Option default values for certain variables that are required for the server, such as MI_DATABASE, MI_USER and MI_PASSWD; or
3. Variables that were set from previous <?MIVAR> and <?**MISQL**> tags. Any variables set with these tags persist for the entire page.

The values of the variables are only substituted when contained within <?**MIVAR**> and <?**MISQL**> tags.

Executing SQL Statements

The <?**MISQL**> tag is used to execute SQL statements. The values of columns fetched from tables are stored in numbered variables—the first column value is fetched into $1, the second into $2, etc. These numbered variables persist until another SQL statement is executed.

If the SQL statement returns more than one row, the tag iterates through each row, applying any supplied HTML formatting. This allows the developer to easily format the entire contents of an SQL query.

The following Web Integration Option tag queries the header information for the entire list of current projects into an HTML table:

```
<?MISQL SQL="
SELECT name, title, proj_type_title, proj_subtype_title,
     region_title, description
  FROM curr_project
 ORDER BY title;">
<TR>
<TD ALIGN="LEFT" COLSTART="1">
<FONT SIZE="+1"><STRONG>
<A HREF="$WEB_HOME?MItab=mis_page&MIval=project-
  details&MInam=name&project_name=$1">
$2</A>
</STRONG></FONT>
</TD>
<TD ALIGN="LEFT"  COLSTART="2">$3</TD>
<TD ALIGN="LEFT"  COLSTART="3">$4</TD>
<TD ALIGN="LEFT"  COLSTART="4">$5</TD>
<TD ALIGN="LEFT"  COLSTART="5">$6</TD>
</TR><?/MISQL>
```

Conditional Logic

The <?**MIBLOCK**> tag is used to code conditional logic on pages. For instance, the existence of the *REMOTE_USER* variable is checked to investigate whether a specific user has authority to use the current page:

```
<?MIBLOCK COND=$REMOTE_USER.nxst.>
<H2><EM>Access violation.</EM></H2>
<?/MIBLOCK><!-- $REMOTE_USER.nxst. -->
```

Also, the <?**MIVAR**> tag can be used to conditionally set the value of variables:

```
<?MIVAR NAME=view COND=$show_expired.eq.no>curr_$table<?/MIVAR>
```

Reusing Sections—Calling WebExplode()

The *WebExplode* function can be called explicitly from an
<?MISQL> tag so that one page can include the interpreted con-
tents of another page. This is helpful when reusing sections of
HTML throughout the Web site—for a consistent look and feel.

For instance, the following code is used to retrieve the header
section for the information management area of the Web site:

```
<?MISQL SQL="
SELECT WebExplode(page,
  'WEB_HOME=$WEB_HOME&page_title=MIS+Project+Header+Management')
  FROM mis_page
 WHERE name='project-hdr';">$1<?/MISQL>
```

The first parameter of *WebExplode* is the column containing
the page to be interpreted, and the second parameter is an
encoded string containing any variables to be passed to the page
for interpretation. The header section is coded as follows:

```
<HEAD><TITLE><?MIVAR>$page_title<?/MIVAR></TITLE></HEAD>

<?MISQL SQL="
SELECT image::text, mime_type
  FROM mis_image
 WHERE name = 'marble4';"><BODY
  BACKGROUND="$WEB_HOME?LO=$1&type=$2"><?/MISQL>

<?MISQL SQL="
SELECT image::text, mime_type
  FROM mis_image
 WHERE name = 'ProjMaintHdr';"><P ALIGN="CENTER"><IMG
  SRC="$WEB_HOME?LO=$1&type=$2" ALT="MIS Website
  Maintenance"></P><?/MISQL>

<H1 ALIGN="CENTER"><?MIVAR>$page_title<?/MIVAR></H1>
```

Note the variables which are passed to *WebExplode*.

Retrieving Images and Documents: large_object

Large database objects database—stored in columns of type *large_text* or *large_object*—can be fetched from the database using a special parameter to *WebExplode: LO*. The *LO* handle is an identifier that is visible when a large object is queried from the database and implicitly or explicitly cast to text.

Using MIME-Types

By passing the correct MIME-type, the browser is provided information on how to format or handle the object. For example, the code to retrieve the icon (which represents the project status) is as follows:

```
<?MISQL SQL="
SELECT image::text, mime_type
  FROM mis_image
 WHERE name = 'ProjectStatus';"><IMG
  SRC="$WEB_HOME?LO=$1&type=$2" ALT="Project Status"><?/MISQL>
```

Keeping Pages Short and Simple

Informix Dynamic Server with Web Integration Option pages can easily become unmanageable. One reason is that HTML was designed as a mark-up language and not a programming language—a page with many conditional blocks is hard to read. Another reason is the statelessness of CGI—many variables might be required to pass the appropriate state values from one page to another.

Following are a few recommendations to keep pages manageable:

1. Keep the user interface simple and HTML forms small. If possible, break larger forms into multiple, smaller pages;
2. Keep conditional blocks to a minimum. Look for opportunities to break a single page with many blocks into multiple, smaller pages; and
3. Off-load SQL complexity to the ORDBMS server—use functions, views, rules, and additional tables to keep the SQL embedded

within HTML simple and compact. As pages are coded, look for opportunities to move functionality to the server.

Implementing Security

Web applications present a special security problem since all pages—and therefore all database access—are executed as a single account: the account that runs the Web server process. Freely-distributed Web servers—such as NCSA and CERN—and commercial Web servers, such as Netscape, often provide a method to secure files and directories with password authentication.

The example is divided into two areas for security purposes. The public area that allows company-wide users the ability to browse project information was not secured. This area has its own CGI executable directory, *Webdriver* and *web.conf* file. The protected area—that allows only project managers, project developers, and Webmasters the ability to maintain the Web site and project information—was secured. A user database[4]—with users' passwords—was built using the administration tools that came with the Web server. The protected area also has its own CGI directory, *Webdriver* and *web.conf* file which are secured by the user database. Once a user logs into that area of the Web site, CGI passes the user account name in the variable REMOTE_USER. The protected pages check for the existence of this variable before continuing to process.

Steps to Success

Following are the steps to the successful development of a Document Management System using the ORDBMS server and

---

[4] The user database is a file built by the Web server administration tools. This file usually resides under the home directory of the web server. This database must not be confused with the ORDBMS server.

Informix Dynamic Server with Web Integration Option module tools:

1. Build a Web infrastructure—incorporate a release process, training, HTML editors, etc.;
2. Ensure user requirements are complete—understand the objectives of the system;
3. Create a rough prototype with static HTML files—explore the flow of the application and review it with end users;
4. Design the data model and build the ORDBMS server—if possible, use modeling tools to visualize the structure;
5. Code Web Integration Option pages and test the result—build ORDBMS server functions and rules to off-load functionality to the server and keep pages simple;
6. Test the completed alpha system and polish the user interface and graphics; and
7. Freeze all page and database changes, release the beta version, and test the results with a handful of users.

Conclusion

The ORDBMS server, Informix Dynamic Server with Universal Data Option, and Web Integration Option provide an excellent development environment for a Document Management system. With careful planning and development, these tools help to ensure a successful pilot project.

Some Helpful Links

The following references provide additional information on some of the topics introduced in this article:

- HTML Information

`http://www.utirc.utoronto.ca/HTMLdocs/NewHTML/htmlindex.html`

- HTML Forms

`http://www.ncsa.uiuc.edu/SDG/Software/Mosaic/Docs/`
`   fill-out-forms/overview.html`

- The Common Gateway Interface (CGI)

`http://hoohoo.ncsa.uiuc.edu`

Server-Side Functions for the Universal Data Option

by Jacques Roy

Introduction

Several examples have been given on the benefits of using Informix Dynamic Server with Universal Data Option's server-side functions. They provide crucial functionality to adapt the database server to the business environment. The result is a more natural problem-solving approach that improves programming productivity and software performance, resulting in faster response time to market changes.

This article describes:

- How server-side functions are executed in Informix Dynamic Server with Universal Data Option's environment;
- How DataBlades can interact with each other; and
- Some finer points of server-side function programming that are essential but often overlooked.

We will start with a brief example of a server-side function declaration and usage to provide a minimum background for the rest of the paper.

Server-Side Functions

Server-side functions augment the database server functionality to better fit your business environment. For example, a simple function can allow a business to perform aggregations in the server in a more natural manner and with improved performance. With the addition of a function that returns the quarter a date is in, quarterly aggregations can be performed. The following statement declaration performs the addition of the `quarter()` function:

```
CREATE FUNCTION quarter(date)
RETURNS varchar(10)
WITH (NOT VARIANT)

EXTERNAL NAME "mylib.bld(quarter)"
LANGUAGE C;
```

This statement creates a function named `quarter` that takes a date as input and returns a variable character string of ten or less characters. The NOT VARIANT modifier tells the system that the function will always return the same result from a specific input. The function is located in the dynamic library `mylib.bld` and the name of the C function is `quarter`.

Once the create statement is executed, the function is available for use. The following SQL statement can then be issued:

```
SELECT branch, quarter(date) Quarter, SUM(total_sales) Total
FROM transactions
WHERE quarter(date) like '1997Q%'
GROUP BY 1, 2
ORDER BY 1, 2;
```

This statement returns the quarterly sales for each branch for the year 1997. There is no need to either issue several separate SQL statements or join with another table to get the right quarter. There is also a performance advantage in addition to the simplicity of the statement.

The result of the function could also be indexed. This could provide additional performance benefits that are transparent to the person issuing statements containing this function.

This brief description raises several questions:

- What languages are supported?
- What are dynamic libraries?
- What other function modifiers are available?

These questions and more are the subject of the following sections.

Programming Languages

Informix Dynamic Server with Universal Data Option was designed from the start to be extensible. This principle also applies to the languages supported in writing server-side functions. Of course, extending the server to support additional languages is a very specialized task that can only be done by experts in the field. Nevertheless, the functionality is there and more languages may appear in the future to better fit the market's needs.

The current version of Informix Dynamic Server with Universal Data Option supports the legacy Informix language SPL (Stored Procedure Language) and the C language.

SPL provides simple programming constructs in the context of an SQL like language. With SPL, it is possible to define variables and use flow control commands like FOR, WHILE, FOREACH, and IF. Here is a simple server-side function written in SPL:

```
CREATE FUNCTION manager_name(mid integer)
RETURNING varchar(20);
```

```
DEFINE mname varchar(20);

IF mid IS NULL THEN
   return " ";
END IF

SELECT name into mname from employee where id = mid;
RETURN mname;

END FUNCTION;
```

This function applies to a specific table. It takes a manager id as input and returns the name of the manager as output. If there is no manager id, a space is returned. This function can simplify statements in which both the employee name and the manager name are required. This is typical of an employee table where each row contains the employee id and her manager id.

For more complex processing, server-side functions are written in C. These functions are referred to as external functions. C functions interface with the server through the DataBlade API library. There is virtually no limit to what can be done through a C function.

Describing the DataBlade API is beyond the scope of this paper. For more information on this subject, please refer to the *DataBlade API Programmer's Manual*.

Dynamic Libraries

External server-side functions are accessed by Informix Dynamic Server with Universal Data Option through dynamic libraries. In UNIX, they are referred to as shared library (.so). In Windows NT, they are called dynamic link libraries (.dll).

In addition to providing the technology required to extend the functionality of Informix Dynamic Server with Universal Data Option, dynamic libraries optimize memory utilization because only one copy of a library is required for all processes using it.

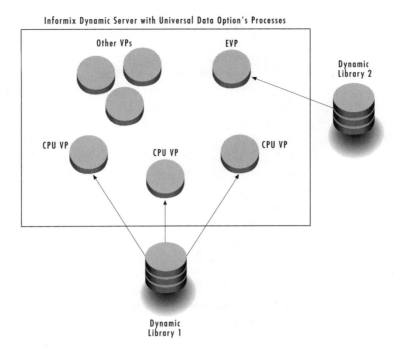

Figure 14–1 *UDO and Shared Libraries.*

In the UNIX environment, each Informix virtual processor is a process. By using dynamic libraries, the physical memory consumption related to their use does not vary with the number of virtual processors. This contrasts dramatically with static libraries that require a separate copy for each separate program.

Before a function within a dynamic library can be used, the library must be loaded and the address of the function must be found. Let's assume we have a library `mylib.so` that contains the function `quarter()`. Here is a code excerpt that would execute the function:

```
void *handle;
char *pquarter, *(fptr)(mi_date);

handle = dlopen("mylib.so", RTLD_LAZY);
fptr = (char *(*)(mi_date))dlsym(handle, "quarter");

pquarter = (*fptr)(date);
```

The `dlopen()` function opens the dynamic library without trying to resolve any symbols. The `dlsym()` functions retrieves the address of the `quarter()` function and the result is cast to the appropriate value. The function is then executed by de-referencing the pointer `fptr`. The `date` argument is a fictitious value of type `mi_date` that is to be processed.

A program can release a dynamic library using the `dlclose()` function call. The Microsoft Windows NT environment provides similar functions for its dynamic link libraries. These functions are `GetModuleHandle()`, `GetProcAddress()`, and `FreeLibrary()`.

The Universal Data Option provides additional error checking and also applies constraints provided in the function definition. Nevertheless, this is a sufficient overview to understand how dynamic libraries are used.

The Fastpath Interface

A DataBlade module refers to a set of user-defined types and the functions that apply to them. This is not entirely true, since a DataBlade module can consist only of functions that apply to existing types. All in all, it is a packaging of functionality.

There are cases where a DataBlade module depends on the functionality of another module. The standard way to take advantage of the functionality of this other DataBlade module is to refer to it through the execution of an SQL statement. For example, if a function wanted to take advantage of the quarter() function provided in a date manipulation DataBlade module, it would include code similar to the following:

```
...
stcopy("EXECUTE FUNCTION quarter('", buffer);
rfmtdate(date, "mm/dd/yyyy", &buffer[26]);
stcopy("');", &buffer[36]);
mi_exec(conn, buffer);
...
```

This is equivalent to executing a statement similar to the following:

Table 14-1 *FastPath API functions.*

```
mi_cast_get()
mi_fparam_get()
mi_routine_end()
mi_routine_exec()
mi_routine_get()
mi_routine_get_by_typeid()
mi_routine_id_get()
mi_td_cast_get()
```

```
EXECUTE FUNCTION quarter('02/14/1998');
```

This way of calling functions from other modules incurs the overhead of parsing, planning, and executing the SQL query. This is followed by the code needed to retrieve the result and manipulate the MI_DATUM return value. Depending on the function usage, the overhead incurred may be insignificant compared to the overall processing. In other cases, it is beneficial to avoid this additional processing.

We cannot execute the function directly because it is located in a dynamic library. Looking back at the way that dynamic libraries work, it is possible to find several reasons why it cannot be done:

- The symbol quarter is not known in the database server and cannot be resolved to the proper function address.
- It is not possible to know if the dynamic library has been loaded.
- We don't have the dynamic library handle.

Opening and using the dynamic library containing the quarter() function can lead to a number of problems. It is better to let the server handle the dynamic libraries' management.

Informix Dynamic Server with Universal Data Option includes an interface that provides the facility to directly call any registered server routine. This facility is referred to as the FastPath interface.

The FastPath interface functions find the right dynamic library and locate the function to execute. It is not necessary for the programmer to handle libraries and functions pointers. For more information on how to use the fastpath interface, refer to the *DataBlade API Programmers* manual.

Well-Behaved Functions

A server-side function executes in the context of a server virtual processor. Informix Dynamic Server implements multithreading within its virtual processors. Informix's threading implementation provides the same benefits as any commercially available thread package.

When Informix implemented its threaded architecture, few if any UNIX systems supported this feature. Over time, UNIX implementations began to support multithreading. Each implementation was different. Even today some platforms do not support multithreading. Even if a standard implementation was available on all platforms, there would be little benefit to change the current implementation.

On the Microsoft NT platform, Informix virtual processors are implemented as NT threads. Regardless, each NT thread is multithreaded using the Informix implementation.

One main advantage of multithreading is the low resource consumption required to schedule the separate threads as compared to the operating system-level process scheduling. One reason is that there is no need to move from the user space to the privilege kernel space. The drawback is that if a user-level thread blocks on some event, then the entire process is stopped until the user thread can resume execution. This is a standard feature of user-level thread packages.

The definition of a well-behaved function is a function that never executes any code which would cause it to block. A function could execute a server API call which would, in turn, cause it to be re-scheduled and placed on a wait queue for a specific event. This has the effect of blocking the thread, but it is done in a collaborative way with the virtual processor, so the virtual processor can then schedule another thread for execution.

Does this mean that it is not permitted to write functions that may block? No. Informix provides the ability to create user-defined virtual processors. These are often referred to as Extended Virtual Processors, or EVPs. The database administrator can define specific EVPs, and the number of EVPs that will be created. The blocking server-side function can then execute in an EVP without impacting the proper execution of the database server.

For example, assuming that your server configuration includes the following Virtual Processor (VP) declaration:

```
VPCLASS myvp,num=1
```

You can declare your misbehaved function as running on that specific extended virtual processor:

```
CREATE FUNCTION newfunc(lvarchar)
RETURNS varchar(10)
WITH (CLASS='myvp', NOT VARIANT)

EXTERNAL NAME "mylib2.bld(newfunc)"
LANGUAGE C;
```

In this way, the server normal processing will not be disrupted.

Function Modifiers

Server-side functions can serve different purposes. The previous section demonstrated that some functions, due to their processing requirements, may need to wait for some external processing. To ensure the proper execution of the database engine, these functions should run on an EVP. This requirement is specified in the function definition through the use of a function modifier. This is reflected in the third line of the previous function creation definition:

. . .
```
WITH (CLASS='myvp', NOT VARIANT)
```
. . .

This declaration contains two function modifiers. Informix Dynamic Server with Universal Data Option currently provides the following modifiers:

- **CLASS**

  This modifier identifies the type of VP that will execute this function. By default, a server-side function executes in a CPU VP. When an implementation includes functions that are not well behaved, the database administrator should create extended VPs. The name of the extended VP is then referred to in the function modifier using the CLASS parameter. This modifier is not used for SPL functions because, by definition, they are always well behaved.

- **HANDLESNULLS**

  By default an external function will not be called if the parameter that it receives is NULL. In this way, no code must be added to the function to test for NULL values. Carefully analyze the way a server-side function will be used and decide if they should handle null values or not. SPL functions handle NULL by default.

- **INTERNAL**

  This modifier indicates that the server-side function is for internal use only. It cannot be called from either an SQL or SPL statement. This modifier is only used for external ("C") functions.

- **ITERATOR**

  This modifier is used to indicate that the server-side function returns a set of values. In this way, the function will be called multiple times until it indicates that no more values are available. In the case of SPL functions, use the "RETURN WITH RESUME" command.

- **PARALLELIZABLE**

  This modifier indicates that the function meets the requirement to be run in parallel. This modifier only applies to external ("C") functions.

- **STACK**

  This modifier is used when an external server-side function requires more space for automatic variables than is provided by the default stack size (default 32 KB; see the STACKSIZE onconfig parameter). You cannot use the STACK modifier for SPL functions.

- **VARIANT**

  When a function is called multiple time with the same arguments, it is assumed that it will return different values. If a function always return the same value when passed specific arguments, it should be declared NOT VARIANT. In this way, the server can cache the result of the call and save the processing of multiple invocation.

When creating a server-side function, it is important to analyze how a function will be used so that the right modifier is specified. For example, if NOT VARIANT is not specified, the processing requirements may increase. Furthermore, it is not possible to create indexes on the result of VARIANT functions.

The MI_FPARAMS Argument

When writing an external "C" function manually, it is natural to assume that the function declaration contains only the arguments which are part of the design of the function. For example:

```
mi_integer my_func(mi_integer value);
```

If you generate the same function using the DataBlade Development Kit (DBDK), you will find the following function declaration:

```
mi_integer my_func(mi_integer value, MI_FPARAM *fparam);
```

This additional argument is called the function parameter. It contains arguments and return type information. The MI_FPARAMS structure is an opaque type and should only be accessed using the provided DataBlade API routines. There currently are 29 API routines provided, all starting with "mi_fp_".

The MI_FPARAM structure is essential for the proper execution of external functions. It allows for the testing of NULL value arguments. It is also the mechanism used to indicate that a function is returning a NULL value. It is important to note that a function should always use the MI_FPARAM structure to indicate that it is returning a NULL value.

The MI_FPARAM structure is also used in the implementation of iterator functions. Iterator functions can return more than one row of values in an SQL statement. They must be able to differentiate between calls so that they can perform the right operation. For this purpose, the MI_FPARAMS structure contains the request information which indicates that the operation is being performed on the current call to the function. The request information can have the following values:

- **SET_INIT**
  This value is used in the first invocation of the DataBlade module function.
- **SET_RETONE**
  This value is used for each subsequent call to the DataBlade Module function.
- **SET_END**
  This value is issued after the last row is returned, providing a means to clean up and shut down the active set.

A review of the MI_FPARAM structure and its API routines is essential to the proper programming of external server-side functions.

Conclusion

The capability to write server-side functions is a powerful way to teach the database server about the finer points of your business environment. Informix Dynamic Server with Universal Data Option provides a flexible implementation which can answer business needs. To take full advantage of this functionality, it is good to have a high-level understanding of how the server-side functions fit into the overall Dynamic Server Architecture.

This article provided an overview of the important features of Informix Dynamic Server with Universal Data Option's environment. These features will help you to take full advantage of server-side functions. The result will be improved responsiveness to your company business needs.

References

- Informix Press, *Extending INFORMIX-Universal Server: User Defined Routines*, Version 9.1, Part No. 000-3803, 1997
- Informix Press, *INFORMIX-Universal Server Informix Guide to SQL: Syntax*, Version 9.1, Part No. 000-3879 and 000-3880, 1997
- Informix Press, *INFORMIX-Universal Server Informix Guide to SQL: Tutorial*, Version 9.1, Part No. 000-3856, 1997
- Informix Press, *INFORMIX-Universal Server DataBlade API Programmer's Manual*, Version 9.1, Part No. 000-4812, 1997
- Informix Press, *INFORMIX-ESQL/C Programmer's Manual*, Volume 1 and 2, Version 9.1, Part No. 000-3671 and 000-3672, 1997

Chapter 15

Aggregations in the Environment of the Universal Data Option

by Jacques Roy

Introduction

Aggregations are an important component of any relational database system. The Informix Dynamic Server with Universal Data Option adds new aggregation functions and functionality. This article provides an overview on aggregations, the aggregation functions provided in the Universal Data Option, and describes a new way to use aggregations in Informix's object-relational environment.

Performance Considerations

Aggregations provide functionality that both reduces application complexity and boosts performance. This performance improvement is mainly due to the following reasons:

- It is not necessary to transfer rows to the database client application. Transferring the rows to a client application involves copying and transferring the rows over a shared memory or network connection, which also involves additional system calls. On network connections, this also has the side effect of requiring more network bandwidth. Furthermore, the network traffic impacts the row-transfer speed. This overhead is significant, compared to the processing required to execute the aggregation. The overhead also increases with the complexity of the GROUP BY clause, since more columns must be transferred for each row.
- The database server can take advantage of parallel processing. In addition, the database server can take advantage of its multithreaded architecture and process the table fragments in parallel. The aggregation function processes each fragment in parallel, thus providing a better response time.

When comparing aggregation in an application and aggregation in the server, a small test using the stores7 demo database has demonstrated a 40-percent performance improvement when aggregating a non-fragmented table using a shared memory connection and the simplest GROUP BY operation possible. For situations where network connections and/or fragmentation tables are used, the performance difference is more significant.

An understanding of the way that aggregations operate is required to take full advantage of the Universal Data Option's aggregation capabilities. Consider the following SELECT statement:

```
SELECT customer_num, COUNT(*)
FROM orders
GROUP By 1;
```

This statement returns a list of customer numbers and the number of their respective orders. For a table that is not partitioned, the operation simply consists of counting the records of a specific type.

To take advantage of the parallelism of the COUNT aggregate on a partitioned table, the Universal Data Option performs the aggregate on each fragment and passes the result to another thread. This final thread must merge the results from each

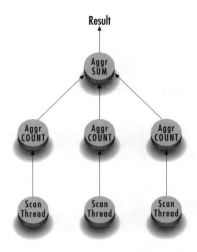

Figure 15–1 *COUNT aggregate.*

fragment into the appropriate aggregation. In our COUNT example, the final processing is a SUM aggregation. The aggregation is illustrated in Figure 15–1.

In the case of a SUM() aggregate, each level must return a summation of the values. However, an AVG() aggregate requires that the lower levels return a composite value of a summation and a count. Every aggregation function must take into account the possibility of running on a partitioned table.

New Aggregations in the Universal Data Option

Informix Dynamic Server supports the following aggregation functions:

COUNT()
This function returns the number of rows that satisfy the query or the number of distinct or unique non-null values in the specified column.

AVG()
This function returns the average of all values in the specified column or expression.

MAX()

This function returns the largest value in the specified column or expression.

MIN()

This function returns the lowest value in the column or expression.

SUM()

This function returns the sum of all the values in the specified column or expression.

The Universal Data Option also supports the following functions:

RANGE()

This function computes the difference between the maximum and the minimum values in the specified column.

STDEV()

This function computes the standard deviation of a specified column. It is defined as the square root of the variance.

VARIANCE()

This function computes the variance of a specified column defined as follows:

```
(SUM(value**2)-(SUM(value)**2)/N)/(N-1)
```

All these aggregation functions can be enhanced by taking advantage of the new features provided by the Universal Data Option, which will be covered in the following section.

Extending Built-In Aggregate Functions

To use the built-in aggregate functions on your user-defined datatypes (UDTs), either provide an implicit cast to a standard type or provide additional user-defined routines to supply the needed functionality. If an implicit cast is provided, the result of the aggregation will return the base type and not the user-defined type. Typically, it is better to provide additional functions to preserve strong typing and return the proper type.

Table 15–1 *Support functions for aggregation.*

Aggregate	Required Functions
AVG COUNT	plus(udt,udt), divide(udt,integer)
MAX	greaterthanorequal(udt,udt)
MIN	lessthanorequal(udt,udt)
SUM	plus(udt,udt)
RANGE	lessthanorequal(udt,udt), greaterthanorequal(udt,udt), minus(udt,udt)
STDEV	times(udt,udt), divide(udt,integer), plus(udt,udt), minus(udt,udt), root(udt)
VARIANCE	times(udt,udt), divide(udt,integer), plus(udt,udt), minus(udt,udt)

Table 15–1 lists the built-in aggregate functions and the support functions which must be added. The return type for built-in aggregates depends on the return type of the last executed function. In the case of AVG, STDEV, and VARIANCE, the return type is determined by the return type of the divide operator.

Grouping

Aggregations operate on sets of values. These sets can be defined by adding a GROUP BY clause to an SQL statement. This is limited by column values. In some cases, the need for specific aggregations force the addition of columns that duplicate information which is already available. This is the case when a quarterly aggregation is needed.

With the Universal Data Option, it is possible to add simple functions that, applied to specific columns, provide additional capabilities for grouping. Consider a user-defined function that takes a date as an argument and returns a string which represents the quarter for a particular date. Let's say that the format is YYYYQN, where "YYYY" represents the year, "Q" simply represents "Quarter", and "N" is the number of the quarter. Thus, the last quarter of 1997 would be "1997Q4."

With this function, it is now possible to perform a quarterly aggregation. The quarterly sales for the year can be expressed with the following SQL statement:

```
SELECT quarter(date) Quarter, SUM(income) Total
FROM orders
WHERE quarter(date) like '1997Q%'
GROUP BY 1
ORDER BY 1;
```

If the company changes its business year, applications do not need to be modified, only the "quarter" function must be redone. In the case of client-server applications, this eliminates the need to update a potentially large number of client machines.

Other functions come to mind easily:

- A function returns if the date is a holiday;
- Another function returns the day of the week with an indication for holidays and non-holidays;
- A function which returns the week of the year, etc.

Accomplishing aggregation in the server instead of within an application provides the following benefits:

- Simplified application: The code to handle all records and perform the aggregation is not needed in the application. Instead, a simpler function is provided in the server.
- Reduced network traffic: Only the result must be sent to the application, thus greatly reducing network traffic. The network can then be used in a more optimal manner.
- Parallel processing: The aggregation can be performed in parallel in the database engine, while the application performs sequential operations.
- Better performance: As mentioned at the beginning of this paper, processing in the server provides a significant performance improvement.

The impact of adding such a function goes further. It is possible to add an index based on the output of a function to speed up processing. The combination of server-side functions and the indexing of their results provides complete functionality that speeds up processing without requiring the maintenance of redundant information.

Aggregation on Functions

The server-side functions can be taken one step further. They can be used to operate on multiple columns within an aggregation function. This provides a way to apply business rules using the content of the row before passing it to the aggregation function. The server-based business rule insures a consistent application of the rules. Any changes are automatically reflected in the existing applications.

Consider the following hypothetical situation. A large bank has a portfolio of loans from its branches. The loans are either personal or commercial. A risk factor is calculated for each loan based on, among other things, the type of loan and the type of business. Over time, the bank may decide to make some adjustments to their formulas to better reflect the risk reality.

Consider the following statement:

```
SELECT branch_id, AVG(risk(A)) as riskfactor
FROM loans as A
GROUP BY 1
HAVING AVG(risk(A)) > 1
ORDER BY 2 DESC;
```

The entire row is passed to the risk function to calculate a risk factor. The AVG function calculates the average risk over all loans for a specific group. It reports the branches that have a risk factor greater than 1 in descending order, assuming that 1 constitutes a warning level. This works fine if you want to calculate the average risk per loan. Instead, a bank may want to calculate an average risk, where each loan is weighed with the amount of the loan. If so, it would be better to implement a new aggregation function to perform the calculation. In our previous example, AVG(risk(A)) could be replaced by AVGRISK(A). The following section demonstrates how an aggregate function is implemented.

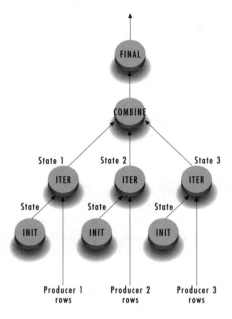

Figure 15–2 *Parallel aggregation.*

User-Defined Aggregates

The Universal Data Option provides the capability to define additional aggregation functions. The aggregate declaration can define up to four functions:

- **INIT**
  This function initializes the data structures required by the rest of the aggregation computation. It takes one or two arguments. The first one is a NULL value of the type of the aggregate column. The second argument may be used to customize the aggregate computation for a particular invocation. The INIT function returns an initialized value of a type (state_t) that will be used internally in the aggregation. The INIT function is optional.

- **ITER**
  This function merges a single value with a partial result, the state_t variable. If no INIT function is defined, then the

initial call to ITER will receive a NULL argument. The ITER function is required for all new aggregates.

- **COMBINE**

  The COMBINE function merges one partial result into the other and returns an updated partial result. The COMBINE function may be the same as the ITER function, if the state_t variable is the same as the aggregated column.

- **FINAL**

  The FINAL function converts a result of type state_t into the result type. It may perform some cleanup work to shut down any resources set up by other functions. If the state_t type is the same as the return type, the FINAL function may be omitted.

Note that the reference to state_t is generic. It simply refers to a type defined in the implementation of a specific aggregation. Assuming that you have a table containing the total purchase of your products for each customer:

```
CREATE TABLE TotalSales (
   customerID      integer,
   productID       integer,
   totalSales      integer
);
```

From this table, you want to find the percentage of the total sales that are allocated to the top "N" products, where "N" could be up to 10. For simplicity in the following example, totalSales has been kept as an integer. In real life, you would probably want to return the top "N" products and the percentage of the total that they each use. We will limit ourselves to the stated problem for the sake of simplicity.

The solution involves finding the "N" largest totalSales and summing up the others. We first define the "state" structure that we will use internally to calculate the result:

```
typedef struct myState {
   mi_integer maxcount;
   mi_integer count;
   mi_integer topN[10];
   mi_integer running_total;
} myState_t;
```

With this structure, we can keep up to ten values. In a production environment, you will want to make this array dynamic. In our array, whichever value does not make the top "N" is summed up in `running_total`.

It is now possible to define the INIT function that will allocate and initialize the structure which will accumulate the information that is required to return the result:

```
myState_t *percenttot_init(mi_integer nil, mi_integer maxi)
{
   myState_t *state;

   state = (myState_t *)mi_alloc(sizeof(myState_t));
   state->maxcount = maxi;
   state->count = 0;
   state->running_total = 0;
   return(state);
}
```

An error should be generated if the `maxi` value is greater than ten. Next, create the ITER function that starts with the first value of the table and the initialized state variable created by INIT. Its role is to insert the value which is passed as an argument into the `state` variable if it is part of the top N or add it to `running_total`. The ITER function is called until all rows are processed:

```
myState_t *percenttot_iter(myState_t *state, mi_integer value)
{
   mi_integer i, j;

   for (i = 0; i < state->count; i++) {
     if (state->topN[i] < value)
          break;
   }
   if (i < state->maxcount) {
     state->count++;
     if (state->count > state->maxcount) {
          state->count--;
          state->running_total +=
               state->topN[state->maxcount - 1];
```

```
    }
    for (j = state->count - 1; j > i; j--)
            state->topN[j] = state->topN[j - 1];
    state->topN[i] = value;
  } else {
    state->running_total += value;
    }
  return(state);
}
```

Depending on the table partitioning and the SQL statement in which the aggregation function is used, we may have several ITER functions. It is now necessary to define a COMBINE function that will merge the partial results:

```
myState_t *percenttot_combine(myState_t *result1,
                                myState_t *result2)
{
  mi_integer i;

  for (i = 0; i < result2->count; i++)
    (void) percenttot_iter(result1, result2->topN[i]);
  result1->running_total += result2->running_total;

  return(result1);
}
```

Once the COMBINE function has processed all the ITER partial results, the processing is completed with a FINAL function which will calculate the result and return it:

```
mi_double_precision *percenttot_final(myState_t *state)
{
  mi_integer i;
    mi_double_precision *retVal;

    retVal = (mi_double_precision *)
          mi_alloc( sizeof( mi_double_precision) );
  for (i = 1; i < state->count; i++)
    state->topN[0] += state->topN[i];
  state->running_total += state->topN[0];
```

```
    (*retVal) = (mi_double_precision)100.0 *
        state->topN[0] / state->running_total;
    return(retVal);
}
```

Once these functions are compiled into a shared library, register the `myState_t` type, functions, and the aggregation function:

```
CREATE OPAQUE TYPE myState_t (internallength = 60);

CREATE FUNCTION percentTot_init(integer, integer)
returning myState_t
with(HANDLESNULLS, parallelizable, not variant)
external name '$DIRLOC/lib.so(percenttot_init)'
LANGUAGE C;

CREATE FUNCTION percentTot_iter(myState_t, integer)
returning myState_t
with(parallelizable, not variant)
external name '$DIRLOC/lib.so(percenttot_iter)'
LANGUAGE C;

CREATE FUNCTION percentTot_combine(myState_t, myState_t)
returning myState_t
with(parallelizable, not variant)
external name '$DIRLOC/lib.so(percenttot_combine)'
LANGUAGE C;

CREATE FUNCTION percentTot_final(myState_t)
returning float
with(parallelizable, not variant)
external name '$DIRLOC/lib.so(percenttot_final)'
LANGUAGE C;

CREATE AGGREGATE percentTot
with (
 INIT = percentTot_init,
 ITER = percentTot_iter,
 COMBINE = percentTot_combine,
 FINAL = percentTot_final
);
```

It is now possible to answer the percentage question (the percentage of total sales that are generated by the three highest selling products per customer) with the following SQL statement:

```
SELECT customerID, percentTot(totalSales, 3)
FROM TotalSales
GROUP by 1
ORDER BY 1;
```

There is a wide range of aggregation functions which can be used, based on business processing requirements. Each business has specific requirements that cannot be met by generic database management systems. The availability of user-defined aggregation functions provide the business the opportunity to apply industry expertise in a more straightforward manner. The addition of aggregation functions simplifies application processing and improves overall performance.

Conclusion

This paper has demonstrated that the Universal Data Option aggregations, coupled with user-defined functions, provide exciting new possibilities. Furthermore, the capability of adding user-defined aggregate functions opens the door to countless opportunities to improve data processing. By adapting the database server to the business environment, there is now the opportunity to simplify applications and improve their performance.

Some developers may have the impulse to throw everything onto the server. However, a careful analysis should be performed to reach the right balance. When used properly, the Universal Data Option can provide a business advantage over standard data processing solutions.

A Case for Informix Dynamic Server with Universal Data Option in Traditional Environments

by Jacques Roy

Introduction

Informix Dynamic Server with Universal Data Option has generated a lot of interest and industry press coverage. Most, if not all, of the attention has focused on the new integration capabilities for Web and multimedia environments. This press seems to suggest that object-relational databases are irrelevant for traditional problems.

However, the premise of this paper focuses on why this technology is important for environments where rich content is not used. The paper begins by looking at the fundamental reasons for object-relational technology and then describes specifically how object-relational features can solve problems in traditional environments.

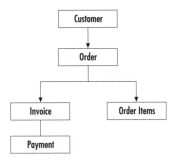

Figure 16–1 *Hierarchical model.*

Why Is Informix Dynamic Server with Universal Data Option Important?

Why is Informix Dynamic Server with Universal Data Option important? To answer this question, we will first take a step back and look at the last revolution in database technology, when hierarchical and/or network database management systems (DBMSs) were replaced by relational databases.

A hierarchical data model always starts with a root node. From this node, an application navigates down the tree in a one-to-many type relationship to a related set of records.

In the example illustrated in Figure 16–1, an application program first finds a specific customer. From the customer record, it then navigates through a set of orders. From a specific order, it is then possible to search for a given invoice or order item.

The network model is a variation of the hierarchical model. It adds flexibility to the node dependencies by removing the constraint of the tree structure.

These models are simple, easy to understand, and very efficient for certain types of problems. On the other hand, the physical database structure is tied to a specific problem. Furthermore, the application program must maintain the links between records, making it closely tied to the physical design. This implies that any changes to the database structure require changes to the application.

A database designed to efficiently answer a specific problem may be unsuited for solving related problems. In our example, determining the quantities of a specific item ordered in one month would require a new application program to traverse the entire database, and this is often impractical for large databases. Thus, hierarchical and network models tie the database and application programs to a specific physical representation.

When the relational database management system (RDBMS) first came out of the research environment, it was viewed as an interesting concept. Because early implementations were quite inefficient in comparison to the established databases, it was believed at the time that specialized hardware would be required to implement the relational model. The RDBMS's viability for large projects was in doubt. It did not help in the early acceptance of the RDBMS model that people applied their hierarchical mode of thinking to RDBMS-based applications.

With improvements in hardware and operating system technology, relational database performance became more competitive. Still, in spite of a performance disadvantage, relational databases have become the model of choice for modern applications.

Over the last 20 years, the cost burden shifted from hardware and software to peopleware. This includes the price of training, development, and maintenance. With an increasing number of people using computers, the user training cost must be considered. Furthermore, rapidly changing business requirements necessitate the evolution of applications and application development.

Relational databases brought two major improvements to application development: a logical database model and a non-procedural language. The logical database model provides the flexibility to access information without forcing users to use a specific physical path. New application requirements may be met by changing the underlying physical storage (mainly indexes) without impacting the logical layer. As the relational model moves away from the physical representation, it moves closer to the business model.

Structured Query Language (SQL) provides a means to express what must be done, and not how to do it. This is essential to the physical layer independence. The database engine is free to decide the best way to execute a query. Any attempt to influence the engine's decision goes against the goal of the physical data model's independence.

Over the years, relational databases have proven to be superior to their predecessors by providing more flexible databases and increasing programmer productivity. However, some shortcomings have been discovered.

To meet performance requirements, the relational model's goal of eliminating redundancy using normal forms required tampering. In some cases, artificial fields were added to satisfy performance needs (indexing).

In many environments, much procedural code was added to the application program to implement the business requirements. This additional code overhead impacts not only performance, but also development, testing, and maintenance, especially in a distributed environment.

While this occurred in the database world, new developments in computer science advanced the concept of object orientation (OO). Since then, OO has become a mainstream technology in analysis, design, and programming. In short, OO extends the type of information which a system can handle by adding the definition of the data and operations permitted on it. Encapsulating data and functions (methods) together provides a higher level of abstraction that frees the designer or programmer from implementation details. Of course, this is a complex subject in itself which is covered in detail in many manuals. Thus, the object-relational model brings us a step closer to the business model.

The object-relational model takes advantage of OO concepts and addresses some of the shortcomings of the relational model. It builds on the relational model foundation by providing an evolutionary path. Existing applications can take advantage of the new technology incrementally, resulting in a faster time to market.

Business requirements are becoming more complex and dynamic. Businesses need to adapt quickly. Keeping the application at a higher level makes it more resilient to change. With Informix Dynamic Server with Universal Data Option, the database adjusts to the application, instead of the converse.

Operating at the business rule level provides several benefits. First, it adds to database independence by providing a richer SQL syntax that simplifies statements and eases maintenance. It restores the non-procedural nature of SQL, simplifying application processing. By taking advantage of business datatypes, the application is more stable, and the changes to business rules are transparent to the application. Informix Dynamic Server with Universal Data Option simplifies SQL queries and provides a more direct way to solve business problems. These benefits are provided by DataBlade modules. DataBlade modules are a packaging of datatype definition and functions, or methods, that operate on them. To facilitate DataBlade module creation, Informix provides the DataBlade Module Development Kit (DBDK).

Are DataBlades Safe?

After a close encounter with the press, Informix was required to provide a sound bite answer: "DataBlade modules are safe." Some people continue to make an issue of this. Instead of answering this question in a vacuum, let's use a more pragmatic approach and look at what has been accomplished in the computer industry over the last few decades.

A database management system (DBMS) relies on the host operating system to provide efficient access to processors, memory, and disk drives, among other things. Every modern operating system provides a device driver interface to add support for third-party hardware, and this concept can be extended to include the addition of new file system management capabilities. One of the most successful third-party file system extensions is Veritas.

Are operating system vendors giving up their responsibility of providing a full-featured product? Are they providing unstable and unreliable environments? Of course not. They are simply making their product more flexible to take advantage of third-party expertise and provide better value to customers.

However, operating systems may prove the exception. What we want to address is mission-critical business applications. In this arena, the uncontested leader is the IBM mainframe environment. IBM has grown with the business community and has answered the business needs of its customers. It is not possible to standardize the world, since every business problem is unique.

IBM has long understood that each customer has different needs. To provide more value to its customers, IBM has added the concept of "user exits" to its software components. A user exit is an entry point into a software package like MVS, CICS, DB2, TLMS, etc. User exits allow the customer to enhance processing by implementing customized functionality. User exits are implemented as object modules that are linked into the software package. In a way, they could be viewed as the conceptual ancestors to DataBlade modules. User exits have been available for decades. It is a proven technology that has benefited IBM customers over the years.

Informix Dynamic Server with Universal Data Option Features

Informix Dynamic Server with Universal Data Option provides added functionality over a standard relational database. These features are listed in Table 16–1.

Table 16–1 *Informix Dynamic Server with Universal Data Option features.*

User defined types:
distinct   opaque
Complex types:
row   set
multiset   list
Implicit/explicit cast operations
User-defined functions
User-defined aggregates
Smart binary large objects (SBLOBs)
Functional indexes
R-tree indexes
Operator overloading
Polymorphism
Type inheritance
Table inheritance
User-defined access method

The two main challenges in using the object-relational database (ORDBMS) model are as follows:

- Our thinking about business problems and the database must change. New data representations can yield major performance improvements. New datatypes could simplify the problem, also resulting in better performance.
- We must strike the right balance between implementing server-side and application functions.

By focusing on the business model, we can define building blocks that will simplify application development and improve performance by providing a more natural way to process information.

The goal of the following section is to open the discussion to new possibilities of problem solving. The provided examples suggest incremental as well as radical changes that can benefit the business community. However, the information only scratches the surface of the potential for new solutions.

Handling Hierarchies

The relational model provided additional flexibility to answer business questions. However, this flexibility comes at the price of performance, especially in cases for which the hierarchical model is well suited.

Consider the following examples:

- **Hospitality Industry**
  Charges for a room are typically represented in the relational model by a separate table containing a room-id, a charge code, the amount, and/or description.
- **Health Care**
  The potential medical procedures performed on a patient are well defined. All performed medical procedures must be linked to the appropriate patient record for billing purposes.
- **Retail**
  An item may be available in different colors. Again, the relational model calls for a separate table with the item key and color.

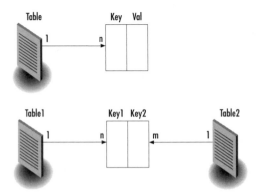

Figure 16–2 *Entity relationships.*

- **Transportation**
  Each carrier has a schedule which includes the day of the week a service is available.
- **Package Shipping**
  Each package has tracking information. It is then possible to locate where a package was at a specific time, and its last known location.

In all of these cases, the typical relational representation is shown in Figure 16–2. The first model represents a one-to-many relationship. For each item in the table, there are zero to N rows in the second table, which typically consists of a key and a value. The two tables could represent a patient record and medical procedures, a product and available colors, etc.

The second model represents a many-to-many relationship. This is accomplished by using an intermediate table that records the keys of related items in Table1 and Table2. The example on medical procedures could fall into this category, with an additional table containing the medical code, description, and fees.

Some of these problems were solved in the relational environment as follows:

- **The Addition of Repeating Fields**
  If the items come only in three or four colors, additional color columns can be added to the table. Such fields will be applied

against the relational model. The application must take into account the different columns which represent the same thing. If a new item is available in ten colors and the table supports up to six, both the database and the application will require modifications. However, for large repeating fields, this approach cannot be used.

- **The Use of a Coded Field**
  In the case of airline flights, the active days can be represented by either a binary vector or a string of seven characters that indicate which day is active. The main drawback of this approach is that the application must know about the internal data representation and is forced to process it.

Informix Dynamic Server with Universal Data Option provides collection datatypes that support unordered sets, ordered sets, and unique sets. A column can be declared as a set of elements of a specific type. These types include the standard relational base types and user-defined types. The use of sets can eliminate the need for extra reference tables.

In the case of large sets, it is not practical to keep the information in a row. Informix Dynamic Server with Universal Data Option provides the capability to create an opaque type and access functions that can be used to solve this problem. An opaque datatype can be represented "in row" up to a determined implementation size and then moved to a large object afterward.

The Informix Dynamic Server with Universal Data Option smart large objects (SBLOBs) provide random access to content. This means that retrieving information out of a large object (for example, 1 GB) does not require reading all of the object's content. The access functions defined with the type can implement more intelligent search and retrieval mechanisms. This provides a significant performance gain over the standard relational binary large objects (BLOBs).

The smart BLOB access solution is well suited for financial instruments in risk management analysis and for stock analysis. Informix Dynamic Server with Timeseries DataBlade Module™ is a good example. By using the Timeseries representation with data represented with a unit of time which is meaningful in the business context, financial institutions can perform their standard business operations on a specifically designed datatype, yielding significant performance improvement and simplified application logic.

As for the coded field solution, simple server-side functions can be created to handle the internal representation and give the application a stable and consistent interface. Informix Dynamic Server with Universal Data Option supports server-side functions written in SPL, C, and Java. If the internal representation is changed, the server-side functions can hide that fact and eliminate the need for application changes.

More Hierarchies

Many systems use hierarchical representations, whether a management hierarchy in an employee table, a part hierarchy in the manufacturing process, or a merchandise hierarchy in retail stores. Informix Dynamic Server with Universal Data Option provides new ways to solve these problems.

Consider an employee table. The standard implementation includes an employee ID, employee name, other employee information, and a manager ID that refers to another row in the employee table. The manager ID may be null in the case of the president or when a manager has not yet been identified. To obtain a list of employee names and manager names, a standard relational implementation would issue the following statement:

```
SELECT e.name, m.name
FROM employee e, OUTER employee m
WHERE e.mgr_id = m.emp_id
```

The outer join is required, or the employees without managers will not appear. This can be a source of error. Furthermore, the outer join makes it more expensive.

By using a server-side function, it is possible to reduce the complexity. Performance testing can be required to measure any additional benefit. The first step is to create a server-side function that performs an index search on the primary key to obtain an employee name:

```
CREATE FUNCTION manager_name(mid integer)
RETURNING varchar(20);
DEFINE mname varchar(20);
IF mid IS NULL THEN
   return " ";
END IF
SELECT name into mname from employee where id = mid;
RETURN mname;
END FUNCTION;
```

With this simple function, the original query can be rewritten as follows:

```
SELECT name, manager_name(mgr_id)
FROM employee;
```

Other hierarchical problems are more complex. For example, a program is required to determine all employees under a manager. The query is repeated each time a manager is found.

Another typical business problem involves parts explosion in a manufacturing application. It can be used to determine the impact of a price change for a part in the manufacture of an object, such as a car.

Paul Brown of Informix Software, Inc., provides a detailed implementation example of this kind of solution in his paper, "Informix Dynamic Server with Universal Data Option and Industrial Applications." The main idea is to define an opaque type that acts as a hierarchy tree.

The functionality required in this type includes comparison operators and the addition operator. By indexing the opaque type, it is possible to resolve the part explosion problem with a simple partial scan of the index. To determine all of the parts included in the 1.2 level of Figure 16–3, the SQL statement can be conceptually represented as follows:

```
SELECT part_name
FROM parts
WHERE part_id > 1.2
AND part_id < 1.3;
```

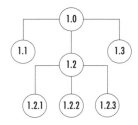

Figure 16–3 Part
number hierarchy.

Parts 1.2.1 to 1.2.3 can have sub-levels. The opaque type offers the needed functionality by properly defining the comparison operators to handle the internal representation and return the correct answer. The complexity is hidden from the application program and the SQL statement is simple.

Paul Brown's solution was implemented at a customer site. Their original solution included an application using object middleware and the data stored in a relational database. The query time was reduced from approximately two hours in the original solution to approximately two minutes using Informix Dynamic Server with Universal Data Option.

By using a new business datatype, the performance improved by a factor of 60 and the overall solution was simplified.

Aggregations

Aggregations are widely used to answer business questions. A typical relational database provides a set of functions that allow the user to express a question directly in SQL. The benefits of this feature include improved performance and simplified implementation.

The performance advantage comes mainly from eliminating the need to transfer the rows to the user application. A simple test with a single table determines that performing the aggregation in the server instead of transferring the aggregation column provides a 40-percent performance improvement with a shared

Table 16–2 *Application aggregation steps.*

Declare cursor
Open cursor
Initialize counters
Loop
Fetch cursor
Test SQLCODE   perform aggegation
Close cursor
Free cursor

memory connection. The difference increases with a network (socket) connection and network traffic. The performance difference also increases if the table is partitioned and the aggregation then runs in parallel on each fragment. Furthermore, duplicating this parallelism in an application program is virtually impossible.

The simplification comes from the fact that the application program must handle one SQL statement and returns only one row of results. Thus, the program is simplified, less error prone, and this leads to faster end-user delivery and reduced maintenance costs.

There are situations where it is not possible to perform an aggregation in SQL. It may be that aggregation functions are not available, such as statistical functions, or the business requirement cannot be expressed in the WHERE clause or the GROUP BY clause.

In order to determine the sales revenue for a year on a day-by-day basis, it is necessary to calculate a total for each day of the week. If you only have a date field, it is necessary to perform the aggregation in an application program. Furthermore, it will be necessary to manage seven aggregation counters. If a function weekday(date) returns the day of the week, the query can be expressed in the following format:

```
SELECT weekday(date) DAY, SUM(sales) TOTAL
FROM sales
GROUP BY 1;
```

This specific function is provided in Informix Dynamic Server with Universal Data Option. Other functions can be added, such as functions that return the corporate quarter that applies to a date, or distinguish whether a date falls between a holiday and a normal workday. Furthermore, these functions can be tailored to suit the handling of dates in the specific business model.

Informix Dynamic Server with Universal Data Option provides the capability to add the functions which facilitate these kinds of queries. In addition, if you require queries such as the following:

```
SELECT weekday(date) DAY, SUM(sales) TOTAL
FROM sales
WHERE weekday(date) = 1
GROUP BY 1;
```

Informix Dynamic Server with Universal Data Option allows you to create an index, called a functional index, based on the result of a function execution. The index can be created with the following command:

```
CREATE INDEX days ON sales( weekday(date) );
```

The implications of this functionality are far reaching. It is possible to perform an index or group by a substring of a field. It is also possible to perform an index or group based on the operations performed on the field. This is one area where object-relational features exceed relational capabilities in a meaningful way for traditional applications.

The previous example clearly shows the benefit of grouping based on an operation on a field (date). Following are the two reasons why it may be useful to use a partial string in a field:

- **Column Containing Sub-Fields**
  Some motor vehicle departments use an extended license plate number that includes the license plate type, vehicle type, and the license plate number. Any grouping on the vehicle type is traditionally accomplished in the application.
- **Slowly Changing Dimensions**
  To handle this issue in a data warehouse, one option is to add a sequence number to an otherwise permanent key. When an

attribute is changed, a new record is inserted with the same key and a different sequence. It then becomes impossible to treat the records as one, requiring aggregation to occur in the application.

Some of these aggregations can be performed using stored procedures. Aggregations also benefit from not transferring the records to the application. However, the complexity of handling the aggregation remains, and the parallelism on multiple fragments is lacking beyond the parallel scan. The aggregation itself would still be single threaded.

Performing aggregations based on a partial key (which does not start at the beginning of the original field) requires an initial sort of the records, and this makes it very expensive, if not impossible, to perform in a stored procedure.

Avoiding Joins

Joining tables is the most expensive operation in the relational model. As was seen earlier in the hierarchy discussion, changing the data representation can eliminate joins and provide significant performance improvement. Research in database technology has greatly improved the performance of joins, however, it still is a general purpose operation that cannot take advantage of the special cases which are data dependent. For this reason, there are still situations where it may be beneficial to remove the join.

Consider the following statement:

```
SELECT company, count(*) Orders
FROM customer c, orders o
WHERE c.customer_num = o.customer_num
GROUP BY 1;
```

The goal of the above query is simply to determine how many orders were placed by each company. In order to return the company name, it is necessary to join the orders table with the customer table. This means that two tables were processed and the temporary rows representing the joined rows were created. Assuming an average of 50 orders per customer, it is possible to process the company name 49 times too often.

Most of this redundant processing can be avoided by using a server-side function. Consider the following function written in SPL:

```
CREATE FUNCTION cname(cnum integer)
RETURNING varchar(20) with (not variant);
DEFINE comp varchar(20);
SELECT company into comp FROM customer WHERE customer_num = cnum;
RETURN comp;
END FUNCTION;
```

This function returns a company name based on the customer number that is passed as its argument. With this function now available, it is possible to rewrite the previous SQL statement as follows:

```
SELECT cname(customer_num) Customer, count(*) Orders
FROM orders
GROUP BY customer_num;
```

Using the Informix stores7 demo database, the first query involved performing a sequential scan of each table, a dynamic hash join, and a temporary file for the group by. The estimated cost of the query was 31.

The second query used the index on customer_num with an estimated cost of 2. Of course, it is necessary to add the 17 select statements from the cname() function on the customer table which used the primary key.

This example may prove a simplification of typical cases; however, it demonstrates the need to investigate this possibility—especially when performance is the ultimate goal. Good candidates for this technique include situations where the denormalization of the relational model is considered for performance reasons.

The object-relational model followed by Informix calls for a reference datatype. It will be part of Informix Dynamic Server with Universal Data Option in a future release. This datatype could replace the `cname()` server-side function. By replacing `customer_num` in the orders table with a reference to the customer table, the previous SQL statement can be rewritten as follows:

```
SELECT deref(customer_num).company Customer, count(*) Orders
FROM orders
GROUP BY customer_num;
```

The `deref()` function returns a row, and in our case, a customer table row. The `company` column is then accessed using the "dot" notation similar to the "C" notation used to access a structure member.

Decision Support Indexes

It is possible to take the previous discussion one step further. If a function is created which obtains information from another table, it is also possible to create an index on a table based on information in another table. In our previous example, the following index can be created:

```
CREATE INDEX company ON orders( cname(customer_num) );
```

This functionality opens the door to new possibilities which were not previously available in standard relational databases. For example, an index can be created on the `orders` table based on the size of the customer's company.

In brief, any attribute from the foreign table can be useful. Of course, this type of scheme should be thoroughly tested before implementation to verify the need for additional indexes and to measure performance improvements.

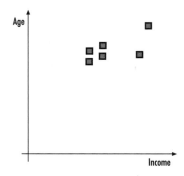

Figure 16–4 *The application of R-trees.*

The Spatial DataBlade Module

A well-documented differentiator of Informix Dynamic Server with Universal Data Option is the Spatial DataBlade module for geographic queries to a database. Many discard this feature simply because they do not intend to use geographic information. However, this functionality can be "re-purposed" for traditional data.

The Spatial DataBlade module provides several new datatypes: point, line, rectangle, circle, ellipse, etc. It also provides functions including overlap, equal, contains, and contained. A point, for example, is represented by two double-precision values. Nothing mandates the values to be longitude and latitude. They could also represent age and income.

An R-tree index can be used to improve performance. To examine the characteristics of customers of age 20 to 30 with an income of $30 K to $40 K, it may be best to use an index instead of performing a table scan by indexing age-income values, and potentially reduce the amount of I/O. The index can also identify a potential group for study. A few count(*) queries with a WHERE clause using the contained() function can identify specific age and income groups.

This new way to look at a problem raises an interesting question. When you have a row that includes a start and an end date, is it better to represent it as a time span? To find out if a specific item is active at a specific date, it is possible to ask which row intersects with the given date. Would the time span more closely represent the business model?

Strong Typing: Semantics versus Syntax

The advent of object-oriented programming has shown us the benefits of strong typing. In the C programming environment, it resulted in the adoption of function prototyping. This single development feature has identified many potential problems in existing applications and prevented errors in development projects.

This also applies to database queries where the syntax may be valid, but the operation incorrect. It becomes even more important in environments where users can execute ad-hoc queries or where reports are modified frequently to meet changing requirements.

Let us consider an international company which tracks the mileage and gas consumption of its vehicles. For domestic operations, units of representation are miles and gallons, however, overseas or in Canada, kilometers and liters are tracked. To list the fuel consumption rate, the following statement executes but returns the wrong answer:

```
SELECT countryname, SUM(mileage) / SUM(gas) mpg
FROM tab1
GROUP BY countryname
ORDER BY 2 DESC;
```

To solve this problem with a relational database, it is necessary to write a program to handle the conversion and re-sort the resulting table.

Informix Dynamic Server with Universal Data Option provides at least two methods to solve this problem: a table hierarchy with distinct types, and cast functions or an opaque type that keeps track of the units used internally.

In the retail supermarket industry, for example, the same item may be measured in different ways: item, package, box, pallet, or truck load. All units may be used in the database. The application must include the logic to handle this situation. Many operations available in SQL may be invalid. By creating specific types that recognize the differences and cast the units appropriately, it is possible to preserve the business view of the information, and still take advantage of the database server storage and access capabilities.

Enhancing the database server with extended datatypes can eliminate errors, reduce application complexity, and improve performance. Furthermore, when business rules change, they can be implemented with minimum or no change to the application, since the application is designed to operate at the business object level.

Conclusion

If object-relational technology is used in the same way as relational technology, it can at best provide comparable benefits and performance. By using Informix Dynamic Server with Universal Data Option to represent business datatypes and using the database engine to operate directly on these representations, application processing is simplified and performance is likely to improve. Informix Dynamic Server with Universal Data Option can be used to simplify queries, streamline specific business processing, and add functionality to the database engine without waiting for the support of new features from the database vendor.

This document suggests new ways to look at old problems. It is a small subset of what is possible with object-relational technology. This is a new opportunity which begs to be explored, and there is a need for additional testing and brainstorming to uncover all the possibilities of this rich environment. The result will be more adaptable environments with improved functionality.

References

The following books provide additional information related to the subject of this article:

Stonebraker, Michael with Dorothy Moore, *Object-Relational DBMSs, The Next Great Wave*. San Francisco: Morgan Kaufmann Publishers, 1996. ISBN 1-55860-397-2.

Kimball, Ralph, *The Data Warehouse Toolkit*. New York: John Wiley & Sons, 1996. ISBN 0-471-15337-0.

Informix, *INFORMIX-Universal Server Guide to SQL: Syntax, Reference, and Tutorial*. Upper Saddle River, NJ: Informix Press, 1997.

The Cyberpublishing Movement

by John Taylor

Introduction

Cyberpublishing tools and processes are rapidly increasing the overall currency of the Internet—making it a more viable source of information, entertainment, and business. Cyberpublishing is achieving this by increasing the ease of collecting, modifying, and publishing information on the Web. This includes all content—text, audio, images, animation, video, or any of the emerging Internet media technologies, such as Java or VRML. As the Internet continues to gain in popularity and significance, Cyberpublishing tools and processes will play an instrumental role in keeping the content on Web sites current and compelling.

This paper takes a closer look at the definition of Cyberpublishing, its current uses, and its benefits. The on-line event—"24 Hours in Cyberspace"—is a case study example which demonstrates the use of Cyberpublishing technology to achieve real-time publishing currency on the Web. To understand the congruence that Cyberpublishing technologies have on the overall market, it is important to take a closer look at the trends in commercial Web site development and production. Finally, this paper outlines the strategy and approach taken by Informix in developing a commercial solution and framework for Cyberpublishing.

Cyberpublishing

Cyberpublishing brings greater currency to the publishing of information on the Internet and represents the first step towards establishing the Internet as the powerful new medium. This is achieved by using emerging technologies and publishing processes to ease—and in some cases automate—the work necessary to publish information and ideas on the Internet. The catalyst for this change is emerging technology and an optimized process architecture that specifically addresses the complexity that is typically associated with publishing and maintaining information on the Internet. The focus is to make the Internet perform in the interactive fashion suggested by its electronic underpinnings.

Cyberpublishing technologies and processes have made the innovative and highly dynamic Web site "24 Hours in Cyberspace" a reality. These same tools and technologies are increasing the richness with which people interact with the Web by enabling the creation of easily updated Web sites with the latest presentation technologies.

What Is Cyberpublishing?

Cyberpublishing refers to the integrated tools and processes involved with the collection, creation, editing and publishing of ideas and information for delivery on the Web. This includes publishing in all of the existing media formats—text, audio, video, still images, and animation—and emerging media technologies, such as Java and VRML. Eventually Cyberpublishing will expand to include delivery on a variety of target media platforms beyond the Web—including traditional print, television, and audio recording formats.

What Is the Benefit of Cyberpublishing?

The benefits of Cyberpublishing are as follows:

- **Rapid Publishing Turnaround**
  Cyberpublishing increases the speed with which various information is collected, edited, and published on the Web.
- **Increased Productivity**
  New Cyberpublishing tools and technologies increase the efficiency and, in some cases, automate the process of gathering, filtering, and modifying information for Web delivery.
- **Collaborative Workflow**
  Cyberpublishing leverages the power of the Web and empowers people to work collaboratively on the creation, modification, and publishing of content.
- **Greater Accessibility**
  Cyberpublishing tools are developed for creatives, as opposed to programmers, improving the ease with which tools are learned and applied. In turn, increased accessibility lowers the training overhead.

Who Benefits from Cyberpublishing?

Cyberpublishing benefits any company or individuals interested in establishing a presence on the Web—for either broad public relations, general business purposes, or internal communications. Anyone who publishes information on the Web benefits from the increased productivity and accessibility of Cyberpublishing technologies. Ultimately, all users of the Web benefit from Cyberpublishing through access to more current information and richer content. Similar to the advent of video tape for news reporting, Cyberpublishing technologies retrieve information on diverse subjects in completely new ways.

Table 17–1 Cyberpublishing advantages by industry.

Industry	Web Service	Advantage of Cyberpublishing
Airlines	Direct-Ticketing Reservations	Constantly updated fares and scheduling.
Banking updates	Home Banking	Rates and services
Entertainment	Reviews	Current catalog listing all reviews.
Financial Services investment	Investment Advisory Services	Query-based guidance.
Healthcare	HMO Selection	Remote authoring and updates by individual HMOs.
Publishing	News Wire Service	Local news and electronic classifieds.
Real Estate	Listings Service	Constantly updated VRML-based Web catalog.
Retail	On-Line Catalogs	Query-driven multimedia catalog.
Shipping	Tracking or Marketing	Customer marketing updates.
Telecommunications	Yellow Pages	Catalog-based yellow pages with multiple-search capabilities.
Travel	Bookings	Updated travel opportunities.

Currently, every major industry is pursuing both a marketing-related and a transaction-related presence on the Web. Consequently, each industry gains by providing richer content and more current information to their customers.

"24 Hours in Cyberspace"

The on-line event "24 Hours In Cyberspace" ("24 Hours") is an excellent case study example of how Cyberpublishing tools and techniques can take a highly complex idea for a Web site from concept to reality.

Overview of the Event

"24 Hours" was held on February 8, 1996. It was considered the largest on-line event ever conducted by many measures. In one day, 110 stories were published with over 300 still images—from a total of over 5,000 submitted stories and over 2,000 photographs. All of the photographs submitted that day were digitally transmitted from the field to "Mission Control"—the name given to the control center of "24 Hours." The stories created for this site were accessed 4-million times by viewers from over 130 countries worldwide.

By looking at the technologies and processes behind this event, it is possible to see how leading-edge Cyberpublishing techniques will revolutionize the entertainment, publishing, and business communications industries. Cyberpublishing tools and technologies are also implemented in the commercial marketplace for the benefit of the entire Web community.

Event Background

Rick Smolan conceived of the "24 Hours" concept to illustrate how computers and on-line cultures are influencing people's lives worldwide. "Painting on the walls of the digital cave" was the event's signature catch phrase. The goal was to create a time capsule—a milestone in the development of a rich new medium called the World Wide Web.

"24 Hours" combined the traditional medium of photojournalism with the newly emerging medium of the Web. This approach was well-suited to the proven storytelling ability of photojournalism and the latest presentation technologies of the Internet. "24 Hours in Cyberspace" set out to integrate the efforts of over 100 professional photographers, professional photo-editors, copywriters, and audio engineers in the publishing of a Web site—all in the course of one day. Along these lines, a photographer in the field photographed his or her subject, transmitted the images electronically to "Mission Control"—where the images were edited, merged with story copy, and published on the Web in pre-designed templates.

By November of 1995, the "24 Hours" plan to build the world's largest one-day network was quickly becoming a reality. In less than three months, the team needed to design, define, and build a network capable of managing the huge volume of information and stories to be submitted to the "24 Hours" Web site on February 8, 1996. The sources of stories—submitted by several hundred sources from all over the world—included text, photographs, graphics, audio streams, and video clips. After successfully launching "24 Hours," a software infrastructure was needed to support the project.

Specifically, the project required a comprehensive system capable of handling the overall workflow of three distinct functions:

- Collecting story data;
- Editing the story elements into refined stories; and
- Publishing the stories into well-presented, HTML-coded Web pages.

"24 Hours" required technologies that would perform the three functions noted above.

"24 Hours" required a database to manage the complex, mixed-media data types and a workflow application environment to manage the overall Cyberpublishing process. The Informix Dynamic Server with Universal Data Option and a complementary set of tools provided the solution to both problems.

The Informix server combines the capability to manage complex datatypes with the necessary extensibility to accommodate new data formats. In addition, the server comes with extensive Web-based tools that provide the framework for a collaborative, workflow application environment which can be implemented and administered on the Web. The database system

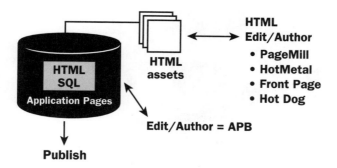

Figure 17–1 *Collecting, editing, and publishing diverse content into Web pages.*

and tools set is optimized to greatly simplify Web site management.

Illustra's technology enabled the "24 Hours" team to design and administer the Web site in a rich and dynamic way.

Process Flow

At its most fundamental level, Cyberpublishing can be broken down into a four stage process: creating, collecting, editing, and publishing content. These four processes are typically represented by disparate technologies and functions, and are often accomplished by different people in various locations. Defining Cyberpublishing by these four processes helps to organize and understand the route that content takes in the Cyberpublishing model. Refer to the following illustration for a detailed technical view of this process flow.

The creating stage is concerned with the location where the creation of the site's content took place—typically, this stage is accomplished in the field. This stage included photographers taking pictures of their subjects around the world, journalists writing the copy, and even the design of the "look and feel" of the site by Clement Mok Designs. The collecting stage describes the process by which the created content originated from points around the world to Mission Control, where the content was received, edited, and published. The editing stage is concerned with the function of editing and readying the photographs, copy

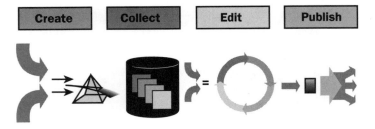

Figure 17–2 *The four processes which comprise the process flow.*

and audio pieces for publication on the Web site. Finally, the publishing stage is involved with the rollout of finished story data to the "24 Hours" mirror Web sites around the world.

Creating

The creating stage took place wherever the creative talent needed to cover their subject. In the case of professional photographers, this meant that it happened in places as far reaching as the outback of Australia and the jungles of Malaysia. Two hundred professional photographers were scattered around the globe to cover numerous subjects. Photographers often used newly developed digital cameras to expedite the process of capturing and transmitting still images to Mission Control. This process enabled photographers to skip the development and scanning of traditional film—an impossibility, given the time constraints. Digital cameras provide a means for the photographers to shoot their subjects and immediately download the images to a laptop computer—used to transmit the digital photographs directly to Mission Control.

Another aspect of the creating stage was the design of the site's templates and general layout. It was imperative to establish these templates and the general layout in order to publish the site within a 24-hour period. "24 Hours" worked with Clement Mok Designs to oversee such aspects as the flow of the site, the design of the site's navigational controls used to move through the site, and the actual graphical design of the pages or templates.

Collecting

In the collecting stage, each photojournalist's story elements were captured, identified, parsed, and stored in Informix Dynamic Server with Universal Data Option's mixed-media server. The "email parser" also ensured that submitted stories adhered to technical guidelines. Stories which did not adhere to the guidelines received an e-mail response. The unique design of Informix's server technology enabled it to intelligently store and query complex datatypes, and to modify and extend the datatypes (for example, the IPTC file constraint).

Editing

It was here that the story elements were reassembled, edited, and recomposed prior to publishing. Each specialist edited the discrete story elements—whether a photograph, an audio stream, or the story copy. Various third-party software tools were used throughout the process. In all cases, however, the tools operated in the Web-based application environment provided by Informix Dynamic Server with Web Integration Option. The tools relied heavily on the module's ability to dynamically generate HTML pages in response to queries.

"24 Hours" underscores the Web's new trend—it is evolving into an application development environment. To envision this trend, consider that each of the edit screens—ten in all—is a form running from a Netscape 2.0 browser across the "24 Hours in Cyberspace" internal net, or Intranet. This trend has powerful implications for all businesses interested in increasing productivity through application development across the Internet.

Publishing

The publishing of fully-edited stories in HTML Web pages was achieved through the joint technology effort of Informix and NetObjects. The combination of the Informix server and the Web Integration Option provided the means of generating HTML pages dynamically and enabled the entire workflow to be achieved within a browser on the "24 Hours" Intranet Editing Web. After completing the editing process, NetObjects used its

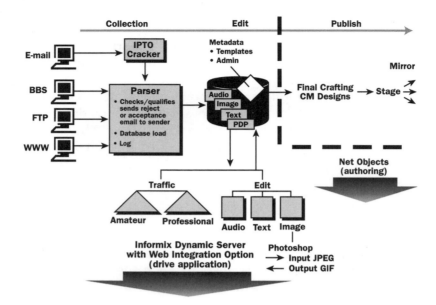

Figure 17–3 *The "24 Hours in Cyberspace" process flow.*

template tool to retrieve the specified story components from the Informix server and to place the components in their chosen template slots. The Informix server's ability to intelligently handle and store mixed-media datatypes empowered the functionality provided by NetObjects. The template data was also stored in the server as metadata.

The Process Summary for "24 Hours In Cyberspace"

Following are the process steps involved in the "24 Hours In Cyberspace" event:

1. Story data is received. Professional JPEG digital images are received via e-mail. The images are then parsed into image and caption information for storage in the server. An IPTC Cracker checks each e-mail, sends either an accept or reject reply, and then logs the submission. Amateur and student submissions are stored in the server.

2. Traffic reviews and assigns a story to a given theme.
3. The editing of audio, text, and image is completed. Text is edited with a basic text editor. Audio is edited with Sonic Solutions' digital audio editing workstation. JPEG images are edited with Adobe Photoshop and saved as GIF images. Pull quotes are also saved as GIFs.
4. The layout template is selected.
5. Text, audio, and GIFs are slotted in the template.
6. Editors preview the completed HTML pages. The pages are then forwarded to senior editors.
7. Senior editors complete the final story review.
8. Stories are staged on a Sun Microsystems Netra server.
9. Proofers and testers check HTML links and pages.
10. Stories are automatically published to eleven mirror sites around the world.

"24 Hours in Cyberspace" Screens

Figure 17–4 is the main menu of the "24 Hours In Cyberspace" Web site, and a description of the other available screens.

Main Menu

The previous screen depicts the main menu of the "24 Hours In Cyberspace" Web site. This main menu serves as the "Control Center" and starting point for the "24 Hours" workflow environment. Three functional areas are color coded: Traffic is purple; Status is red; and Edit is yellow.

Professional Inbox

Professional photographic images are reviewed in the Professional Inbox, and either assigned or moved to the Story Inbox. The Professional Inbox enables users to perform searches by photographer and story.

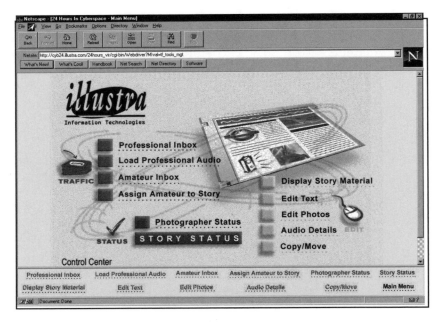

Figure 17–4 *The main menu of the "24 Hours in Cyberspace" Web site.*

Load Professional Audio

This screen selects and loads professional audio clips into the server.

Amateur Inbox

This screen facilitates the review and rating of student and amateur story submissions.

Assign Amateur to Story

This screen provides the means to assign a student or amateur story submission to a theme for editing and publishing.

Photographer Status

This screen allows a search by photographer as a means to determine the status of a photographer's digital image transmissions.

Story Status

This screen serves as the checklist monitor for the position of a story in the editing process. As a story progresses through various stages, the corresponding box is checked-off. There are boxes for Audio, Traffic, Edit, Proof, Approve, and Publish. There is also a field for Version number and a flag for the new data received for a given story. Searches are available by Theme, Sort by Story, or any of the above stage labels.

Display Story Material

This screen shows all data for a given story: Images with corresponding captions and descriptions, Audio, and Text. Searches are available by Theme and Story.

Edit Text

The Edit Text screen provides the means to edit story copy. Text is copied from the text window at the left of the frame. Subsequently, text is pasted into the text window at the right of the frame. All original story copy remains in the server—along with the newly edited story copy. Searches are available by Theme and Story.

Edit Photos

This screen enables the user to expand thumbnail images for review and editing. Double-clicking on a photographic image in this screen automatically launches Adobe Photoshop, which retrieves the image from the server for image editing. The photo is cropped, color corrected, and saved as a GIF image in a selected template slot which corresponds to its cropped size. Searches are available by Theme and Story.

Audio Details

This screen shows the properties related to a given audio clip.

Copy/Move

This screen provides the ability to either copy or move a given story's data from one story to another. Searches are available by Theme and Story.

Core Technology in "24 Hours in Cyberspace"

Informix Dynamic Server with Universal Data Option and Web Integration Option provided the core technology for the above process flow. Additional technology—such as the Image DataBlade module—also played an integral role in the system design. It is helpful to see how these technologies contributed individually to the overall implementation.

The Informix Server

The Informix server provided the technology infrastructure to support the myriad of features and functionality required by the "24 Hours" operating environment. The Informix server enabled the collection, storage, and management of the multimedia objects associated with the "24 Hours" project. Specifically, these multimedia objects included JPEG and GIF images, audio files, text files, Java applets, and the metadata associated with pre-designed HTML templates. These complex datatypes were stored in the server in their original forms. The server had an intrinsic knowledge of each object class—whether a JPEG image file, GIF image, or Real Audio file. This capability was critical to the sustainability of the "24 Hours" operating environment and was made possible by the Informix server's unique and substantial extensibility.

ORDBMS Architecture

The Informix server was designed to support user-defined objects or datatypes. All knowledge of data stored in the server is contained in tables of metadata that describe each datatype—whether defined by the system or user. This design gives the system its extensibility for existing complex datatypes and its guaranteed adaptability to forthcoming datatypes.

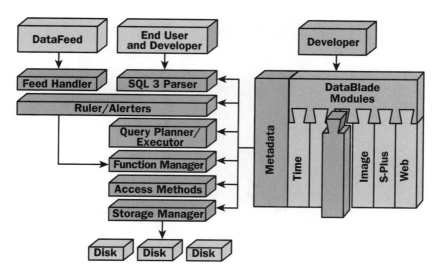

Figure 17–5 *Object storage in the Informix server.*

Versioning support is an intrinsic design element of the Informix server and played a significant role in the "24 Hours" editing workflow environment. As is the case with most multimedia editing, a trail of edit versions is typically left for the final edit of all media components. Each collected and published photographic image passed through an edit stage. A photo editor often completed three to six edits per each still image before completing the processes of color correcting, cropping, and sizing for a given page layout or template. In the course of these intensive processes, the server maintained the progressive evolution of image edits—enabling the photo editor to automatically access the appropriate image edit version to finalize the task at hand.

Informix Dynamic Server with Web Integration Option

Informix Dynamic Server with Web Integration Option served as the enabling technology to implement the "24 Hours" editing workflow environment within a Netscape Browser on the "24 Hours" intranet. The Netscape 2.0 browser acted as each user's window into the workflow of the editing and publishing operation at Mission Control. Each image arrived at Mission

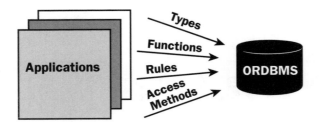

Figure 17–6 *Data type extensibility.*

Control, and was sent on to the Traffic person who reviewed and sent the image to an edit pod. Finally, photo and text editors worked to build the stories. Through all these processes, all image processing occurred in a browser using a front-end designed around the Informix Dynamic Server with Web Integration Option.

Architecture of Informix Dynamic Server and the Web Integration Option

Three basic technologies provide the overall functionality of the Informix Dynamic Server with Web Integration Option to dynamically generate HTML pages: Webdriver, Application Page, and WebExplode.

The Webdriver manages the connection to the appropriate database and the retrieval of the specific Application Page. This includes a request by the Web server for the specific Application Page from the server. Following the WebExplode function and the formatting of the dynamic HTML page in the server, the page is rendered back to the Web server and on to the Webclient.

An Application Page is an HTML document with embedded Informix Dynamic Server with Web Integration Option tags that have corresponding SQL statements. These Informix Dynamic Server with Web Integration Option tags are SGML-compliant tags and attributes which enable SQL statements to be executed dynamically within HTML pages. Application Pages can be created with the Data Director for the Web and stored in the Informix server as rows in a table.

The WebExplode function automatically parses the Informix Dynamic Server with Web Integration Option tags from the

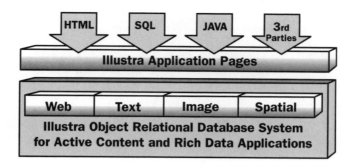

Figure 17–7 *The Informix server processes rich data types.*

Application Page, and dynamically builds and executes the corresponding SQL statements. The results are formatted according to instructions, and the formatted page is returned to the Webdriver for final delivery to the Webclient.

The Informix Dynamic Server with Web Integration Option—with its unique versioning, rules, and multimedia support—enabled this Web-centric approach to collaborative application development. The Informix Dynamic Server with Web Integration Option supports "application pages"—which are stored within the server, and provide for the dynamic generation and update of HTML pages based on standard SQL queries. This functionality makes Web-based applications like "24 Hours in Cyberspace" possible—while simplifying the overall maintenance of Web sites.

In the "24 Hours" operating environment, the Image DataBlade module provides support for JPEG, GIF, and IPTC/JPEG formats. All photographic story elements were digitized and transmitted as JPEG files. Standard JPEG file structures are easily managed by the Image DataBlade module—which was designed to accommodate standard image formats, like JPEG. However, professional news photographers utilized a modified JPEG file constraint (IPTC)—enhanced to encapsulate information specific to a photograph. The Informix server's open and flexible handling of diverse datatypes enabled the application developers to quickly extend the Informix Dynamic Server with Web Integration Option to decode the IPTC file and parse it into its original JPEG photographic image and its related captioning information.

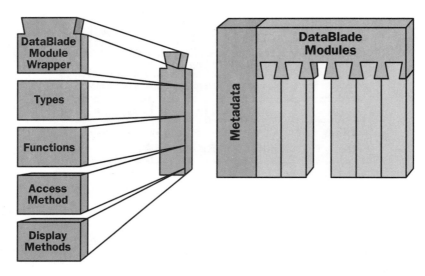

Figure 17–8 *The Informix Dynamic Server with Universal Data Option architecture.*

The Informix server's ease in accommodating the IPTC image format indicates its power to handle complex and diverse data types. The "24 Hours" event is just one example of the server's unique power to manage mixed media.

Technology Partners

To make this event possible, it was necessary to collaborate with the top creative professionals in the publishing industry, and integrate these professionals' efforts using the leading technology providers. "24 Hours In Cyberspace" integrated the technical efforts of more than 50 high-technology companies.

Table 17–2 is an abridged list of the companies and descriptions of their contributions.

Mission Control: The Operations Center

The physical center of the "24 Hours In Cyberspace" operation was referred to as "Mission Control" and took place in a specially outfitted 6,000 square-foot loft in San Francisco's south side.

COMPANY	TECHNICAL CONTRIBUTIONS
Informix Software, Inc.	Multimedia database, editing workflow environment, underlying management platform.
Sun Microsystems, Inc.	Workstations, servers, and firewall technology.
Kodak	Digital cameras, film, scanners, and printers.
Adobe Systems, Inc.	Adobe Photoshop and Adobe Acrobat.
Netscape Communications	Web browser and web server technology.
MFS Communications	Internet connectivity. Local and long distance communication services.
Power Computing	Macintosh operating system compatibles.
NEC Technologies	Notebook computers.
NetObjects	Web publishing software.
Claris Em@iler	E-mail management software.
Sonic Solutions	Audio-editing technology.
Software Construction Company	Image-caption software tools.
Internet MCI	Internet peering services.
Polaroid Corporation	Portable film scanners.
BBN Planet	Mirror site.
Best Power	Uninterruptible power supplies.
US Robotics	High-speed modems.
Cisco Systems	High-speed routers.
Bay Networks	High-speed hubs.
Farallon Computing	Routers, ethernet hubs, and cards.
Telos Systems	Telephone interface services.
Progressive Networks	RealAudio technology.
Wildfire Communications	Intelligent telecommunication services.
Dallas Semiconductor	Data rings.
Spider Land Software	Telefinder BBS software.
Adaptive Solutions	PowerShop high-speed accelerator boards.

This space became the workplace for 100 creative and technical professionals. At any time throughout the event, this space also included photo editors, copy editors, senior editors, designers, programmers, and systems administrators.

Technical Set-Up

Two Sun Microsystems SPARCServer 1000s acted as the operation's database servers. The servers served not only as the repository for all "24 Hours" media elements, but also enabled the collection of incoming images and integrated the entire editorial workflow process. Collectively, these two servers provided over 900 MB of RAM and 400 GB of disk storage. One server was configured with a 4-processor CPU, while the other was configured with an 8-processor CPU.

Sun Microsystems Netra Servers provided the FTP and e-mail support. In addition, 60 UltraSPARC workstations, along with 40 NEC Pentium PCs, were used throughout Mission Control's editorial workflow environment.

Operating Layout

The layout of Mission Control was essentially split up by function into three separate work areas: Editing, Traffic, and Technical Support.

Editing was organized within each "theme pod" by function: image edit, text edit, and story layout. There were six editing stations, or theme pods, which corresponded to the six topical themes of the "24 Hours in Cyberspace" event:

- **Pod 1**
  Power Points;
- **Pod 2**
  Digital Leapfrogging;
- **Pod 3**
  Earthwatch;
- **Pod 4**
  Faster, Cheaper, Better;

- **Pod 5**
  Cyberfrontiers; and
- **Pod 6**
  A Better Place.

Each editing pod contained four machines, two Sun Micro-systems workstations, and two NEC PCs. The editors worked at these machines to accomplish all image editing, story editing, and page layout for all stories assigned to a particular theme.

Traffic was divided into two areas: Professional Inbox and Amateur Submission. Professional Inbox was responsible for the scanning of incoming images from professional photographers and for assigning the images to an editing pod. Amateur Submission was responsible for reviewing and selecting amateur submissions from students and the general public, and assigning those stories to a specific edit pod.

Technical Support was responsible for overseeing all technical aspects of the operation. This included the maintenance of e-mail and FTP traffic, LAN and WAN operation, database support, and continued software and integration support. Technical Support was also responsible for all training and also provided general hands-on help.

Mission Control's Local Area Network (LAN) consisted of a 100 Base-T ethernet running behind Sun Microsystems' Firewall-1 security technology. Mission Control's LAN was segmented into three separate sections: the Clean LAN, the DMZ LAN, and the Press LAN. The Clean LAN was behind the firewall—in the same location as the database and the editing systems. The Clean LAN was responsible for the highest volume of traffic on the LAN. The DMZ LAN represented the part of the LAN with access to the public Internet—in the case of "24 Hours"—for the collection of story data. The third section of the LAN was the Press LAN—where the press or third parties received demonstrations of the workflow process without access to live editing systems. Like the Clean LAN, the Press LAN does not have access to the public Internet.

Extensive use of mirror sites was used in order to balance the more than four-million hits to the "24Hours" site in the first day. Three mirror sites in the United States (U.S.)—located in Mountain

View, California; Atlanta, Georgia; and Baltimore, Maryland—
and eight international mirror sites were used. The international sites were provided through the 1996 Internet World Exposition's (IWE) "Central Park" servers. It is claimed that IWE essentially tripled the world's Internet traffic on February 8—with the use of its Central Park Servers.

There were two physical Internet connections into Mission Control. A local ISP, Cyberports Inc., installed the lines into the building and worked with MFS Datanet for all connections to the Internet. MFS Datanet is the largest private owner of fiber-optic data transmission lines in the U.S., and owns MAE West and MAE East—two major Internet backbones in the U.S. Each line consisted of a Private Virtual Channel (PVC) over a DS3 line comprising a nationwide 10 Mbps backbone.

Installed network hardware included the following:

Table 17–3 Installed network hardware.

AT&T	1100CAT5 Modular Jack Panel
Bay Networks 100BaseT Hub (8 x 12 port)	Model 28104 100BaseT Switch
Cisco Systems	Cisco 2500; Cisco 7010 Router
Digital Link	Prelude Encore T1 DSU/CSU
Grand Junction	FastSwitch 2100 25-port Fast Ethernet 100 Mbps
Net Edge Systems	ATM Connect
Ortronics	24-port panel (RJ11 Jack Support)
US Robotics	12 X Quad V.34 Modem Cards Network Management Card 2 x AC PSU 45A
Westwell	DS1 Mounting

Implications for Today's Organizations

The tools, technologies, and processes which were developed and implemented for "24 Hours in Cyberspace" have direct benefits to organizations in the management of communications and business transactions. Whether an organization derives all of its revenue from its Web site—or simply uses the Web for internal communications—the technologies used to make "24 Hours in Cyberspace" a reality produce richer and more responsive Web sites.

Evolution of Commercial Web Sites

To put Cyberpublishing in its proper perspective, it is necessary to look at the general trends regarding the Internet and commercial Web site development. Internet usage continues to grow unabated. Recent studies conducted by the Gartner Group indicate that the Internet is doubling in size every 57 days. Other studies by Morgan Stanley and Alex, Brown and Sons indicate that Internet connections have an annual growth of more than 100 percent. Regardless of the exact numbers, almost all studies agree that the growth of the Internet is accelerating relative to all metrics: Internet connections, aggregate bandwidth allocation, Internet-based application development, and host server deployment.

Higher Bandwidth and Multimedia Support

As available bandwidth increases throughout the Internet, there is a greater demand and propensity to build Web sites with rich multimedia data elements. The days of file system-based HTML pages are rapidly giving way to Web sites that use audio streams, video, animation, still images, and other complex datatypes expressed with newly developed languages, or standards—like Java, VRML, and QuickTimeVR. Available bandwidth adds to the complexity of managing the site, and is a significant factor in the operation of the site. For example, a file size of 5 KB

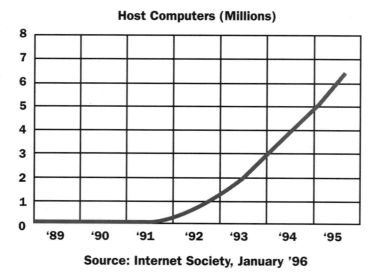

Host Computers (Millions)

Source: Internet Society, January '96

Figure 17–9 Chart of Internet growth.

can comprise a basic HTML page that describes a new car. However, the richer the media type, the greater the requirements for file space. For example, a Shockwave file illustrating the car in its movie format may require 300 KB, while a streaming MPEG file (for video) can easily require a file size in excess of 1 MB. The trend in using multimedia components to illustrate concepts or to increase the overall attractiveness of the Web site not only persists, but is quickly becoming the standard for all Web sites.

The Complexity of Web Site Applications

The complexity of Web site applications is increasing sharply to accommodate the demands of multimedia, increased content currency, and transaction processing. As organizations realize the importance of Web sites as valuable communications tools, new ways are sought to constantly update Web-resident content—which drives the need for CGI programming or dynamically generated pages. This is a logical outcome and serves as a driver for new tools and development practices that ultimately add to the overall complexity of the Web site.

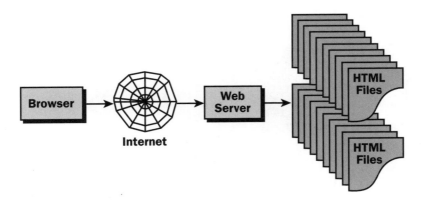

Figure 17–10 *The first-generation site.*

The Evolution of Web Site Development

With its inception in 1992, the Web has been rapidly maturing from a collection of basic HTML text files to a constantly updated medium comprised of multimedia and interactive applications. The content management system requirements necessary to keep pace with change have been enormous and such requirements have brought about a generational shift in Web server application development. Following are descriptions of the generational shifts.

The First-Generation Site

A first-generation site is simply represented by a group of static HTML documents—typically stored in a computer's file system. The process of requesting a specific HTML document or Web page is simply evoked by the user's Web browser as it requests the specific page or URL. This process is simple, but can only accommodate rudimentary Web sites that utilize simple datatypes—typically, text with few images—and are relatively static.

The Second-Generation Site

The requirement for more dynamic content served as a catalyst for the development of the CGI. CGI enabled programmers to design static HTML pages with hooks to an outside data source

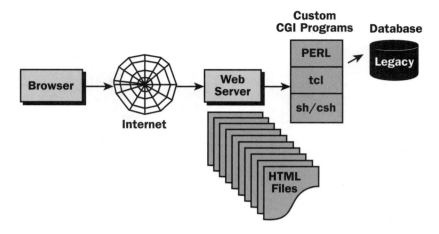

Figure 17-11 *The second-generation site.*

as a means to generate dynamic content. CGI requires customized programming—which is usually performed in languages, such as Perl, Tcl, or C. Second-generation sites have served many Webmasters' needs—with several short-comings. To begin with, CGI-based sites are difficult to develop and maintain. They also provide minimal support for the storage and management of rich datatypes—such as video, audio, animation, and images. Furthermore, this approach offers little extensibility for the support of new datatypes—resulting in poor adaptability to new technologies like Java, VRML, or Shockwave.

The Third-Generation Site

A third-generation site utilizes Informix Dynamic Server with Web Integration Option to create highly dynamic Web sites that utilize complex datatypes in a database-driven model. This approach allows the entirety of a Web site's content to remain as discrete data elements which are stored in the database. Using the functionality of Informix Dynamic Server with Web Integration Option, pages are dynamically generated—based on the user's query and the site's pre-determined page layout.

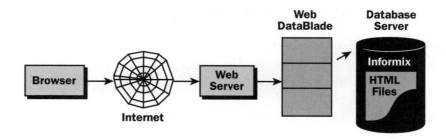

Figure 17–12 The third-generation site.

A good example of the power of a third-generation site is a computer company's catalog listing of software solutions. Prior to implementing this solution using Informix Dynamic Server with Web Integration Option, the organization used a Web site based on fixed HTML pages. This Web version was not vastly different from the original physical catalog. Maintenance of the static HTML pages was onerous and the on-line catalog was never entirely current.

Using the third-generation model, the organization was able to build a site that generated each page based on the user's interest. All catalog content is stored in the server as discrete data elements. The content is presented only in response to a specific query. This dynamic query capability enables a richer and more efficient system to present the appropriate software solution content. It also facilitates data update—by either the organization itself or its software solution partners.

Functional Services

The functional services of Web sites are growing in both quantity and complexity as organizations attempt to accomplish more with their on-line presence. In this context, functional services refer to the technical processes necessary to support the following functions: Cyberpublishing, advertising, electronic commerce, multi-user on-line games, chat services, interactive multimedia, and user registration.

Characteristic	Description
Open	The Cyberpublishing solution must comply with existing standards for web servers, database, and communications protocols.
Extensible	The Cyberpublishing solution must be designed to accommodate existing tools and datatypes with the utmost in extensibility—so that it can adapt to any forthcoming tools or datatypes.
Scalable	The Cyberpublishing solution must be able to scale across Web sites—regardless of size or functional requirements.
Efficient	A commercial Cyberpublishing solution must be easy to learn and maintain, and provides a synergistic workflow environment of the tools that are used to create, edit, and publish content.

A Commercial Solution to Cyberpublishing

A commercial solution to Cyberpublishing must be open, extensible, scalable, and efficient. Note Table 17–4.

Conclusion

Illustra supports Cyberpublishing by providing the progressive ability to manage mixed-media data types quickly and intelligently—while offering the ability to dynamically generate HTML pages from queries to its database. The combination of these two capabilities is essential in maximizing the currency of a Web site. These capabilities help to bring an optimal level of currency and overall interactivity to the "24 Hours in Cyberspace" Web site. This same solution for Web site development is utilized by hundreds of commercial organizations in building Web sites that provide users with richer content and more compelling interactive experiences.

The Application Services Approach

The capabilities of the Informix Dynamic Server with Web Integration Option are extended to include the core functionality required for a commercial Cyberpublishing solution. These application services address the core requirements common to most Cyberpublishing solutions. Over time, the base of application services will grow to drive an ever more powerful Cyberpublishing solution that will continue to address the needs of the market. Application services will be developed by third-parties, customers, and Informix Software, Inc.

Chapter 18

Informix Digital Media Solutions: The Emerging Industry Standard for Information Management

by Howard Greenfield

Introduction

The ever-increasing use of digital media is transforming the way information is utilized in business, entertainment, and communications. Companies that seek more effective communications and better market recognition now turn to digital media to make the greatest impact.

Yet despite these developments, companies still face many challenges in the management of content and information on demand. Despite the explosive growth in the use of digital tools, services, and the World Wide Web (Web), today only a small fraction of a company's information assets are managed.

That is why the future of content management will be as much about powerful, scalable, multimedia-enabled databases as it is about networking. Whether text strings and numbers, Web pages, or digital media applications, storing and managing rich media content has become the critical challenge of the database.

Table 18–1 *Media information management is required in a variety of industries.*

MARKET	APPLICATIONS
Publishing, Web Sites	Content management
Broadcast/Cable	Catalog, edit, deliver
Corporate Multimedia	Intranet training, communications
Electronic Commerce	Browse, "shop before you buy"
Telecommunications	Content provider, yellow pages, Media Broker™
Post-Production	Edit, search, transcode

With the introduction of Informix Dynamic Server with Universal Data Option Informix now delivers the only truly extensible object-relational database architecture designed to provide native support for dynamic multimedia content, interactive Web applications, and core business transactions. Informix Dynamic Server with Universal Data Option combines Informix's Dynamic Scalable Architecture™ (DSA) with innovative plug-in DataBlade modules to provide comprehensive support for any type of data. This breakthrough technology now creates unlimited possibilities for Informix and partners to deliver digital media solutions for fast and intelligent searching, indexing, and management of rich content.

Informix's technological lead over competitive offerings, as well as broad industry support, makes Informix Dynamic Server with Universal Data Option and DataBlade module technology the emerging standard for managing digital media. This paper will introduce the key technologies, partnerships, and solutions.

Information Management Challenges for Rich Media Content

The rapid accumulation of digital assets in all areas of business today creates a critical demand for information management. No matter what the business, companies today require a content management strategy that includes the storing, cataloging, managing, and deploying of rich media.

Increasingly, businesses use digital media and the Web to enhance key business applications, deploy new products or services, reach new markets, and improve organizational

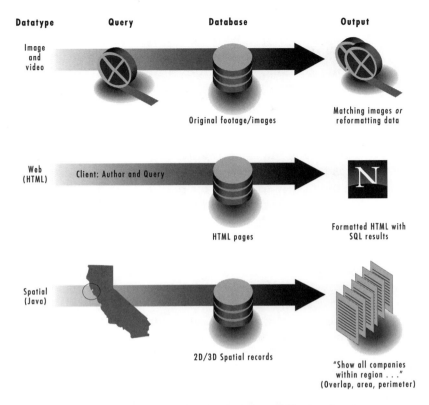

Datatype	Query	Database	Output

Image and video — Original footage/images — Matching images *or* reformatting data

Web (HTML) — Client: Author and Query — HTML pages — Formatted HTML with SQL results

Spatial (Java) — 2D/3D Spatial records — "Show all companies within region . . ." (Overlap, area, perimeter)

Figure 18–1 Media applications query using different datatypes.

effectiveness. In entertainment or broadcasting, digital media now redefines how content is created, used, and manipulated. Digital media puts a premium on an organization's ability to manage assets for competitive advantage and creative potential.

Until recently, the most commonly used databases were only capable of managing text and numeric data. However, as information evolves to include rich media, companies require a broader content management strategy that provides secure access and the sharing of vital media assets. The database architecture required to implement this type of broad information management is fundamentally different than anything that has existed in the market until recently.

To keep pace, companies must link text, images, and other rich media information with the process-driven database transactions of core business applications. For example, many corporations—ranging from retail to manufacturers and service organizations—want to incorporate digital video for electronic commerce, internal training, and corporate communications. Companies also plan on using images in human resource applications to display photos of employees along with data based on benefits and payroll information.

At the same time, the entertainment and broadcasting industries demand a full spectrum of content management capabilities which include full media search capabilities instead of mere queries on limited keywords or catalog indexes. These companies want the ability to search for photos or images based on content, color, or texture. Yet most conventional approaches limit searches solely to keywords associated with a photo, image, or video. As an example, a video production site or a corporate video producer should be able to search and retrieve portions of a video sequence. This means having the ability to access video archives—enabling broader creative choices, as well as reductions in cost and time.

However, it still remains necessary to provide investment protection for many video production facilities which must manage both digital and analog video inventory. Along with the opportunity to repurpose existing published information in new digital forms, the protection of copyrights has become a critical issue for any organization with valuable media assets—especially those companies who distribute or publish assets on the Web. Publishers now require a method to embed identification information into any content provided to an end user or buyer. These challenges and others are forcing this industry to look for more efficient and powerful solutions to help manage the vast amount of information published each day.

With the growing acceptance of the Internet as the network infrastructure for electronic commerce, it is now clear that the increased use of integrated database and Web technologies will become the vital enterprisewide computing mechanism that enables both people and applications to work together more effectively. Gone are the days of command-line interfaces. Users today want color, sound, animation, and intuitive navigation. Companies also demand the ability to manage all the content that is involved in doing business, such as corporate documents or financial reports, images and graphics designed

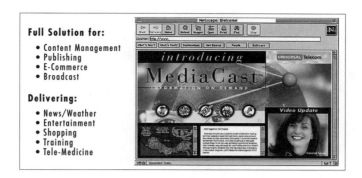

Full Solution for:
- Content Management
- Publishing
- E-Commerce
- Broadcast

Delivering:
- News/Weather
- Entertainment
- Shopping
- Training
- Tele-Medicine

Figure 18–2 A dynamic Web solution enabled by diverse media types on Informix Dynamic Server with Universal Data Option.

for marketing collateral, and complex financial objects, such as stock portfolios and derivatives.

The challenge in the years ahead is to deliver a solution that can be used to manage the rich content of business, entertainment, and publishing. Clearly, the Web's influence has demonstrated the need for a powerful, scalable data management system that addresses the storage and delivery requirements of rich media-based applications. The following section provides an overview of Informix's comprehensive solution for digital media.

Informix's Digital Media Solutions

Informix today offers the most effective solution for managing digital media in business, entertainment, publishing, communications, electronic commerce, and interactive Web applications. This is accomplished via the world's first enterprise-capable object-relational database management system (ORDBMS) designed to fully support rich media content, as well as core business transactions.

To understand the importance of the Informix solution to digital media professionals, it is necessary to review the recent history of database management systems in general. ORDBMSs,

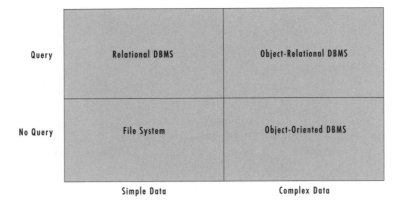

	Simple Data	Complex Data
Query	Relational DBMS	Object-Relational DBMS
No Query	File System	Object-Oriented DBMS

Figure 18–3 *The figure above shows the contrasting approaches of relational and object databases, and illustrates the benefits of converging these two technologies.*

such as Informix Dynamic Server with Universal Data Option, bridge the gap between relational and object-oriented database approaches, each of which are designed to address vastly different data management requirements.

Relational versus Object-Oriented

Built for traditional corporate database requirements, relational database management systems (RDBMSs) operate by organizing numerical and fixed-length text fields into two-dimensional tables. Users can query, sort, and manipulate the rows and columns which represent different records in a variety of ways. Queries can be submitted in structured query language (SQL) or through the Microsoft Object Database Connectivity (ODBC) API. Most RDBMSs are designed to handle large volumes of text and numeric information, and simultaneous operations. The primary benefits of a relational database include stability, speed, and power.

Yet the very structure which provides stability and speed is also the greatest limitation of a relational database. Complex data, such as geospatial information or multimedia data, is not easily or quickly broken down into the numerical coordinates that a relational system can handle. As a result, most complex data, such as photo images or video clips, are stored as binary large objects (BLOBs). A BLOB can be stored and accessed only as a complete entity, which eliminates the possibility of native content queries. This approach also complicates the process of adding new media types to the database, resulting in reduced overall performance, more lines of code, and needless complexity for database administrators (DBAs).

Rather than use the table model, object-oriented database management systems (OODBMSs) use hierarchical models as the database design. Consequently, OODBMSs are more adept at handling spatial and multimedia data, such as CAD files, animation, and time series or composite data. They can also be adapted more easily to include new datatypes. Conversely, object-oriented database systems are often criticized for their unreliability, limited or slow search capabilities, failure to support industry standard SQL, and lack of robustness in a multiuser environment.

The evolution of the ORDBMS arose out of the need to combine elements of both relational- and object-oriented database management technology. Building on the object-oriented development environment which defines datatypes as objects, ORDBMSs recognize and manage native content, rather than operating to simply store and manage BLOBs. In addition, an ORDBMS can use developer-defined functions to manipulate data. Drawing from the capabilities of the relational database, ORDBMSs support industry standard SQL, are considerably more stable than OODBMSs, and are extremely powerful for the fast and easy manipulation of complex data, and the processing of multiple operations.

In early 1996, Informix purchased Illustra Information Technologies, gaining the Illustra DataBlade Module architecture integral to the development of a truly parallelized object-relational database system—optimized to fully support rich new multimedia, and Internet and/or Web applications. The integration of Informix Dynamic Server with the Illustra object-relational database represents a turning point in the balance of power within the database industry.

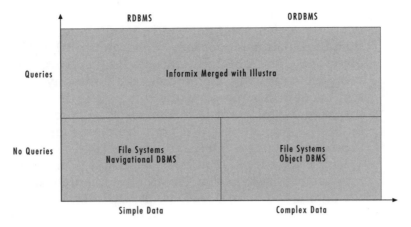

RDBMS ORDBMS

Queries Informix Merged with Illustra

No Queries | File Systems Navigational DBMS | File Systems Object DBMS

Simple Data Complex Data

Figure 18–4 The merging of Informix Dynamic Server with the Illustra Server.

Informix Dynamic Server with Universal Data Option and Digital Media

Informix Dynamic Server with Universal Data Option brings together the speed, reliability, and flexibility of the DSA architecture with the broad support for digital media types enabled by Informix DataBlade module technology.

This capability allows companies to use Informix Dynamic Server with Universal Data Option's unique object-relational database architecture to manage either industry or company-specific datatypes, as well as rich media. Companies may use either one or more DataBlade Module(s) simultaneously to create a unique, integrated information management solution that is customized for specific business requirements.

A growing number of partners, such as Kodak, NEC, VXtreme, Virage, and Muscle Fish, supply DataBlade modules to address enhanced digital media support in Informix Dynamic Server with Universal Data Option. In addition, strategic partners— including Netscape Communications Corporation (Netscape); Silicon Graphics, Inc. (SGI); Avid; Sun Microsystems, Inc. (Sun Microsystems); and The Bulldog Group, Inc. (Bulldog)—deliver comprehensive solutions based on Informix technology. These partners, in addition to many others, contribute to provide

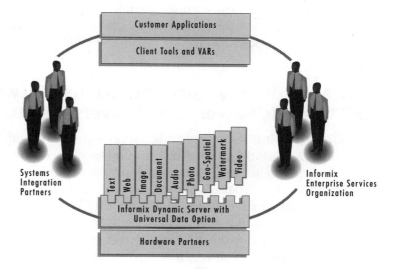

Figure 18–5 *Informix Dynamic Server with Universal Data Option, DataBlade module technology, and Informix partners enable extensibility and provide full digital media solutions.*

Informix customers with the most powerful and extensible information platform in the industry.

Informix DSA provides unsurpassed scalability and break-through performance for the mission-critical data processing requirements of on-line transaction processing (OLTP), batch, and decision-support applications. DSA was designed with parallel pro-cessing at the core of its architecture. As part of the fundamental rewrite of its engine in 1991, Informix added the "hooks" which facilitated the smooth integration of Illustra technology. These hooks were built as part of the core engine in the Informix extensibility project. That is why merging Illustra extensibility to any RDBMS other than Informix DSA would have been prohibi-tively difficult and time consuming. The project's goal was to ready Informix for future extensions. By adding Illustra, the promise of an object-relational architecture became a reality.

With Informix Dynamic Server with Universal Data Option, it is now possible to quickly add third-party, reusable software plug-ins which extend the capabilities of the core database server. Unlike competitive approaches, Informix Dynamic Server with Universal Data Option does not rely on a middleware layer that impacts performance, manageability, and integration. Instead, it is optimized for the performance and critical integration of database server operations.

DataBlade Modules Enhance the Extensibility of Informix Dynamic Server with Universal Data Option

Together, Informix Dynamic Server with Universal Data Option and DataBlade module technology provide a powerful, integrated object-relational database solution capable of extension by various developers, whether independent software vendors (ISVs), customers, or Informix, to handle any kind of information. The combination of Informix Dynamic Server with Universal Data Option and DataBlade module technology renders the harnessing of digital media simple and expedient.

Companies can mix and match shrink-wrapped DataBlade modules from third parties and Informix—or write their own—to create innovative business applications. These professionally certified extensions to Informix Dynamic Server with Universal Data Option are designed specifically to enable users to efficiently store, retrieve, update, and manipulate on demand any new kind of data, regardless of its nature.

Produced by Informix and ISVs to deliver breakthrough technology to organizations worldwide, DataBlade modules encapsulate new abstract datatypes and access methods, and add greater intelligence to the database server, thus enabling users to manage any kind of information. In addition, DataBlade modules can be used individually or in conjunction with other DataBlade modules to offer maximum flexibility.

For developers, Informix Dynamic Server with Universal Data Option database application programs are easier to write since they take advantage of the technology embedded in DataBlade modules. Access to data is more efficient, since DataBlade modules provide native access methods for optimizing the search and retrieval of complex data. But most importantly, with new DataBlade modules providing extensibility, the database can grow to accommodate new business requirements. DataBlade modules allow customers to leverage existing investments in database technology while preserving an extensible growth path.

The structure of Informix Dynamic Server with Universal Data Option and DataBlade module technology gives users the ability to handle digital information within a database in a way that more closely mirrors how users might manipulate data in the real world. For example, users can search for photos or images based on actual content, color, or texture, and not solely keywords. As new file formats and standards emerge, such as MPEG-4, VRML, and Java, DataBlade modules will provide extensible support for these technologies in Informix Dynamic Server with Universal Data Option.

Dynamic Web Support

In 1996, Informix announced its Universal Web Architecture, a collection of Informix and third-party servers and tools for building and managing interactive Web sites and applications. The products that constitute the Informix Universal Web Architecture allow users to store and manage an entire Web site in an Informix database, including its application logic, application templates, and content.

Storing sites in an Informix database offers an alternative to saving sites as flat files and scripts in a Web server. The challenge of merging text and multimedia-intensive Web pages has overwhelmed many users of traditional relational databases. Instead, the Informix Universal Web Architecture allows complex, data-rich Web content to be combined with the highly scalable Informix Dynamic Server with Universal Data Option. The Informix Universal Web Architecture includes Dynamic Informix server and Web Integration Option to allow developers to store Web site content and application logic in an Informix server. Informix Dynamic Server with Web Integration Option is a platform that enables third-party developers to write Web applications for Informix databases.

DataBlade modules within Informix Dynamic Server with Universal Data Option enable user-defined datatypes, functions, and access methods, and support true *dynamic* Web sites with digital media, HTML, and Java as part of the ORDBMS. This expands the information management capability, and allows all forms of multimedia information to be handled natively in the core engine. The result is higher performance, better access, and secure administration of an organization's precious digital assets.

DataBlade Modules and Partner Profiles

DataBlade Partners: A Key Success Factor

DataBlade module partners represent one of the key factors in the success of the Informix Dynamic Server with Universal Data Option strategy. Informix has a commitment to developing mutually beneficial relationships with DataBlade module partners, and DataBlade module development represents a tremendous business opportunity for ISVs, VARS, systems integrators, and consultants. The strong response from the industry shows Informix's strategy is working.

Many DataBlade module partners already bring to Informix a demonstrated expertise in technology areas such as compression technology, text search and retrieval capabilities, voice-recognition algorithms, multimedia content management, Internet/intranet management, geospatial mapping, electronic commerce, and more.

The following profiles offer an overview of some of the digital media DataBlade module technologies which were developed for Informix Dynamic Server with Universal Data Option.

Informix Video Foundation DataBlade Module

The Informix Video Foundation DataBlade Module addresses the long-standing need companies have for storing, searching, and utilizing analog and digital video resources. This DataBlade module offers a solution for companies who need to access video assets for use in corporate messaging or training, entertainment industry video needs, or wherever video is needed. This module provides an opportunity for customers to take full advantage of existing video resources, since it provides storage and recall

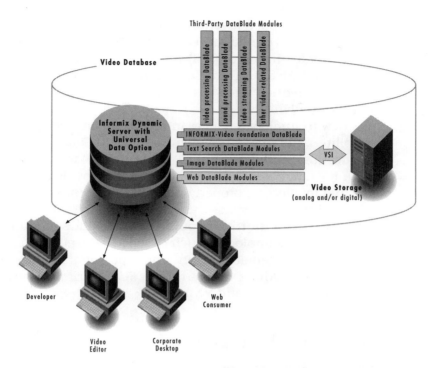

Third-Party DataBlade Modules

Video Database

video processing DataBlade
sound processing DataBlade
video streaming DataBlade
other video-related DataBlade

Informix Dynamic
Server with
Universal
Data Option

INFORMIX-Video Foundation DataBlade
Text Search DataBlade Modules
Image DataBlade Modules
Web DataBlade Modules

VSI

Video Storage
(analog and/or digital)

Developer

Video
Editor

Corporate
Desktop

Web
Consumer

Figure 18–6 *The Informix Video Foundation DataBlade Module
architecture.*

capabilities for the entire video segment, or allows searches
based on image, sound, or text elements within the video itself.

The Informix Video Foundation DataBlade Module also serves
as the backbone to a new class of advanced video applications
which give customers more opportunities to use their valuable
video assets across multiple channels such as the Web, broadcasting, and publishing. The module is based on an open and
scalable software architecture that allows strategic third-party
development partners to incorporate specific video technologies
into Informix Dynamic Server with Universal Data Option.

With the Video Foundation DataBlade Module, metadata is
stored in the Informix Dynamic Server with Universal Data
Option, while the actual video content can be maintained on
disk, video tape, video server, or other external storage devices.
By using indexes and cataloging applications that run on
Informix Dynamic Server with Universal Data Option, both digi-

tal and analog video inventory can be efficiently managed. The Informix Video Foundation DataBlade Module also includes a Virtual Storage Interface (VSI) that links Informix Dynamic Server with Universal Data Option to a video server of the user's choice. This feature offers the ability to both store and play video from that server.

As new technologies deliver Internet support and interactive possibilities, the Informix Video Foundation DataBlade Module provides customized access and query to the video segments stored within the database. These capabilities are provided, while still enforcing intellectual property rights for the entire video segment, or for each frame if necessary. In addition, partners who endorse Informix as a platform are building DataBlade modules for video-specific technologies, such as video servers, video streaming, and video scene detection. These partners include Sun Microsystems, EMC, Excalibur, IBM, SGI, Starlight Networks, Virage, Vivo, Vosiac, and VXtreme.

VXtreme Video DataBlade Module

Video is an important part of the media which is transmitted via the Internet and corporate intranets. However, companies increasingly face barriers to accessing real-time video due to low bandwidth. The VXtreme Video DataBlade Module, built on the Informix Video Foundation DataBlade Module, allows real-time video to be streamed on demand, so users can view video without waiting for the entire file to download.

VXtreme's target application environments are the Internet and corporate intranets. For the Internet, this means providing video capabilities for news, entertainment on-demand, catalogs, and consumer support. Primary intranet video streaming applications include on-demand training, corporate communications, sales support, and on-line executive messages which can be delivered to the desktop. With the introduction of its Web Theater product, VXtreme supports three important capabilities: video serving, plug-ins for viewing and delivery, and authoring—enabling the integration of HTML and graphics at any point in a video segment.

In addition, corporate training on-demand for a vast and often global workforce has become a critical requirement at large

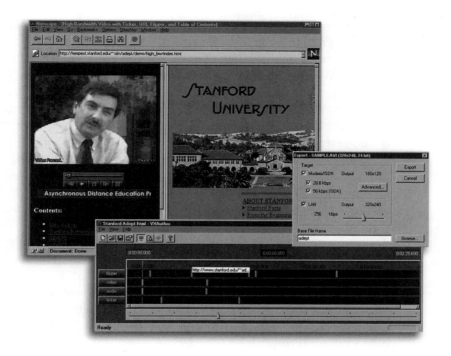

Figure 18–7 The VXtreme Video DataBlade Module allows real-time video to be streamed on demand.

corporations. Intranet video-enabled training captures the knowledge of a company and makes it accessible to every employee.

To offer this level of video support on the Web, VXtreme utilizes an extremely high-compression ratio that scales up to 500:1. This innovative compression technology enables high-quality video to be delivered on the Internet, while minimizing demands on network bandwidth and server storage. This technological advantage results from VXtreme's ability to scale to different bandwidths—allowing flexibility in the size, quality, and the frame rate of the video transmission.

Muscle Fish Audio Information Retrieval

Utilizing audio segments in a variety of applications is a necessity for industries as diverse as entertainment, advertising, and law enforcement. Previously, audio files were handled as BLOBs, and qualitative queries of any kind were only possible if the database developer manually entered keywords or textual descriptions for every audio file in the database. The Muscle Fish Audio Information Retrieval (AIR) DataBlade Module leverages the Informix Video Foundation DataBlade Module to enable database applications to automatically analyze and translate raw audio data into a meaningful form for storage in tables.

With the AIR DataBlade Module, sound files are automatically analyzed for acoustic-perceptual and file attributes when inserted into the database. The module enables the development of audio databases and sound browsers with a totally intuitive approach, providing powerful, and insightful tools to sound designers and editors, while offering cost saving advantages to producers of films and multimedia titles. Television and radio advertising agencies can also benefit from content-based sound browsers, since they rely on quick access to innovative sounds in order to deliver a specific message to an audience. Adding the AIR DataBlade Module is effectively similar to attaching a pair of ears to one's database.

Kodak PixFactory DataBlade Module

Transporting high-resolution images over a network can be time consuming and can result in the reduced quality of images. This is a problem, as businesses increasingly rely on high-quality graphical images for use in all aspects of print and Web-based publishing.

The Kodak PixFactory DataBlade Module addresses the traditional challenges of incorporating digital image technology to supplement analog (film) based processes by introducing FlashPix technology, and associated metadata content, to Informix Dynamic Server with Universal Data Option. A FlashPix image is a resolution-independent file which allows the quick transmission of lower-resolution images via traditional network services, while maintaining the integrity of higher-resolution image files. The FlashPix file format is a collaborative initiative between Microsoft Corporation, the Hewlett-Packard Company, Kodak, and Live Picture.

The Kodak PixFactory DataBlade Module introduces FlashPix image content information to Informix Dynamic Server with

Universal Data Option. Once imported, this information is complementary to other DataBlade module technologies, that is, digital full-color images used in conjunction with audio information. With this module, businesses can import metadata content from FlashPix images and subsequently manage the content associated with the images, for fast and efficient image search and retrieval.

NEC TigerMark DataBlade Module

Since the advent of the Internet, ensuring the security of intellectual property and published assets has become a growing concern for many businesses. NEC TigerMark Technology provides powerful watermarking technology for content protection and identification, and offers the most robust, secure, and stable image-sensitive watermarking technology available.

Digital watermarks are tags, or serial numbers, which are embedded in rich content. Three properties make these tags extremely valuable:

- They are invisible and do not degrade the quality of the content;
- They are indelible. That is, they survive common processing and are not removable, even through illegal means;
- They are embedded directly into the content; thus, wherever the data goes, so does the watermark.

Watermarks help to protect copyrights in important ways, such as authenticating ownership. By embedding owner, user, or buyer identification directly into content, such as a still image, the watermark helps to track illegal use. This is a critical feature, since images that are stored in Informix Dynamic Server with Universal Data Option can be automatically and seamlessly watermarked as they are sent out to the Internet. As a result, the NEC TigerMark DataBlade Module fulfills an important role for emerging content management applications.

Excalibur Technologies Corporation DataBlade Modules

To support Informix Dynamic Server with Universal Data Option, Excalibur Technologies created a suite of DataBlade modules which transform the various forms of information into usable knowledge. One of these modules is detailed below.

SceneChange DataBlade Module

Motion picture studios, advertising agencies, and television news departments must keep storyboards for their libraries of video clips. Instead of investing hours or days of unproductive time in navigating through archived video assets, and deciphering manually indexed film tables, users need to quickly locate the footage required for film trailers, merchandising, or retrospective presentations.

Utilizing the Informix Video Foundation DataBlade Module, the SceneChange DataBlade Module enables users to index and access every scene change in a digital film archive. Once the film has been indexed, the SceneChange DataBlade Module allows users to review the film as a storyboard—compressing hours of video review into a manageable number of keyframes.

The SceneChange DataBlade Module consists of the following components:

- Storyboarding, and the search and retrieval of QuickTime, ActiveMovie, and MPEG video files;
- Various functions that allow users to create and search new tables and cursors based on the Histogram; and
- An SQL interface for client application development. The SQL API allows third parties to develop database applications which incorporate tables derived from the histograms produced by the SceneChange DataBlade Module.

Virage Visual Information Retrieval DataBlade Module

As technology evolves in certain vertical markets, such as medicine and satellite imaging, the vast amounts of data collected cannot be effectively managed with the current industry-standard tools. With Virage's Visual Intelligence application, companies can manage their visual assets with viewing, annotation, archiving, retrieval, and modification tools.

Virage's Visual Information Retrieval (VIR) DataBlade Module allows users to search and retrieve graphics files, based on the content of the stored image. The images can be stored in a wide variety of graphic formats. Users can also combine searches on image content with traditional string searches using text to describe the images. The multifaceted search-and-retrieval capacity of the VIR DataBlade Module renders it suitable for animation, video, and other multimedia applications, as well as for still photographs, scanned images, and more conventional graphic files.

The VIR DataBlade Module is already essential for SGI and Bulldog applications. SGI has found that with Visual Intelligence running on its media servers, users can quickly search through terabytes of visual information with differing address schemes, file names, and file formats. Several media asset management products use VIR to provide for the enterprisewide control of digital assets, and their integration with workflow and other enterprise processes, such as network publishing.

Verity Text DataBlade Modules

While adequate database storage is certainly a concern, the ability to appropriately search and access textual information is of even greater importance to most businesses. The Verity Text DataBlade Module is an embedded extension to Informix Dynamic Server with Universal Data Option, and provides the most flexible, extensible way to search, store, and manage full text. The Text DataBlade Module supplies a fully functional document searching mechanism, allowing for effective searching on complex concepts.

By integrating the Verity engine, Informix combines database queries with full-text queries to deliver highly accurate, relevance-ranked results to the user. The Verity Text DataBlade Module supports custom datatypes which can be further extended by the user to fit changing business needs. These types can be combined with other types, whether user defined or supplied by Informix, to create entirely new constructs. The Verity DataBlade Module is fully internationalized, supporting 11 languages right out of the box and allowing for the full-text search of documents in multiple languages.

Informix Digital Media Strategic Partnerships

Informix has a long history of successfully teaming with partners, and it is leveraging this history in its digital media strategy. For example, Informix is participating in the Creative Artists Agency (CAA)/Intel Media Lab, a high profile showcase for digital media solutions for Hollywood. Examples of three Informix partners are Bulldog, SGI, and Netscape.

The Bulldog Group Partners with Informix for Digital Media Management

The Canadian-based Bulldog Group offers an enterprise-wide media asset management solution which integrates workflow processes to better manage digital media, including video, audio, HTML, text, and graphics, and integrates the processes into an overall business process. This solution is built on Informix's Illustra content management system. The combination of Bulldog's media asset management software and Informix's technology allows businesses to manage all of their information assets into a single, elegant information management solution.

Bulldog Media and Workflow Management software is particularly appealing to the "Media 200"—the top 200 media rich organizations which span entertainment, publishing and pre-press, advertisers, and communications/broadcasting networks. Designed specifically to enable users to centralize, control, and manage digital media assets, key features of Bulldog software include:

Centralized Digital Media Assets

Bulldog manages digital media assets in an enterprise-wide, distributed database architecture. This allows for the easy access, secure sharing, search, retrieval, and repurposing of these assets.

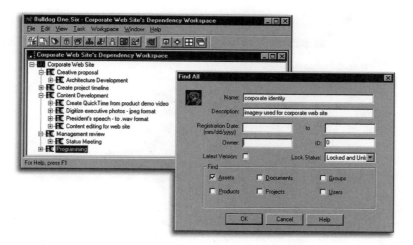

Figure 18–8 *The Bulldog Group's asset management software keeps track of an entire project in the database.*

Mapping Assets Against Workflow

Bulldog's asset management software allows project managers to utilize resources more effectively by tracking the status of projects and allocating tasks according to users' skill sets.

Automatic Indexing for Easy Search and Retrieval

With Bulldog's software, Media assets are automatically indexed to a particular task and project—simplifying and accelerating search and retrieval. Documentation, such as copyrights, trademarks, and licensing agreements, can also be attached to assets.

Video Streaming

Through Bulldog, users can view MPEG1 and MPEG2 in real-time, without waiting for time-consuming video downloads.

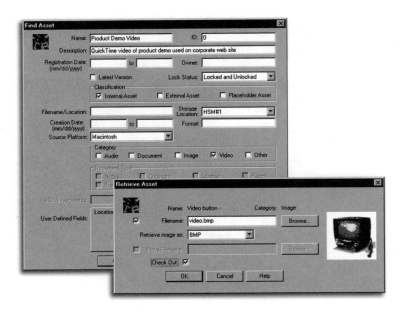

Figure 18–9 *Individual media files can be tracked by format, deadline, and datatype.*

In addition, Bulldog is now integrating its media asset management technology into a DataBlade Module which will provide broad content management capabilities for a wide range of Informix users and applications.

Avid Technology Utilizes Informix Technology

Avid Technology is the leading supplier for capturing, editing, and distributing digital media on disk. Today, Avid Technology supports over 1,100 broadcast facilities and over 60,000 journalists worldwide with disk-based editing, newsroom computer systems, and commercial production and playback applications. Leveraging its experience in non-linear editing and newsroom computer systems, Avid is revolutionizing the digital news-gathering process by offering the only client/server production system available to take broadcasters all the way from camera, to editing, to playback—without using tape.

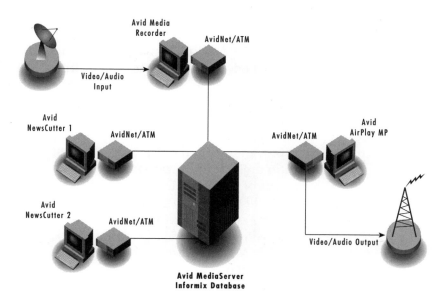

Figure 18–10 The Avid network topology is based on the Informix database engine.

The Avid Digital News Gathering (DNG) system provides broadcasters with an efficient, reliable, and fast means to produce top-quality, up-to-the minute newscasts. The Avid MediaServer Database is an integral component of the DNG system. Avid made the decision to build this application using Informix database technology. Avid believes that the Informix engine offers the best combination of robustness and functionality for the demanding DNG environment, and the specific requirements of video management.

Avid's fully integrated production environment allows broadcasters to work on media simultaneously, as is not possible with stand-alone systems. For example, one editor can work on a hard-news story, while a second works on repurposing the story for distribution, and a third works on a news tease. Each editor can pick and choose the needed shots from the same source media in the library.

Informix provides state-of-the-art database technology for Avid's Digital News Gathering system. The combination of these two industry-leading products offers unprecedented media management capabilities for the broadcast industry.

Silicon Graphics Builds Video Solutions with Informix

As a leading supplier of high-performance, interactive computing systems, SGI embeds Informix database technology into its Cosmo MediaBase software to fully leverage its RISC microprocessors and IRIX operating system for digital media applications. SGI's WebFORCE Media Server with Cosmo MediaBase is a powerful platform for video serving, and incorporates a complete solution for storing, managing, retrieving, and delivering high-quality, streaming digital video content.

With the support of Informix Dynamic Server with Universal Data Option, SGI will provide specialized video management capabilities to their existing client base and to leading companies in the industry, as well as entertainment fields. Cosmo MediaBase provides Web integration to allow URLs and cgi/bin scripts to reference video content and metadata, and to enable the playback of real-time video streams to Web browsers with fully interactive VCR controls. In addition, plug-ins, such as the Cosmo Stream Player, offer full motion MPEG1 and MPEG2 video playback for Web browsers and helper applications on a wide variety of platforms. These tools provide systems administrators and content management specialists extended capabilities to efficiently install and manage large volumes of rapidly changing video and other digital content.

SGI also plans to support direct database access to Informix Dynamic Server with Universal Data Option from MindSet, the company's flagship product for exploratory data analysis. MindSet provides an integrated, interactive tool for data access and transformation, data mining, and visual data mining.

Informix Digital Media Customer Profiles

Warner Brothers Online

In November of 1996, Warner Brothers Online (Warner Bros. Online) based its intelligent Web applications on Informix Universal Web architecture, an open Web development environment that supports Informix Dynamic Server with Universal Data Option. Warner Bros. Online selected Informix products because the company's dynamic Web site demanded fast, efficient performance to provide visitors with real-time, interactive experiences. Also, Informix's extensibility allowed Warner Bros. Online to store multiple datatypes, such as images, audio, and video, in both current and future applications.

Warner Bros. Online has a history of using Informix products, including the Informix Web, Text, and Image DataBlade Modules, and Informix database technology. Specific applications include the Virtual Lot Web site, the WB Animation site, the Rosie O'Donnell talk show site, and the Six Flags Online site. In addition, Informix technology is used to support rotating content on the Warner Bros. Online home page, creating a unique experience upon each visit to the site.

Sun Microsystems Teams with Informix

Using Informix and the Internet as the foundation for an on-line partner catalog, Sun Microsystems found a way to help its partners and customers, while improving the productivity of Sun employees. It was necessary to locate the catalog on the Web—so that partners, customers, and employees could access and update information in real-time. Sun Microsystems selected the Illustra Server from Informix as the foundation for its on-line catalog due to its demonstrated ability to manage many different types of data.

The on-line Catalyst Catalog runs on a Sun Microsystems SPARCstation, and is accessible by any browser from any platform. The Informix server gives customers the ability to perform full text and ad-hoc searches on keywords, simplifying the process of finding applications to meet specific needs. The implementation of this system comes from a real-world situation faced in 1996, when Sun received a request to deliver 300 copies of a European version of the Catalyst Catalog to Barcelona, Spain within 10 days. Prior to instituting the on-line catalog solution backed by Informix, fulfilling this request would not have been possible. Sun Microsystems is also adding support of the Informix DataBlade Module API in its Media Server offering to deliver extensibility for the broad base of DataBlade modules.

The Seattle Times

When the largest daily newspaper in Washington State and the Pacific Northwest sought a database to provide robust functionality for their new interactive entertainment Web site, the Seattle Times selected Informix database technology and the Informix Dynamic Server with Web Integration Option.

Based on Informix database technology, the Seattle Times created the "Datebook," an intelligent Web site which allows visitors to plan their leisure activities by searching on area events and creating personalized "datebooks" on the fly. Visitors can add appointments and scheduled activities to their personal datebook, which can be modified throughout the week to create an on-line or hardcopy social planner.

The site utilizes Informix technology to manage complex datatypes such as graphics, images, and HTML. The Informix Dynamic Server with Web Integration Option, a Web application development tool, allows visitors to create the personalized planners on line. The Personal Library System (PLS) DataBlade Module is used to search and retrieve restaurant reviews, scan movie listings for favorite actors, or group all theaters which show a particular performance. The Image DataBlade Module allows for intelligent image retrieval, including still images of movies, performers, venue seating charts, and other graphic elements. In future releases, the 2D Spatial DataBlade Module will enable the geo-mapping of queries such as "show the closest restaurant to this concert."

The Emerging Industry Standard for Information Management

Through its proven, open, and extensible database architecture, Informix enables customers, DataBlade module developers, and channel partners to create a new generation of digital media-based applications, and to easily extend the functionality of existing applications with plug-in modules. Thus, all the leading tools for creating graphics, video, images, and text in the industry can now be enhanced by the broad data management and dynamic Web support capabilities of Informix Dynamic Server with Universal Data Option.

With hundreds of companies worldwide in various stages of DataBlade module development, it is now widely acknowledged that Informix delivers the emerging industry-standard platform for information management and rich media applications. In fact, DataBlade module support extends beyond images and video to include text and document management, the Web and electronic commerce, data warehousing, and geospatial data such as maps. According to Patricia Seybold Group's Eckerson, "Informix's strategy is clear: make the DataBlade module API a de-facto industry standard for database extensibility by creating a broad following of ISVs and corporate developers. So far, Informix has had great success recruiting ISVs to write DataBlade modules."

In years to come, many companies will base data management extensibility in applications, operating systems, and the Web on Informix's standard DataBlade module plug-in module approach. This is a critical step in the establishment of Informix's technology specifications as the industry's premier solution for a wide range of critical information management applications.

For Informix customers, broad industry endorsement of Informix translates into greater opportunity, flexibility, and investment protection. Informix Dynamic Server with Universal Data Option users will be able to plug in diverse DataBlade modules to meet ever-changing business requirements. With high performance and scalability assured, customers can rely on Informix Dynamic Server with Universal Data Option as an open data management server which will always support industry-leading solutions. Informix Dynamic Server with Universal Data Option extends the functionality of existing client/server and business applications, while evolving into the Web-enabled platform for dynamic electronic commerce and content management.

For ISVs and channel partners, Informix Dynamic Server with Universal Data Option represents an opportunity to leverage existing or new application modules on an open data management platform that addresses the future of network computing. This is critical since companies that rely on business applications and effective communications look for new functionality that results from the integration of rich media and data management. For those developers, Informix Dynamic Server with Universal Data Option now emerges as the vital link that integrates database-enabled interactive applications, dynamic Web sites, and core business transactions for comprehensive digital media solutions.

Informix's database technology, application development tools, superior customer service, and strong partnerships enable the company to be at the forefront of the information technology revolution—delivering solutions which address today's core business requirements and the promise of tomorrow's content-rich applications.

Enabled by Informix Dynamic Server with Universal Data Option and DataBlade module technology extensibility, rich media will allow a new generation of applications that change how people live, work, and communicate. That is why Informix's vision for digital media is based on a future that all can see, hear, and feel.

Chapter 19

Java Database Connectivity

by Kingsley Idehen

The Java Programming Language

Java is described by its creators (Sun Microsystems) as an operating system independent, object-oriented, programming language. "Write once and run it anywhere"—this is a compelling proposition for the emerging world of Internet-based distributed computing.

Imagine your corporate information system (IS) being written in Java and usable by all employees, irrespective of individual, departmental, or divisional preferences for graphical user interfaces (GUI), or computer hardware (PCs, notebooks, palmtops, PDAs, etc.). Then, imagine embarking on a corporate Internet/intranet/extranet project without restrictions. This is what makes Java so compelling and explains why it has caught the attention and imagination of IS corporate managers, developers, and end users worldwide.

A secondary proposition is the development of "Zero Admin" Java applications and applets. Picture the ability to notify every user of your corporate IS system about system revisions or enhancements by simply sending a Uniform Resource Locator (URL) to access the new version of the IS. The cost savings would be phenomenal, at the very least.

Java's Implementation and Architecture

Java is implemented through a virtual machine (VM). A VM is a software implementation of a computer (sort of) that runs within a host operating system, which then runs on an actual computer device. You might also refer to this as the runtime environment for Java applications (apps) and applets.

The Java VM (JVM) is written in a combination of 'C' and Java (some assembler code has also made its way into the more recent releases). Java apps and applets are compiled into Java byte code during development and executed within the JVM, which plays the role of byte code interpreter. Java byte code is a machine-independent intermediary machine code format. This machine code format isn't device-specific; hence the JVM's much vaunted platform independence.

Java objects are built using Java classes, and these classes are the compiled end product of Java class interface definition and implementations (contained in Java language source code files).

Java Object Assembly Steps For the "HelloWorldObject" Java Object

Note the following Java Object assembly steps:

1. Source file extract (filename is HelloWorldObject.java):

```
Import java.*
Class HelloWorldObject {
  Public static void main(String[] args) {
    System.out.println("Hello World!!!");
  }
}
```

2. Compilation of source file (from host operating system command line):

```
javac HelloWorldObject.java
```

3. Java class file produced:

```
HelloWorldObject.class
```

4. Execution of Java application (object instantiation):

```
java HelloWorldObject
```

Java apps, applets, and beans typically comprise of numerous other Java objects which work in concert through an object-messaging protocol (and this has nothing to do with messaging communications middleware). A Java developer typically constructs his or her own objects, or incorporates those of others. Once constructed, the developer devises a messaging protocol between these objects. This is what the end user experiences as a Java app, applet, or bean.

Using Java

Apps

Java apps fit into the traditional application model in the sense that they are executed from a command line and must be installed on, or migrated to, each application's host machine, and then executed within that machine's JVM using the following command line construct:

```
java myappclass
```

Applets

Applets do not live in a page, as is commonly perceived. Applets are actually Java classes identified via HyperText Markup Language (HTML) tags within Web documents; it is these HTML tags which are embedded within Web documents. Java applets are loaded from Web servers somewhere on the Internet, or within corporate intranets or extranets.

Java Beans

A prefabricated Java component is known as a Java bean. The Java bean API provides a specification through which Java objects are fabricated (using the Java beans' interface specification) into component objects. These component objects are usable by Java beans compliant container environments. Typical examples of such container environments include documents, application assembly environments, and other software component specifications, such as OpenDOC and ActiveX.

Java beans facilitate the development and implementation of operating system independent, prefabricated application components. These components include graphical widgets, query engines, process engines, and full-blown applications, etc. To date, this has been an operating system specific experience, as demonstrated with OpenDOC (predominantly Macintosh OS and OS/2 based) and ActiveX (predominantly Microsoft Windows based).

Note

Please keep in mind that software components do not need to be visible at runtime in order to fit into the definition of a "prefabricated component."

Java Class Migration Methods

The Java VM, as explained earlier in this document, plays the role of an execution environment for Java objects. Thus, before any Java app/applet/bean can be instantiated, their constituent classes must first make their way to the relevant VM from which their services are to be consumed. The process is described in this article as "Java class migration." This process is one of the key elements that drives the perception of Java, in terms of performance and stability.

Java classes are typically migrated using one or more of the following methods:

- Web servers and HTTP;
- Push-based replication; or
- CORBA-based Object Request Brokers (ORBs) using the Internet Inter Orb Protocol (IIOP).

Web Servers and HTTP

The HyperText Transport Protocol (HTTP) is an Internet protocol that addresses the transfer of files between Web browsers (HTTP clients) and Web servers (HTTP servers).

Java applets, by their very nature, are inextricably linked to HTML documents and the HTTP file transfer protocol. This linkage exists because applets are identified via HTML tags within these documents, and it is these HTML tags which instigate the browser into sending an additional HTTP message to the relevant Web server which requests a Java class file.

The following steps illustrate this process:

1. A user enters the URL string into the browser, for example:

```
http://oplweb.openlinksw.com/demo/JDK1.1/WebScrollDemo.htm
```

2. The browser passes the URL and determines that it will use the HTTP protocol to request a document called "WebScrollDemo.html," located within the directory called "Demo/JDK1.1," on a server machine named "www," within the domain "openlinksw.com," and running a server process (the actual Web server) that speaks HTTP.

3. The Web server receives file requests from the browser and proceeds to locate the file called "WebScrollDemo.html." Once the file is located, the server sends the file across the network to the requesting browser.

4. On receiving the file "WebScrollDemo.html," the browser proceeds to process the HTML tags contained within the document, as follows:

```
<html>
<head>
<title>WebScrollDemo</title>
</head>
<body>
<hr>
<applet
   code=WebScrollDemo.class
   id=WebScrollDemo
   width=600
   height=400 >
</applet>
<hr>
<A HREF="WebScrollDemo.java" >
   <I>The Java Source</I></A>
</body>
</html>
```

5. The "<applet>" tag within this document indicates to the browser that it needs to send another request to the server machine "www," within the domain "openlinksw.com," and requests the file named "WebScrollDemo.class" (actual Java class), which is situated within the "Demo/JDK1.1" directory.
6. The Web server locates the file "WebScrollDemo.class" and sends it back to the browser.
7. On receiving the Java class file, the browser executes it using its own version of the Java virtual machine.
8. The user interacts with the Java applet.

Disadvantages of HTTP

The disadvantages of HTTP includes the following:

1. HTTP is insensitive to the format of the files that it transfers—every file is treated the same.
2. HTTP is a stateless protocol; it doesn't know or particularly care where you are in the processing cycle while using it.
3. It is a simple protocol built to accomplish very basic things.
4. It is inherently inefficient due to the fact that each response results in a new connection.

Advantages

The advantages of HTTP include the following:

1. HTTP is in wide use due to the popularity of Web browsers.
2. HTTP facilitates the centralization of resources, such as Java objects and HTML documents.

Push Technology

In response to some of the obvious shortcomings of HTTP, an alternative approach to Java class migration has recently emerged, which is popularly known as "push technology."

Push technology (PT) involves intelligent caching and file replication schemes, whereby Java byte code is copied to the host machine (a client, in this instance) from a remote application server machine, and then cached (a local copy is kept for subsequent use). Subsequent modifications to the application classes are addressed by the server notifying the relevant JVM client about these changes, and after obtaining approval from the client machine, it sends (the push process) the updated application classes across the network to the appropriate client JVM.

PT products always involve client and server software components and, as a Java byte code migration mechanism, can substantially increase the perceived performance of your Java app. The perceived performance of your Java app increases significantly because the class migration frequency between the client and server is much lower in comparison to HTTP.

Advantages

The advantages include the following:

1. Improved performance of Java apps.
2. Removes dependency on Web browsers as a medium through which Java objects are utilized.
3. Removes dependency on HTTP as the sole or dominant protocol for Java class migration.
4. It provides reduced administration, basically reinforcing the "Zero Admin" value proposition.

5. Java apps are centrally administered on the server and propagated out to requesting clients.

Disadvantages

The disadvantages include the following:

1. A majority of push servers aren't written in Java (at the time of writing, none were found), as a result the "write once, run anywhere" value proposition is compromised. The push servers available today typically run on Solaris and Windows NT.
2. The client parts of a push technology solution must still be installed on each client that seeks to use this technology; thus, the "Zero Admin" is not really being achieved.
3. Push products can rapidly consume the limited disk resources currently available in today's PC-dominated Internet client world. It is a known fact that Internet client devices and local storage will get smaller, not larger.

Object Request Brokers

A few years ago the Object Management Group (OMG)—http://www.omg.org—commenced work on the development and definition of a standard known as the Common Object Request Broker Architecture (CORBA). This is a very broad, powerful, and well-defined standard which addresses the issues of locating, binding, and consuming objects, and the services that they provide, in a distributed computing environment. As we all know, the Internet has become the critical backbone of distributed computing, thereby accelerating the appreciation of CORBA-compliant ORBs.

ORBs locate objects locally or across a network. Then, ORBs bind these objects such that, when using these objects, their physical location is insignificant to the consumer of the objects. An ORB is the most natural and coherent mechanism for locating and consuming Java objects.

Today, we use the term "Web browsing" to describe the experience of visiting a Web site and viewing the contents of the HTML documents stored on various Web servers. Unfortunately, what we are really doing is "Web fetching," because the documents we view are transferred via HTTP (see the previous section on HTTP) to the PC (or other Internet client devices), running our so-called Web browser. The same applies when these HTML documents contain references to other data formats, such as Java applets, multimedia clips, etc.

In the future, the Web we know today will evolve into an "InterGalactic object Web," and we will conduct true Web browsing using ORBs that support the Internet Inter Orb Protocol (IIOP). A Web site will become more like a dynamic multidimensional object-relational database, capable of storing the entire spectrum of usable human information. HTML documents and Java classes will no longer be migrated in their entirety to client Internet devices—thereby allowing powerful servers to process the bulk of the work associated with these objects.

Advantages

The advantages include the following:

1. Increased performance and resilience of Java-based solutions, due to the reduced network hoops associated with Java class migration.
2. The "write once, run anywhere" value proposition is reinforced, and in situations where apps aren't written in Java, implementations already exist for all major operating environments. CORBA is much broader than Java and is language independent. Thus, COBRA allows the object Web to be comprised of objects that are built using a variety of object-oriented programming languages.
3. IIOP is a stated oriented protocol, unlike HTTP, and implies that distributed Java solutions can be implemented without compromising resilience or sophistication.
4. Some Web browser vendors are shipping ORBs along with the browser.

Disadvantages

The disadvantages include the following:

1. Although IIOP has become the defining standard for Inter-ORB communication, a majority of implementations from different vendors remain incompatible.
2. ORBs require a fair degree of administration, however, this will change as Java orblets (the client or proxying element of an ORB) become commonplace.

Java Trouble Spots

Java Development Kit (JDK) Version Incompatibility and Cross-Platform Availability

Java is made available to users via the JDK. In recent times, JDK has been upgraded to version 1.1.6, which now includes Java Database Connectivity (JDBC). As you can imagine, Java-compliant apps and environments haven't kept pace.

The "write once, run anywhere" value proposition is JDK version specific; today this applies primarily to JDK 1.02, as it is the most widely implemented version of the JDK. Unfortunately, the more exciting and mature aspects of Java reside in version 1.1 JVM and higher.

Java Class Migration

HTTP was primarily built to handle document migration, not application state management—a vital element when utilizing or writing an even moderately sophisticated application. Therefore, HTTP is not the foundation on which to build enterprisewide business systems. Of course, applets can make a strong claim in the "Zero Admin" proposition space, as they are written once and will run anywhere. However, in what "STATE" remains the bigger and certainly more important question.

Push technologies typically require a client and server apiece, and are not typically written in Java, which means that they potentially compromise the Java value proposition—unless ported to all major operating environments. These products have an administration overhead which potentially compromises Java's other important value proposition, "Zero Admin."

ORBs, like TV remote controls, may not work with objects from other manufacturers. Imagine being forced to buy both the TV and the remote control from the same vendor. This is great for the vendor, but a pathetic situation for the consumer. Luckily, there are generic remote controls available today in the consumer electronics world and generic ORBs are certainly on their way, too (this is basically what IIOP facilitates).

Java DataBase Connectivity

Java Database Connectivity (JDBC) is a database-independent API that facilitates the development of database-independent Java apps/applets/beans. It is a Java abstraction layer that is based on the X/Open SAG CLI specification.

The JDBC Value Proposition

The JDBC value proposition is simple: "Write your Java apps, applets, and beans independent of the database once, and run anywhere."

The potential of JDBC in a Java-dominated distributed computing world is only limited by the boundaries of our individual imaginations.

Architecture

JDBC drivers are exposed to JDBC-compliant Java apps via the JDBC driver manager.

The JDBC driver manager is a Java class implementation. This means it is an interface used by JDBC service consumers (apps/applet/bean developers) and services providers (JDBC driver developers). The JDBC application developers call upon the JDBC driver manager for JDBC driver association (or binding). JDBC driver developers then build the JDBC classes to the specification, as depicted by the JDBC driver manager class implementation.

Driver Formats

JDBC drivers fall into four main categories: JDBC driver type 1, JDBC driver type 2, JDBC driver type 3 (formats A and B), and JDBC driver type 4.

JDBC Driver Type 1

The JDBC-ODBC bridge provides JDBC access via most ODBC drivers. Note that some ODBC binary code, and in many cases, database client code, must be loaded on each client machine that uses this driver. This kind of driver is most appropriate on a corporate network, or for application server code written in Java using three-tier architecture.

Advantage

An advantage is the following:

1. If an organization has made an enterprisewide commitment to ODBC as its data access standard, then this JDBC driver format will simply fit into the existing infrastructure.

Disadvantages

The disadvantages include the following:

1. It compromises the "write once, run anywhere" value proposition. ODBC is a Microsoft operating system specific database connectivity standard. The JDBC-ODBC bridge is implemented using native methods (operating system specific calls).
2. This approach forces a three-tier architecture on organizations in which the middle tier must be a Windows NT or Windows

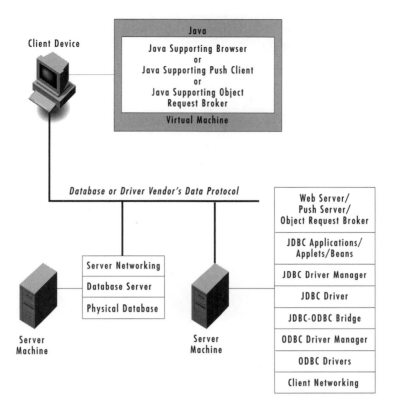

Figure 19-1 JDBC driver type 1.

95 machine, should you attempt to implement solutions as Java applets.

3. The "Zero Admin" value proposition is also compromised, as ODBC drivers and ODBC-JDBC bridging software (and in some cases, additional expensive DBMS vendor provided networking software) must be installed and configured in addition to the JDBC drivers on each client machine.

4. JDBC driver performance and sophistication is solely dependent on the performance of the underlying ODBC driver.

5. This, ultimately, is an expensive approach to JDBC, both in tangible (actual and hidden networking product costs) and intangible (administration, training, implementation) terms.

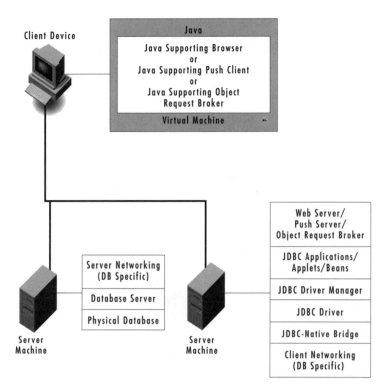

Figure 19–2 JDBC driver type 2.

JDBC Driver Type 2

Whether a native Application Programming Interface (API), for example, INFORMIX-ESQL or INFORMIX-CLI, or third-party Java-based drivers, that implement JDBC driver classes via native methods, these methods are typically direct bridges to the C-based Call Level Interface of the relevant database engine (for example, INFORMIX-OnLine Dynamic Server). As such, the methods do not require the intermediary layer provided by ODBC drivers.

This driver format requires the relevant database vendor's CLI libraries and native bridge libraries to be installed on each client and making use of JDBC compliant applications/applets/beans, as these libraries (for example, DLL files under Windows-based operating environments) are not transportable over HTTP. Examples of the middleware required on each machine are INFORMIX-Net and INFORMIX-Connect.

Advantages

The advantage includes the following:

1. If an organization has made an enterprise-wide commitment to a single database engine, and also subscribes to the "ODBC is slow" opinion, then this JDBC driver format will simply fit into the existing infrastructure (native driver based).

Disadvantages

The disadvantages include the following:

1. It compromises the "write once, run anywhere" value proposition, since database vendor CLIs provide zero database independence. The JDBC-native bridge is implemented using native methods.
2. This approach forces a three-tier architecture on organizations in which the middle tier must be a machine running database-specific networking software (the hidden high-cost element), should you attempt to implement solutions as Java applets.
3. JDBC driver performance and sophistication is solely dependent on the performance of the underlying native API and its database-specific networking software.
4. This, ultimately, is a very expensive approach to JDBC, both in tangible (actual and hidden product costs) and intangible (administration, training, and implementation) terms.

JDBC Driver Type 3 (Format A)

A net-protocol all-Java driver translates JDBC calls into a DBMS-independent network protocol that is then translated to a DBMS protocol by a server. This net server middleware is able to con-

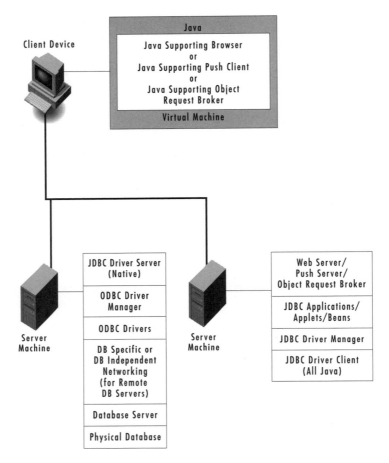

Figure 19–3 *JDBC driver type 3 (Format A).*

nect all its Java clients to many different databases. The specific protocol used depends on the vendor. In general, this is the most flexible and open JDBC alternative. It is likely that all vendors of this solution will provide products suitable for intranet use. In order for these products to also support Internet access, they must handle the additional requirements for security, access through firewalls, etc., that the Web imposes. Several vendors are adding JDBC drivers to their existing database middleware products.

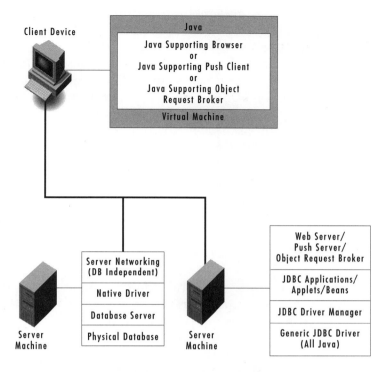

Figure 19–4 JDBC driver type 3 (Format B).

JDBC Driver Type 3 (Format B)

This JDBC driver format differs from the previous architecture, based on JDBC's use as the "across the wire" data protocol, as opposed to the use of ODBC.

Advantages

The advantages include the following:

1. Reinforces the "write once, run anywhere" Java value proposition. This is a generic format in which the JDBC driver contains no native methods, and isn't bound inextricably to alternative data access standards, such as ODBC or database-specific networking software provided by database vendors.

2. Facilitates the implementation of JDBC-compliant applets without a three-tier architecture, thereby reinforcing the "Zero Admin" Java value proposition.
3. Performance and sophistication become sole features of the JDBC driver, as opposed to underlying dependencies on the capabilities of ODBC or database-specific networking software.
4. Reinforces the JDBC value proposition by enabling the development of database-independent Java applications/applets/beans.
5. This is a very cost-effective way to implement JDBC within the Internet/intranet/extranet.

Disadvantages

The disadvantages include the following:

1. Performance and sophistication (security, configuration management, etc.) depend on the underlying capabilities of the database-independent networking aspects of the JDBC driver. If this is slow or unsophisticated, then the perception of the JDBC experience within your organization will also be slow and unsophisticated, albeit independent of the underlying database.
2. An ODBC-based "across the wire" protocol, or a JDBC server component that is totally ODBC-based, ultimately limits the scope of JDBC drivers to those of the underlying ODBC drivers. This ultimately, once disentangled, compromises the "write once, run anywhere" Java value proposition.

JDBC Driver Type 4

A native protocol all-Java driver converts JDBC calls into the network protocol used by DBMSs directly. This allows a direct call from the client machine to the DBMS server, and is a practical solution for intranet access. Since many of these protocols are proprietary, the database vendors themselves will be the primary source for this style of driver. Several database vendors have these protocols in progress.

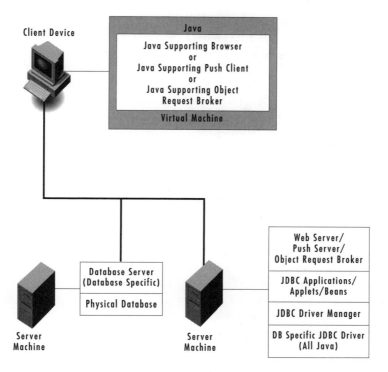

Figure 19–5 *JDBC driver type 4.*

Advantages

The advantages include the following:

1. If an organization has made an enterprise-wide commitment to a single database engine, and also subscribes to the notion that the database vendor should provide all relevant interfaces to the database, then this JDBC driver format will simply fit into the existing infrastructure (native-driver based).
2. It supports the implementation of "Zero Admin" JDBC-compliant applets.

Disadvantages

The disadvantages include the following:

1. It compromises the database independence of JDBC in the sense that the behavior of JDBC-compliant applications/applets/beans are far less predictable across different database engines, primarily in the area of JDBC API implementation, as opposed to core database functionality (the right place where DBMS engines can differentiate themselves).
2. JDBC driver performance and sophistication is solely dependent on the performance of the underlying database-specific protocol implemented in Java by the relevant DBMS vendor.
3. This is ultimately a very expensive approach to JDBC, both in tangible (actual and hidden product costs) and intangible (administration, training, implementation) terms. The back-end DBMS licensing will remain excruciatingly painful, although the front-end JDBC driver might initially appear to be very cost effective. JDBC, like ODBC, is about database engine commoditization, and naturally, most DBMS vendors will resist this for as long as the market remains unaware of this ulterior motive.
4. It attempts to perpetuate the soon to be obsolete "one-stop shop" mindset, amongst technology vendors and consumers.

JDBC Utilization Mechanics

In JDBC parlance, a source of data is a resource and since JDBC is an Internet-centric data access mechanism, it is imperative that it emulates the existing resource binding mechanisms used by other Internet protocols and technologies. JDBC drivers locate and bind to data sources via JDBC URLs, and take the following format:

```
<Protocol>:<Sub-protocol>:[<sub-name>]:
  [//<host name or address>[:port number]]
  [/Driver Attribute 1 ……./Driver Attribute n]
```

The URL structure above is driver dependent, i.e., it is the driver's responsibility to parse and interpret the areas represented in square brackets. Thus, the JDBC drivers provided by different JDBC driver vendors require different URL formats.

Example JDBC URLs

Sun's JDBC–ODBC Bridge

The URL below connects to an ODBC Data Source Name (DSN) called "Accounts" which already exists on the machine from which this JDBC driver is to be loaded (typically your PC):

```
jdbc:odbc:Accounts
```

OpenLink Software's JDBC Driver

The URL below connects to a logical Data Source Name (DSN) called "Accounts" which already exists on a server machine (host name Jupiter) from which this JDBC driver is to be loaded:

```
jdbc:openlink://jupiter:5000/DSN=Accounts
```

JDBC Utilization Today

JDBC is currently used by Java application and applet developers to build Internet- and intranet-based database-independent apps/applets. The applet classes are predominantly transported to the calling JVM via HTTP, while application classes increasingly make their way to the calling JVM via push technology products.

JDBC Utilization

The Java/CORBA juggernaut is gathering tremendous momentum and in the coming year, there will be a substantial shift to Object Request Broker (ORB)-based binding to remote Java classes using the OMG's IIOP protocol. ORB-IIOP based Java class binding will have a much smaller data transfer footprint than push technology and none of the HTTP dependencies of applets, without compromising Java and JDBC's respective value propositions.

Javasoft has also provided an additional Java-specific based remote binding and method execution mechanism called Remote Method Invocation (RMI). RMI is conceptually very similar to the ORB-IIOP approach; however, it is a Java-only solution, whereas the ORB-IIOP standard binds to a range of object implementations. Nevertheless, it is expected that RMI will be discontinued, as Javasoft favors the CORBA implementation.

JDBC Trouble Spots (Value Proposition Break Points)

The JDBC value proposition is currently very vulnerable and once compromised, its relevance and usability will always come into question. These vulnerability, or value proposition, break points take many shapes and forms, most of which are addressed in the sections below.

HTTP Dependence of Applets

JDBC applets are currently the rage: we all want "Zero Admin" Java solutions that are independent of database, which we develop once and run anywhere. But what does "anywhere" really mean in this instance? At the present time, it means "anywhere" there is an HTTPD (Web server) process running, with your JVM being a part of the Web browser that you use to view the pages that host your JDBC-compliant applets.

JDBC is not part of JDK 1.02, and a majority of Java-supporting Web browsers (especially Netscape, and Microsoft Explorer) currently ship with the 1.02 JVM. Java support by a browser vendor typically means the JDK 1.02 core classes are pre-installed on the Internet device (typically a PC) in use. It also means that the browser will not expect to load core Java classes from a remote server, irrespective of the transport mechanism (HTTP or IIOP). Thus, attempts to load applets that have been developed using core Java classes which are not part of the local JVM implementation are rejected, and these rejections are communicated as "applet security model" violations.

JDBC is part of JDK 1.1, but the browser vendors are all currently working on JDK 1.1-based JVM implementations for their browsers. Until JVM 1.1 browsers are developed, it isn't possible to develop or use JDBC-compliant Java applets.

Push Technologies

Push technologies provide one of the methods in which the browser and HTTP dependencies, referred to previously, can be circumvented. However, the push technology method introduces its own set of value proposition break points. For example, these products are not written in Java on the server side, so writing once and running anywhere is more of a "somewhere" type of proposition.

These products subscribe to the concept of total object migration, as opposed to object referencing, since they have no appreciation or understanding of matters such as physical disk real estate on the Internet device (the products presume that the PC has lots of disk space and memory). The products certainly speed up the initialization time of your JDBC-compliant Java application, but do not truly preserve the value proposition.

Object Request Brokers (ORBS)

ORBs, like real life brokers, bind you to service providers. However, like one of the most ubiquitous real-life providers of all (Remote Controls), ORBs do not migrate the service provider (TV set), or the actual service (the program being viewed), in its entirety to you. Instead, you remotely control and consume the service provided.

Java and ORBs are coming together at a frenzied pace, but questions remain regarding cross-ORB interoperability. The IIOP standard is a major step in the right direction in addressing this problem. However, the standard still does not guarantee that Java objects, and the ORBs that broker these objects, are independent. Thus, it is safe to conclude that Java application developers must currently write to numerous ORB interfaces in order to pursue any possibilities of real ubiquity. This certainly breaks the Java and JDBC value proposition.

Very few ORBs are written in Java. This introduces yet another potential value proposition break point, as your Java objects might not have an ORB implementation for the host operating environment in which the JVM resides.

Performance

If JDBC drivers do not deliver acceptable performance consistently across multiple platforms and database engines, then the JDBC value proposition will be broken.

ODBC Links

In recent times, Microsoft's Open Database Connectivity (ODBC) standard and JDBC have become inextricably linked for the wrong reasons. Of course, it is important that JDBC drivers are able to exploit the plethora of ODBC drivers available today, but it isn't mandatory that ODBC must be in the mix when dealing with JDBC. Unfortunately, a majority of the current JDBC technology adopters fail to see or, more importantly, understand the impact of this misconception.

ODBC is operating environment specific—it was devised with Windows in mind and that's it. Although implementations on other platforms exist, tangible use outside of the Microsoft operating system space has been sparse, to say the very least.

Inextricably linking ODBC with JDBC certainly breaks the JDBC value proposition.

Record Scrolling and Data Sensitivity

JDBC, unlike its operating system specific counterpart ODBC, currently lacks the ability to scroll through records. The JDBC Record Set Object only has a "Next" method, and this is a gaping hole in the JDBC definition itself, which makes it practically unusable for the development of data-sensitive enterprisewide solutions. Currently, most JDBC developers and driver vendors implement scrolling capabilities by abstracting above the base JDBC level, while others attempt to use the embedded SQL hooks provided by the specification for locating cursor names, etc. Unfortunately, this approach is outdated and, more importantly, a far cry from the real solution. If it is not possible to write sophisticated data-sensitive JDBC-compliant applications/applets/beans, then JDBC's use becomes much reduced.

JDBC developers and users cannot be expected to enjoy writing or using JDBC solutions that only deliver on the core JDBC value proposition if the data access elements of their solutions are static in nature. The world is becoming a smaller and more dynamic place everyday, driven primarily by the information revolution and connected global marketplace—both of which are driven by the access and manipulation of dynamic data.

Proxying and Security

The Internet, intranet, and extranets define three of today's TCP/IP-dominated, distributed computing formats. The Internet is the all-encompassing infrastructure, intranets are the segments of the Internet which reside behind corporate firewalls, and the extranets are the portions of the intranets which are exposed to the wider Internet.

To use JDBC drivers within any of the distributed computing formats mentioned previously, these drivers must be capable of providing access to the databases behind corporate firewalls—but not at the expense of security. The JDBC drivers that possess proxying capabilities address this requirement.

If JDBC drivers are not usable within the Internet, intranets, and extranets, then the JDBC value proposition will be broken.

User and Organization Diversity

One of the greatest weaknesses of any technology is its failure to anticipate diversity among its consumers. For instance, it is no secret that there is a range of computer skill levels within organizations, and these skill levels typically transcend departments and divisions. It is also no secret that even if we were all computer technology wizards, the very existence of our employing organizations would rest not on the chaotic application of our wizardry, but on the orderly application of this wizardry through the coherent development, acquisition, and application of the organizations' business systems.

JDBC must allow the development of applications that appreciate user diversity within an organization, and without this capability, JDBC applications/applets/beans become inherently inflexible—due to fixed assumptions about JDBC technology consumers. JDBC must bind itself to the consuming organization logically, as opposed to physically—without this integration, it inevitably breaks its value proposition.

OpenLink Generic High-Performance JDBC Drivers

OpenLink generic, high-performance JDBC drivers provide transparent access to data sources from JDBC-compliant applications/applets/beans which are resident on the Internet, or within intranets or extranets. These drivers are an integral part of the commercial offering known as the "OpenLink data access drivers suite."

The OpenLink JDBC Value Proposition

The OpenLink JDBC Value proposition is as follows:
"Write once, independent of the database, and run anywhere, without compromising usability, security, performance, or any aspects of the Java value proposition."

Implementation and Architecture

OpenLink Software provides type 1, type 2, and type 3 JDBC drivers. The type 1 and 2 drivers are integral parts of the OpenLink Data Access Drivers Suite (Lite Edition), while the type 3 drivers are integral parts of OpenLink Data Access Drivers Suite (WorkGroup and Enterprise Editions).

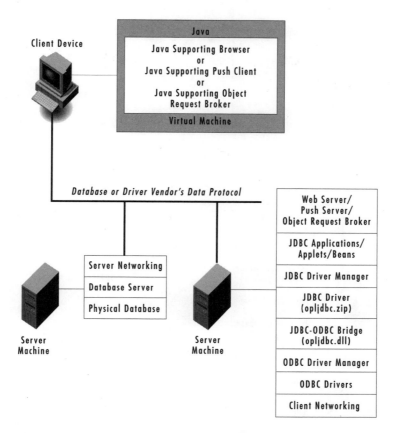

Figure 19–6 OpenLink JDBC Lite (type 1 JDBC driver).

OpenLink JDBC Lite Type 1 JDBC Driver

The OpenLink JDBC Lite type 1 JDBC driver is a JDBC–ODBC bridged driver, implying an inherent dependency on the existence, features, and capabilities of the ODBC driver manager and ODBC drivers installed on the machine that hosts your JDBC-compliant applications/applets/beans.

The JDBC driver classes are implemented via native methods, and this implies that the methods implemented within the JDBC driver are implemented via mappings to C functions, or C++ objects in a separate dynamic or shared library (depending on the host operating system); these libraries are basically ODBC-compliant service consumers (clients).

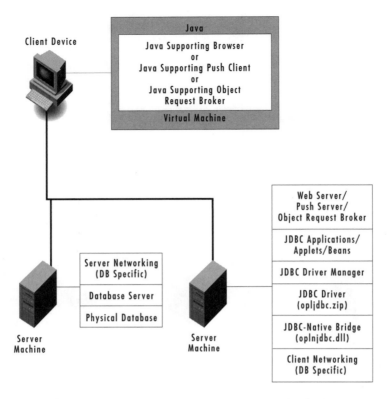

Figure 19–7 *OpenLink JDBC Lite (JDBC-native bridge).*

OpenLink JDBC Lite Type 2 JDBC Driver

The OpenLink JDBC Lite type 2 JDBC driver is a JDBC-native database interface bridged driver, implying an inherent dependency on the existence, features, and capabilities of the relevant database vendors' client interface and database-specific network middleware on the machine that hosts your JDBC-compliant applications/applets/beans.

The JDBC driver classes are implemented via native methods, and this implies that the native methods within the JDBC driver are implemented via mappings to C functions or C++ objects in a separate dynamic or shared library (depending on the host operating system). These libraries are built using the native call-level interfaces of the relevant database server.

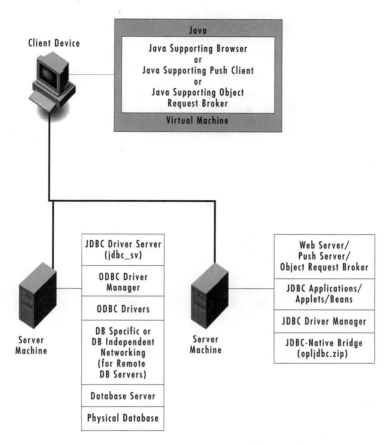

Figure 19–8 OpenLink generic JDBC driver (multi-tier architecture—ODBC server).

OpenLink JDBC–ODBC Type 3 JDBC Drivers (Format A)

The OpenLink JDBC–ODBC type 3 JDBC (format A) driver is a generic driver implementation with the JDBC driver methods written entirely in Java—negating the need for native methods. It is also a multi-tiered implementation that facilitates a very thin client layer implementation that also incorporates a database-independent networking layer. This driver format uses ODBC drivers for its lower-level data access services.

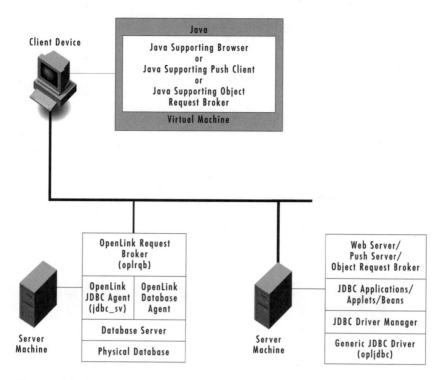

Figure 19–9 OpenLink generic JDBC driver (multi-tier architecture—native server).

OpenLink JDBC Drivers Type 3 (Format B Drivers)

The OpenLink JDBC Drivers type 3 (format B) driver is a generic driver implementation with the JDBC driver methods written entirely in Java—negating the need for native methods. It is also a multi-tiered implementation that facilitates a very thin client layer implementation, and also incorporates a database-independent networking layer. This driver format uses native database drivers (OpenLink database agents) for its lower-level data access services.

Conclusions

Informix User Implications

Java and JDBC set the foundation upon which a new generation of "Zero Admin" and operating-system independent Informix applications will be built. The administrative overhead and desktop complexities associated with the old desktop and "fat client" client-server applications models will rapidly become a thing of the past—primarily due to the rapid migration from two-tier to N-tier distributed computing models.

Informix Developer Implications

Vertical market application development remains a stronghold for Informix, the emergence of Java, JDBC, and N-tier distributed computing simply creates broader markets—with much reduced product maintenance, support, and implementation overhead. Java is fast becoming the application server lingua franca, due to the rapid emergence of Java application frameworks that sit atop JDBC, thereby providing reusable templates and components that dramatically increase product "time to market." Java and JDBC provide a much broader market for Informix application developers.

Industry Implications

Java has caught the imagination of the world, and for the right reasons. The JDBC and the Java beans specification certainly bolster Java, both technically and commercially. The coming of age of CORBA-compliant ORBs and the IIOP protocol, applied in tandem with Java, basically set the stage for the next major quantum leap in IT.

The age of distributed, component-based computing is near. Failure to accept or understand its potential and ramifications can only be detrimental to IT developers and end users alike.

Anticipating the manifestation of this IT prophecy can only yield good things for your organization's critical success factors—increased profits, reduced staff turnover, leaner and meaner enterprises, increased freedom to innovate on the part of software entrepreneurs, improvements in software quality via componentization, ultimately leading to much better returns on IT investments.

Chapter 20

Using Informix DataBlades to Facilitate E-Commerce

by Bo Lasater

Introduction

Industry visionaries have heralded e-commerce for several years and yet, until recently, few established companies committed the resources to create e-commerce implementations that were more than pilot projects. Now, due to the success of several highly visible Web sites, a general improvement in technology, and an ever-growing Web community, e-commerce is entering maturity. Dataquest has called 1998 the year of e-commerce. Companies are no longer asking, "Why e-commerce?" but rather, "When and how?"

In spite of the massive interest in e-commerce, there's no shrink-wrapped, one-size-fits-all e-commerce solution. However, there are many good solutions for specific areas of the e-commerce problem. The challenge is to tie these best-of-breed solutions together in a seamless, scalable, and extensible way.

One solution is to use Informix Dynamic Server with Universal Data Option.

Characteristics of a Full E-Commerce Solution

A full e-commerce solution orchestrates all aspects of the traditional buying experience:

Advertising and Marketing

Advertising and marketing includes all of the demand creation activities and devices, from the ubiquitous banner ads and brochureware, to cross-promotion with conventional marketing, to community creation, to the emerging one-to-one marketing paradigm.

Merchandising

Merchandising deals with the way product is presented, aggregated, priced, and sold. If a Web site is to be considered a serious sales vehicle, it must be able to support a large number of merchandising methods such as coupons, rebates, membership discounts, affinity programs, sweepstakes, bundles, volume discounts, frequent purchase discounts, hot products, trial periods, and demo products, to name a few. More importantly, a Web site with a mature merchandising model must be flexible enough to easily integrate new merchandising methods as they arise.

Payment Processing

Several good solutions exist for vendors to take credit card orders over the Internet, although the problem still remains of convincing the public that they are secure. However, even this area is still in its infancy. Web site owners are currently experimenting with ways to extend payment processing to purchase orders, digital wallets, subscriptions with automatic and semi-automatic renewals, and other more esoteric payment protocols.

Price Calculation

Determining the appropriate tax and shipping charges for a user at the time of purchase is not a trivial activity. Several companies, notably Taxware, UPS, and Federal Express are committing many resources to tackling these problems. Would-be site designers are well advised to incorporate these solutions rather than to try to build their own.

Order Fullfillment

Customers expect information about their order, such as whether a product is in stock and when it can be expected to arrive. In short, sophisticated Web sites of the near future require a high level of integration with the host company's conventional order fulfillment systems.

Tracking

It's critical to capture information about user activity. Some of the information currently measured are click paths, referrals, and activity by the hour of the day.

Profiling

Although most tracking solution providers include a number of reports with their products, they rarely offer the market segmentation analysis that marketing professionals desire. Good profiling is a keystone technology for making the promise of one-to-one marketing a reality.

Customer Service/Resale/Upsale

To convert one-time purchasers into loyal customers, users of the site must feel that the company is responsive to their needs. The

Web offers many wonderful ways to establish this perception, yet it does not happen automatically. FAQs, forums, news-groups, and e-mail are all ways to establish this perception.

The Datablade E-Commerce Solution

In order for a platform to support e-commerce, it must bring many systems together in a scalable, manageable way. This is a lot to demand of a platform and few of them are up to the task. Informix Dynamic Server with Universal Data Option provides the integration, scalability, flexibility, and manageability required of a world-class e-commerce application.

Integration

Through its DataBlade technology, Informix Dynamic Server with Universal Data Option can elegantly bind in almost any functionality or datatype imagineable. The technology is well-suited at wrapping third-party data and functionality so that it behaves syntactically and semantically like built-in datatypes and functions. The gateways to other databases are good exam-ples of this seamless binding, as are many of the advanced image and video processing blades that encapsulate advanced graphics algorithms in user-friendly interfaces. For e-commerce purposes, payment processing, and complex entities—such as customers, products, companies, and transaction types—are great candidates for DataBlades. The graphics, videoprocessing, and other rich data manipulation blades are especially useful for many sites where added value is sophisticated access to rich content.

Scalability

By making external systems part of the database, system design-ers are able to leverage all of the scalability features afforded by a mature, industry-leading enterprise RDBMS-features like repli-cation and distributed server environments.

Performance

E-commerce solutions which are built on Informix Dynamic Server with Universal Data Option perform for the same reasons that the solutions are scalable—they leverage the features of a mature enterprise RDBMS. Furthermore, Informix Dynamic Server with Universal Data Option solutions provide more ad-hoc solutions because they tend to conserve bandwidth better, and provide better query optimization.

Bandwidth Conservation

Imagine a financial application that must run a complex statistical analysis on a massive amount of data. In many implementations, the data would have to be piped out of the database in which it is stored and placed in the server that contains the logic for the calculation. By co-locating the logic with the data, no data piping is required and only the results need to be sent over the wire.

Query Optimization

When a query must take place across several datatypes, Informix's integrated approach really shines. Consider a Web site that offers the harried gourmand the ability to find a favorite meal in her vicinity. She wants to sample Penne ala Vodka in an Italian restaurant near 1st and Main streets. To return results to the query, the backend of the Web site must join results from a traditional RDBMS search for the enumerated value 'Italian', with results from a text search on the keywords 'Penne' and 'Vodka' on the menu field of the restaurant records, and results from a spatial search on restaurants within a mile radius of 1st and Main.

In other systems, the non-standard searches would occur outside of the database, and therefore, outside of the purview of the query optimizer. With Informix, all searches are equal and subject to optimization. Sometimes the spatial search will occur before the text search and sometimes it's the other way around. This ability to switch orderings on a per-query basis can reap huge performance over a system that evaluates queries in a fixed order.

Flexibility

Since Informix Dynamic Server with Universal Data Option is an object-relational database, most of the benefits in terms of code re-use and ease of code modification can apply. Polymorphism is especially useful for defining interfaces to which future modules can be written.

Unlike object-relational approaches taken by other vendors (with the exception of IBM's DB2), Informix Dynamic Server with Universal Data Option doesn't glom object-oriented features onto a relational underpinning through plug-in code that makes function calls to other applications, or through the addition of separate APIs and server subsystems.

Manageability

In an Informix Dynamic Server with Universal Data Option e-commerce implementation, everything from Web assets to third-party functionality resides in the database. This characteristic not only means that content is much more accessible than if it resided on a file system, but further, it ensures that the interface to the content is consistent across the site. The learning curve for clients to become familiar with the details of a Web site driven by Informix Dynamic Server with Universal Data Option is, consequently, shorter than that of Web sites powered by alternative technologies.

The DataBlade Model

To understand why Informix Dynamic Server with Universal Data Option is a good fit for e-commerce, it is critical to understand the DataBlade model. This section addresses the Data-Blade model and presents a simple e-commerce application to illustrate these principles.

The DataBlade architecture embodies the modifications necessary for an RDBMS to become an object-relational database system, or universal server. The two terms are essentially synonymous, but emphasize different features. "Object relational" highlights the fact that the paradigm supports inheritance and polymorphism, as well as standard relational concepts. "Universal server" emphasizes the fact that data of any type can be supported in a uniform way. As per Dr. Michael Stonebraker, chief technology officer at Informix and founder of Illustra Technologies, the following components of a traditional RDBMS must be modified in order for it to become truly object relational: access methods, executor, parallelism system, optimizer, and parser.

Not only must the b-tree method of index access be generalized in order to support new types of comparison methods, but entirely new access methods must be allowed to support datatypes that don't lend themselves to b-tree searches. B-tree is short for binary tree—a tree with two branches per node. At each node, a piece of data exists. Throughout the tree, the following criteria are maintained—all the descendents on the right branch of a node are greater than the value at the node itself, and the descendents to the left of the node are less than the value at the node. R-trees are more complicated to explain. Essentially, they are b-trees except that the comparison operator uses X-axis data on even levels and Y-axis data on odd levels of the tree. Suffice it to say that it is a variant of the binary tree that can handle 2-D data. R-trees can be generalized to handle data of any dimension.

Likewise, indices on functions of data are also important. Consider a field of graphic data. Few meaningful indices could be made directly on the bits themselves, however, ranking the images by statistical functions could make lots of sense.

The executor must be able to solve queries that contain user-defined functions and datatypes. Moreover, a good implementation must allow dynamic linking and unlinking of functions, as it is undesirable to stop and start a system whenever new datatypes and functions are added.

The parallelism system must be extended to support user-defined aggregates. The optimizer must be able to use dynamic statistics to run its heuristics rather than hard-coded ones. In addition, the optimizer must take into account the CPU cost of functions on functional indices in addition to the typical considerations of record number.

And of course, the parser must be extensively re-written to accomodate the notions of inheritance, and to handle the dynamically loaded metadata in the system catalogs that are created.

Spacely Publishing On-Line Catalog

To illustrate how Informix Dynamic Server with Universal Data Option's database-enabling technology can be used in e-commerce solutions, this section examines an implementation of a simple on-line catalog for a publishing company.

Application Description

The creator of our sample application, Spacely Publishing, Inc., is a company that publishes trade journals, text books, presentation aids, conference proceedings, and other materials intended for a professional accounting audience. Spacely wants to create an e-commerce presence, and has opted for a simple catalog application with credit card payment to get started in a quick, yet conservative way. Eventually, Spacely wants the application to grow into a much fuller e-commerce installation.

The basic page flow of the application is straightforward, refer to Figure 20–1. On the first page of the site, users pick categories of the catalog to browse through and/or enter keyword searches. Search results appear in groups of nine thumbnail pictures of products with accompanying text. Users can further drill down into the details of a product and, if they choose, add the item to their shopping cart for subsequent purchase. When a user decides to purchase, he or she must submit credit card information along with other registration information. A purchase confirmation screen appears, reiterating what the user has purchased. When the user accepts, the purchase is consummated.

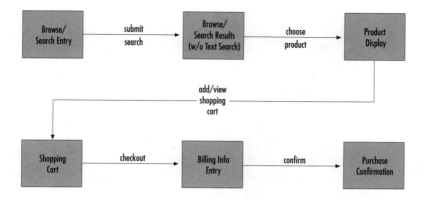

Figure 20–1 The user chooses some criteria to get a hit list of interesting products. From this list, the user can get more details about a particular product and, eventually, buy one or more.

Web Connectivity

Thanks to the Web DataBlade, any Web asset required by the Web site—HTML code, images, sound files, video clips, Java applets, etc.—could be stored in the database, although it doesn't need to be. The Spacely publishing site stores all its assets in the database. Here's how these assets make it to the user's browser: when the user requests a page from the application's Netscape Enterprise Server, the request is translated into a call to the Web Driver shared object through NSAPI (CGI versions of Web Driver are also available). Web Driver produces an SQL statement from the input parameters and calls it into the database, Figure 20–2 illustrates this process. The database returns an HTML page that the Web server then streams to the client.

For instance, the user requests:

```
http://www.spacely.com/open/
  Webdriver?Mival=product_display&prod_id=10023
```

Web Server ——→ Cache ——→ IDS/UDO

Web Driver ←——

webExplode

Figure 20–2 *Web DataBlade architecture—the Web Driver generates an SQL statment from the user's input parameters and queries the database. In response, the database generates an HTML page that is sent through the Web server to the client.*

The Web Driver intercepts this request and generates the following query:

```
select webExplode(object,"prod_id=10023") from webPages
where ID='product_display';
```

WebExplode is a function written in C that executes during query processing, just as any standard SQL function would. "Object" is a text field that contains HTML with embedded WebBlade tags. WebBlade tags can contain environment variable definitions and any legal SQL commands. WebExplode parses and executes the WebBlade tags to the effect of replacing the commands in the tags with content from the database, modifying the Web server environment, or modifying data in the database accordingly.

Payment Processing

For its first foray into cybercommerce, Spacely wants to keep it simple. It focuses on credit card payments in phase 1. To collect payments, it utilizes some of Informix Dynamic Server with Universal Data Option's DataBlade creation ability to bind CyberCash functionality into the database.

CyberCash links the Web sites with credit card processors to provide authorizations in real time at the time of purchase. After the sale, CyberCash provides a full HTML interface for capturing and settling transactions.

Integrating Cybercash into Informix Dynamic Server with Universal Data Option is a simple matter of wrapping the functions from the Cybercash API with datatype conversion code, compiling the wrapped functions as a shared object, and registering it into the database.

Following is the wrapping function:

```
#include <mi.h>
#include "credit.h"

int authorize (tsorder_id, tscurrency_amount, tscard_number,
  tscard_type, tscard_exp, tscard_fname, tscard_lname,
  tscard_address, tscard_city, tscard_zip, tscard_state,
  tscard_country)
        mi_text * tsorder_id;
        mi_text * tscurrency_amount;
...
        mi_text * tscard_country;
{
  char * csorder_id=mi_lvarchar_to_string(tsorder_id);
  char *
cscurrency_amount=mi_lvarchar_to_string(tscurrency_amount);
  ...
  char * cscard_country=mi_lvarchar_to_string(tscard_country);
  char * transtype = "auth";

  credittransaction *ct;
  ct = (credittransaction *) mi_alloc(sizeof(
     credittransaction));
  ct = transaction(ct, transtype, csorder_id,
    cscurrency_amount, cscard_number,
    cscard_type, cscard_exp, cscard_fname,
    cscard_lname, cscard_address, cscard_city,
    cscard_zip, cscard_state, cscard_country);
  return stcmp(ct->ravs_code;
}
```

Code is compiled into a shared object. For example, the make file might contain some of the following text:

```
create function function name(input para)
return data_type;
```

After the function is created and compiled, it must be registered:

```
create function authorize(transaction_t)
returns integer
as external name 'MI_HOME/functions/authorize.so';
```

Text Search

Spacely has a large number of manuscripts and its categorization is not intuitive, especially for Spacely's customers. For this reason, Spacely wanted to offer enhanced text search in Phase One, in addition to a hierarchical search. To implement the search, Spacely is using the Excalibur Text Search DataBlade Module, refer to Figure 20–3.

```
...where etx_contains(description, row('multimedia'));
```

The text search blade is the most complete DataBlade I've examined yet. It defines new types, operators, and access methods within the database, among other things.

In the application, I enable searching on the description field of products by defining it as a certain type:

```
CREATE TABLE products (
...
dscrpt     IfxDescDoc,
...
);
```

Next, I index the field:

```
CREATE INDEX desc_idx ON products (description etx_doc_ops)
USING etx in sbsp1;
```

"Etx" is a custom access method created for the text search blade. In creating an index with it, several ancillary data

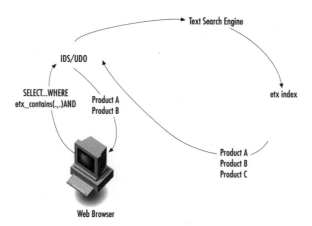

Text Search Engine

IDS/UDO

SELECT...WHERE
etx_contains(.,.)AND

Product A
Product B

etx index

Product A
Product B
Product C

Web Browser

Figure 20–3 *Text search blade—Queries with the text search operation are executed by functions in the text search blade, which in turn utilizes the special text search index. The text search engine and etx index are part of Informix Dynamic Server with Universal Data Option, but are shown separately for clarity.*

structures are formed including hashtables and word orderings by frequency. The details of the arrangement aren't known to Informix Dynamic Server with Universal Data Option, nor do they need to be, since whenever the index is used, it is called using another function supplied by the DataBlade:

```
...where etx_contains(description, row('multimedia'));
```

By using etx_contains and other included operators, the search designer can add Boolean, keyword, phrase, proximity, and fuzzy searches to an application and rank the results by relevancy.

Planning for the Future

As Spacely develops Phase One of its application, the management team comes up with many enhancements they would like to see in Phase Two. For instance, Order Processing would like to more closely tie the Web site to their back-end systems, and Marketing would like to see a greater variety of merchandising on the site.

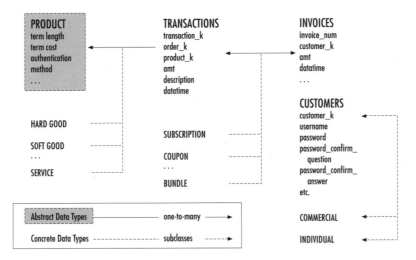

PRODUCT
term length
term cost
authentication
method
...

HARD GOOD
SOFT GOOD
...
SERVICE

TRANSACTIONS
transaction_k
order_k
product_k
amt
description
datatime

SUBSCRIPTION
COUPON
...
BUNDLE

INVOICES
invoice_num
customer_k
amt
datatime
...

CUSTOMERS
customer_k
username
password
password_confirm_
    question
password_confirm_
    answer
etc.

COMMERCIAL
INDIVIDUAL

Abstract Data Types —————— one-to-many ——→
Concrete Data Types -------- subclasses ----→

Figure 20–4 *Object-relational schema for the Spacely catalog.*
The design is flexible enough to incorporate future enhancements
because it employs object-oriented programming.

The designers pave the way for the inevitable enhancements by
employing object-oriented programming practices in their design.
Through inheritance and polymorphism, the designers keep their
Web page code clean, high-level, and stable by isolating subtype-
specific code in the methods of those subtypes, see Figure 20–4.

As an example of how this might work, consider potential
code to extend the notion of product:

```
create table products of new type product_t (
id   text,
dscrpt    IfxDescDoc,
price    numeric(6,2)
);
create table products_hard of new type product_hard_t (
size numeric(6.2), —cubic inches
weight numeric(6.2) —lbs.
) under type product_t;
create table products_soft of new type product_soft_t(
sizeinteger —bytes
) under product_t;
```

Shipping costs are handled differently for different types of products. For simplicity, we are assuming shipping costs are a function of product only.

```
create function get_shipping(product_t)
returns numeric(6,2)
as return 0;

create function get_shipping(product_hard_t)
returns numeric(6,2)
as   return (((.2)*$1.size * $1.weight) /20+10) ;

create function get_shipping(product_soft_t)
returns numeric(6,2)
as return $1.size/1048576;
```

Then, when total shipping costs should be displayed for the items in a customer's shopping cart—keeping in mind that $cust_id is a Web DataBlade environment variable—the call might look as follows:

```
select sum(i.qty*get_shipping(p)) from products p,
  shopping_cart_items i
where p.id = i.prod_id and i.cust_id = $cust_id;
```

This code operates for any mix of hard and soft goods in the user's shopping cart, is easily understandable, and will not change when new types of products are added.

Conclusion

Doing e-commerce fully means combining a large amount of capabilities into a coherent whole—it's an undertaking that demands a lot of the underlying platform. The platform must integrate disparate parts seamlessly. Marketing and merchandising, payment processing and order fulfillment, tracking and profiling, and customer service functions must work together on the same data. The platform must scale—popular e-commerce installation can expect millions to tens of millions of hits per day. The platform must be flexible and extensible. It must grow with the needs of the organization and keep pace with the competition in a rapidly evolving marketplace. It must also perform. Patience of Internet users is a well-documented diminishing commodity. Most of all, the platform must be manageable. A system that requires programmers to update products, change promotions, or edit banners is doomed to failure.

Informix Dynamic Server with Universal Data Option can deliver on these requirements. The fact that it's built on a robust enterprise RDBMS means it can scale and perform. Its ability to pull any data and functionality into the database as a first-class datatype gives it the ability to integrate well. Because all data can be in the same database and handled in a consistent way, a system based on Informix Dynamic Server with Universal Data Option is manageable. Since it's object relational—allowing a separation of interface from implementation—Informix Dynamic Server with Universal Data Option is flexible and extensible.

About the Authors

Paul Brown

Paul Brown is a member of the Chief Technology Office, Informix Software, Inc., Oakland, California.

Malcolm Colton

Malcolm Colton is a frequent contributor of articles to *Tech Notes* and is a widely published author of articles related to object-relational technology.

Terence A. Di Benigno

Terence A. Di Benigno is director of Business Development for IsoQuest, Inc., and heads the DataBlade Module and Informix Partnership programs for IsoQuest.

About IsoQuest, Inc.

With headquarters in Fairfax, Virginia, IsoQuest specializes in developing advanced text analysis software systems. These systems are designed to enable corporate users to quickly locate specific business and competitive information on the Internet, corporate intranets, and other natural text-based environments. IsoQuest aims its products toward information-dependent organizations, such as publishers, market research firms, content providers, the financial and legal communities, government and regulatory agencies, and other organizations which can benefit from rapid, cost-efficient access to information.

IsoQuest is located at 3900 Jermantown Road, Suite 400, Fairfax, Virginia, 22030. To contact IsoQuest, call 703-293-2350 or visit the IsoQuest Web site at www.isoquest.com

Matthew Eichler

Matthew Eichler is a an expert in the fields of management and object-relational technology. He is a frequent contributor of articles to *Tech Notes* and other publications.

Howard Greenfield

Howard Greenfield is the senior manager of Interactive Media Products at Informix, Menlo Park, California. He is responsible for corporate strategy in the areas of digital media and content management. Prior to Informix, he worked at Sun Microsystems for seven years, where he managed Interactive Media systems development, and served as product manager for Solaris-related products. Upon completing graduate studies at Stanford University in Interactive Technology, Mr. Greenfield worked in Apple Computer's Advanced Technology group, focusing on research and development. In the past, he ran his own consulting practice focused on business systems, software development, and instructional technology.

Eric Horschman

Eric Horschman is director, Product Marketing, at Premenos Corporation, and is responsible for the marketing of products from Premenos' Prime Factors unit.

About Prime Factors, Inc.

Founded in 1981, Prime Factors, Inc., is an internationally recognized and trusted producer of information security and data encryption systems. More than 250 major banks, corporations, and high-level government organizations rely on Prime Factors' innovative systems to guard sensitive information from internal and external threat. Prime Factors' Descrypt and Psypher product families provide easy-to-use encryption and authentication for electronic commerce, financial applications, and general security requirements.

Prime Factors was acquired by Premenos Corporation in 1996. The Prime Factors products integrate tightly with Premenos' electronic commerce product set to offer the highest levels of security for business-to-business commerce.

Prime Factors is located in Eugene, Oregon and can be contacted via phone at 541-345-4334, fax at 541-345-6818, or Web at www.primefactors.com. Premenos Corporation is located in Concord, California, and may be contacted at 800-426-3836 or via the Web at www.premenos.com

About Premenos Corporation

Premenos Corporation is a leading provider of electronic commerce solutions for established and emerging trading communities. Its standards-based business applications leverage the strengths of traditional EDI systems, TCP/IP networks, secure information and Web technologies. Premenos has a history of market-proven innovation, including the first open-network technology for secure, auditable data transmission over the Internet. Through partnerships with leading application and integrated solutions vendors, Premenos empowers businesses to lower costs, shorten trading cycles and increase competitive advantage. For more information, access the Premenos home page on the Web at the following location: www.Premenos.com

Kingsley Idehen

Kingsley Idehen is president, founder, and CEO of OpenLink Software, Inc. OpenLink Software is an industry-leading developer and deployer of secure, high-performance database connectivity software independent of operating system, network protocol, and underlying database engine. Its technologies adhere to key industry data access standards, such as Java Database Connectivity (JDBC), Open Database Connectivity (ODBC), and Universal Database Connectivity (UDBC).

Kingsley Idehen became familiar with information technology as an end user, developer, and consultant. While working at Harrods of Knightsbridge in London, he became involved in the early computerization of the accounts department ledger accounting system. He later moved on to join Orthet & Laybrand (holding company of Giorgio Armani's designer fashion boutiques), where he began his tenure as an accountant. Shortly thereafter, Kingsley was given total control of the Orthet & Laybrand IT infrastructure due to his enthusiasm and talent for integrating computer technology with business management processes. It was in this role that he encountered the technology issues that OpenLink Software, Inc. solves today.

Upon leaving Orthet & Laybrand, Kingsley joined the Moss Brothers Group as a project accountant. He was initially given the assignment of designing and developing a fixed asset accounting module for the corporate organization. Much later, he joined Unisys as a database and Fourth Generation Language (4GL) consultant. At Unisys, Kingsley was exposed to a wide range of database and 4GL technology. Having gained much satisfaction from utilizing computer technology for productivity advancements, and realizing the potential of the emerging client-server computing model, he departed Unisys to create P.A.L. Consulting, Ltd.

Within several years, Kingsley Idehen realized that the corporate enterprise, to remain independent, successful, and sound, needed the availability of an open platform in database access technology. With this vision in mind, Kingsley employed his experience and talent to develop a conceptual and technical architecture, the very ideals that OpenLink Software, Inc. has been founded upon.

About OpenLink Software

OpenLink Software is an industry-leading developer and deployer of secure, high-performance database connectivity technology, independent of operating system, network protocol and underlying database engine.

OpenLink offers a suite of drivers, comprising of ODBC, JDBC, and UDBC data access drivers with support for all major databases and operating systems. ODBC data access drivers are available in single-tier and multi-tier formats, providing end users with a transparent but controlled, high-level interface between desktop applications and corporate data sources. JDBC drivers are equipped with a sophisticated bi-directional scrollable cursors engine that support empowering OpenLink and non-OpenLink ODBC and JDBC drivers.

OpenLink's high-performance database connectivity middleware provides developers and users of Internet/intranet/extranet solutions products with a consistent database interface for developing and implementing database driven Web servers, Java applications/applets/bean components, and ActiveX-based components across multiple operating environments.

Bill Kelley

Bill Kelley received his MEE in computer science from Rice University. Working in leading-edge software technology ever since, his contributions include three years of service on the ANSI SQL standards committee, ANSI representative to ISO SQL, board member of Object Data Management Group, contributing author to "Modern Database Systems" (ACM Press), and founder of Wind Traveller Consulting.

About Wind Traveller Consulting

Wind Traveller Consulting was founded to supply the growing demand for high-end database consulting and outsourcing. The company offers expertise in emerging object-relational technology, DataBlades, SQL, and integrated database and internet solutions, and is also an Informix DataBlade partner.

Bo Lasater

Bo Lasater is a founding member of Fort Point Partners, where he oversees the implementation of e-commerce installations for several Fortune 1000 companies. Prior to joining Fort Point Partners, he was the director of Research and Development at Morgan Interactive, a prominent multimedia and object-oriented development firm where he evaluated and implemented business and technical strategies. Prior to Morgan Interactive, Bo was a management consultant for KPMG Peat Marwick, where he was involved in re-engineering business processes through technology. He has a degree in mathematics from Princeton University and an MCS/MBA from Rice University.

About Fort Point Partners

Fort Point Partners specializes in the planning and development of high-volume, database-driven, Internet commerce applications. The consultants and developers at Fort Point have unparalleled experience in large-scale Web application planning and development, including Internet commerce and site management application development, strategic planning and Internet technology analysis, and high-speed networking and high-availability Web deployment. Fort Point Partners is located at 612 Howard Street, Suite 300, San Francisco, California, 94105. For more information, contact Fort Point Partners by phone at 415 546 5700, via fax at 415 882 4246, or access their Web site at: http://www.ftpoint.com

Craig O'Connor

Craig O'Connor is a senior consultant with Panttaja Consulting Group, Inc. He has over six years of experience in building client/server systems that are based on relational database management systems. He has developed Web sites using Informix Dynamic Server with Universal Data Option, the Illustra Server, and DataBlade Modules. Craig can be reached via e-mail at craigo@pcgi.com

Jim Panttaja

Jim Panttaja is vice president, Technology, at Panttaja Consulting Group, an Informix Consulting Solutions partner with extensive experience in design and implementation using the technology of the Informix Dynamic Server with Universal Data Option. Jim has over 25 years of experience in software design, database development, and database tuning experience. Before joining Panttaja Consulting, he was director of Compiler Products Development at MicroTech Research. Prior to MicroTech Research, he was the manager of Languages and Tools at Tandem Computers and a manager of compiler development at IBM. He was also the ANSI COBOL Committee Chairman from 1979 to 1981.

Jim has previously appeared in *Tech Notes*, Volume 7, Issue 1, as the author of the article entitled "DataBlades for the Informix Dynamic Server with Universal Data Option."

Mr. Panttaja's current focus is on relational and object-relational database development technology, including Informix, Illustra, Sybase, and Microsoft SQL Server. He is a sought after database instructor, lecturer and author, and served as co-author of both the Sybase SQL Server Survival Guide and the Microsoft SQL Server Survival Guide books. Mr. Panttaja combines technical expertise with the rare ability to communicate both knowledge and solutions that expand the limits of his teams' capabilities. He can be reached via e-mail at pcg@pcgi.com

About Panttaja Consulting Group, Inc.

Panttaja Consulting Group, Inc. (PCG) is a premier service organization with extensive experience in design and implementation using the technology of the new Informix Dynamic Server with Universal Data Option. PCG offers key services within their Universal Server practices including DataBlade Module design and development, Web site development with the Web DataBlade, Universal Data Option and DataBlade Module development training, and system integration for Universal Data Option object-relational database applications. In addition to experience with Universal Data Option technology, PCG provides extensive experience in relational database, client/server, and object-oriented development to assist clients in gaining a competitive edge through the effective use of advanced information technologies.

The Panttaja Consulting Group is located at 103 Plaza Street, Healdsburg, California. They may be contacted via phone at 1 707 433 2629, facsimile at 1 707 431 0549, e-mail at pcg@pcgi.com, or the Web at http://www.pcgi.com

Jacques Roy

Jacques Roy is a member of the Advanced Technology Group at Informix Software, Inc., Denver, Colorado. He can be contacted via email at jroy@informix.com

David W. Sharpe

David W. Sharpe is a co-founder and president of Consistency Point Technologies, Inc. He has been involved in optical storage since 1987. He can be reached at sharpe@cpt.com

About Consistency Point Technologies, Inc.

Consistency Point Technologies, Inc. provides innovative storage management solutions for the expanding storage requirements of today's multimedia database systems. The focus of the company is to develop products and services that enable the capture, storage, and retrieval of multimedia and relational data objects through database storage extension technology. Consistency Point Technologies is located at 528 Glasgow Court, Milpitas, California, 95035. For additional information regarding OptiLink or consulting services, please contact Consistency Point Technologies via phone at 1 408 263 4278, facsimile at 1 408 263 0925, or the Web at http://www.cpt.com

Michael R. Stonebraker

Dr. Michael R. Stonebraker is a co-founder of Illustra Information Technologies, Inc., and Chief Technology Officer of Informix. A noted expert in database management systems, operating systems, and expert systems, Dr. Stonebraker is Professor Emeritus of Computer Science at the University of California, Berkeley, where he joined the faculty in 1971. Illustra Information Technologies, Inc. represents the commercialization of Dr. Stonebraker's POSTGRES research project. In 1996, Informix acquired Illustra Technologies, Inc.

Dr. Stonebraker founded INGRES Corporation (now the INGRES Products Division of ASK Computer Systems) in 1980 and served on the company's board of directors until 1993. Dr. Stonebraker recently authored the book entitled *Object-Relational DBMSs: The Next Great Wave.*

John Taylor

John Taylor is a consultant in the Internet/Intranet business unit of Informix in Oakland, California.

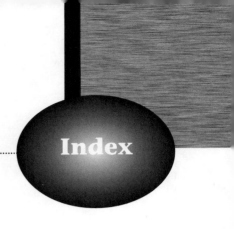

Index

A

Accessibility, and cyberpublishing movement, 285
ActiveX, 344
Administration, data warehouse, 42–43
Adobe, 38–39
Advertising, and e-commerce, 374
Aggregations, 272–75
    aggregation on functions, 253–54
    built-in aggregate functions, extending, 250–51
    grouping, 251–52
    performance advantage, 272–73
    performance considerations, 247–49
    and the Universal Data Option, 247–59
        AVG(), 249
        COUNT(), 249
        MAX(), 250
        MIN(), 250
        RANGE(), 250
        STDEV(), 250
        SUM(), 250
        VARIANCE(), 250

    user-defined aggregates, 254–59
        COMBINE function, 255, 257–58
        FINAL function, 255
        INIT function, 254, 256
        ITER function, 254–57
Aggregation values, handling, 169–76
AIR DataBlade module, 327–28
Amateur Inbox screen, 294
Analysis phase:
    Web DataBlade project lifecycle, 83–87
        deliverables, 83–84
        tips, 85–87
Analysis prototype, 84
Andyne, 39
Angoss, 40
Applets, 343–44
    HTTP dependence of, 362–63
Application development, DataBlade modules for, 64–65
Application development tool, 88
Application services approach, 311
Assign Amateur to Story screen, 294
Audio Details screen, 295
AVG() function, 250

Avid Technology-Informix partnership, 334–35

B

Binary large object (BLOB), 21, 48, 122, 319
BladeManager, 64
BladePack, 64
BladeSmith, 63–64
Body frame, 204–5
BPWin (LogicWorks), 84
Brio, 44
Broadcasting industry, and content management capabilities, 326
Brown, Paul, 137, 389
b-tree, 61
b-tree index, 8, 379
Built-in aggregate functions, extending, 250–51
Built-in key, 220–21
Bulldog Group-Informix partnership, 332–34
   automatic indexing for easy search and retrieval, 333
   centralized digital media assets, 332
   mapping assets against workflow, 333
   video streaming, 333–34
Business datatypes, implementation of, 57
Business Objects, 44
Business process analysis, 83
Business process modeling tool, 84

C

Casting, 29
CGI "stub" program, 210
CICS applications, 10
CLASS function modifier, 242
Class migration methods, 344–50
   Object Request Brokers (ORBs), 348–50
   push technology, 347–48
   Web servers and HTTP, 345–47
Client-based business objects, 52
Client-side architecture, extending, 29–30
Closure phase:
   Web DataBlade project lifecycle, 91–92
      deliverable, 91
      tips, 91–92
Closure presentation, 91–92
Coding, 223–29
   conditional logic, 226
   large_object, 228
   pages, keeping short/simple, 228–29

SQL statements, executing, 225–26
variables, 225
WebDriver, 224–25, 229
WebExplode(), 227
Cognos, 44
Collaborative workflow, and cyberpublishing movement, 285
Colton, Malcolm, 17, 389
COMBINE function, 255, 257–58
Commercial Web site evolution, 305–9
   complexity of Web site applications, 306
   evolution of Web site development, 307
   first-generation site, 307
   functional services, 309–10
   higher bandwidth/multimedia support, 305–6
   second-generation site, 307–8
   third-generation site, 308–9
Common Gateway Interface (CGI), 194–95
Common Object Request Broker Architecture (CORBA), 10, 149, 348–49
Complex datatypes, 27–29
Complex data warehouse:
   database background, 45–46
   DataBlade modules, defined, 46–47
   data format, 49
   functional index, 48
   and Informix Dynamic Server with Universal Database Option, 45–57
      features, 47–48
   r-tree index, 48
   smart large objects, 48
   strong typing, 55
   table/type inheritance and polymorphism, 48
   type-based integrity check, 55–56
   universal data warehouse, 48–52
      client-based business objects, 52
      data integration, 51
      difficulty in maintaining code, 51
      integrated data server, 52–54
      multiple data sources, 49
      multiple technologies in use, 51
      object mapping, 50
      object-oriented design and implementation, 54–55
Composite datatypes, 27–28
Consistency Point Technologies, Inc., 397
Copy/Move screen, 296
CORBA, 10, 149, 348–49
Cost/benefit analysis, 82
COUNT() function, 249

cpt_clearVolume, 133
cpt_close, 133
cpt_connect, 133
cpt_disconnect, 133
cpt_export, 133
cpt_getFamily, 133
cpt_getOpticalOid, 133
cpt_getSize, 133
cpt_import, 133
cpt_info, 133
cpt_inventory, 133
cpt_label, 133
cpt_ls, 133
cpt_mount, 134
cpt_optiLinkStatus, 133
cpt_read, 133
cpt_setFamily, 133
cpt_setTimeOut, 133
cpt_setVolume, 133
cpt_unmount, 134
cpt_write, 133
CREATE CAST syntax, 166–67
Custom DataBlades, 67–73
    costs, 73
    key enabling technology, 71–72
    three-tier architecture:
        factors influencing, 70–71
        typical, 67–69
    transaction processor/monitor, benefits of,
        69
Customer service, and e-commerce, 375–76
CyberCash, 382–83
Cyberpublishing movement, 283–311
    and accessibility, 285
    advantages of, 285
        by industry, 286
    application services approach, 311
    commercial solution to, 310
    commercial Web site evolution, 305–9
        complexity of Web site applications,
            306
        evolution of Web site development, 307
        first-generation site, 307
        functional services, 309–10
        higher bandwidth/multimedia support,
            305–6
        second-generation site, 307–8
        third-generation site, 308–9
    and collaborative workflow, 285
    defined, 284–85
    and productivity, 285

and publishing turnaround, 285
"24 Hours in Cyberspace," 287–310
    Amateur Inbox screen, 294
    Assign Amateur to Story screen, 294
    Audio Details screen, 295
    collecting stage, 291
    Copy/Move screen, 296
    core technology in, 296–300
    creating stage, 290
    Display Story Material screen, 295
    editing phase, 291
    Edit Photos screen, 295
    Edit Text screen, 295
    event background, 287–89
    implications for today's organizations,
        305
    Informix Dynamic Server with Web
        Integration Option, 297–300
    Informix server, 296
    Load Professional Audio screen, 294
    main menu, 293–94
    Mission Control, 300–304
    ORDBMS architecture, 296–97
    overview of, 287–89
    Photographer Status screen, 294
    process flow, 289–93
    process summary for, 292–93
    Professional Inbox screen, 293
    publishing phase, 291–92
    screens, 293–96
    Story Status screen, 295
    technology partners, 300–304
who benefits from, 285–86

D

Database extensibility:
    aggregation values, handling, 169–76
    CREATE CAST syntax, 166–67
    date datatype, 139
    external extension implementation diffi-
        culties, 140
    fuzzy searching, 142–50
    and industrial applications, 137–78
    parts number management, 150–61
    rapid/multimarket interest in, 138
    Soundex() algorithms, 143–50
    temporal queries, 161–69
        CHECK syntax, 163–65
    time datatype, 139
    user defined types, 153–54, 160–61

Hierarchical storage management (HSM),
and Open/C, 132
High-performance Web application design,
179–92
database management, 184–86
adding indexes, 185
datatypes, 185
fragmentation, 184
indexes, 184
index maintenance, 184–85
index statistics, 185
memory, 184
nulls, 185
number of indexes, 185–86
selective denormalization, 186
selective relax referential, 186
separation, 184
table keys, 185
time of maintenance, 186
database servers, 181
memory utilization, 183
network environments, 181
page outs, 183
performance monitoring by symptoms, 183
performance tuning areas, 181
by application impact, 182
performance tuning methodology, 180–83
Web browsers, 180
Web DataBlade architecture, 186–87
Web DataBlade tuning, 187–92
development tips, 191
isolation levels, 189–90
large object caching, 188–89
minimizing network traffic, 190
tracing/reviewing query plans, 191–92
using NSAPI/ISAPI, 187–88
Web servers, 181
Windows NT, monitoring resources on,
184
Hilbert() function, 168fn
Horschman, Eric, 95, 391
HTML, See HyperText Markup Language
(HTML)
HTML editing tool, 84
HTTP, See HyperText Transport Protocol
(HTTP)
Hyperlinks, 209
HyperText Markup Language (HTML), 194,
343–44
HyperText Transport Protocol (HTTP), 194,
345–47, 349, 350, 362
advantages of, 347
disadvantages of, 346

I

IBM DB2/6000 Common Server, 14, 16
Idehen, Kingsley, 341, 392–93
Illustra Server:
data modeling with, 216–19
See also High-performance Web applica-
tion design
Indexes, 33, 184
adding, 185
maintenance, 184–85
number of, 185–86
statistics, 185
Information management, emerging indus-
try standard for, 338–40
Informix digital media solutions, 313–40
customer profiles, 336–38
Seattle Times, 338
Sun Microsystems Catalyst Catalog,
337
Warner Brothers Online, 336–37
DataBlade modules, 322–23
Excalibur Technologies DataBlade
Modules, 329–30
Informix Video Foundation DataBlade
Module, 324–26
Kodak PixFactory DataBlade module,
328–29
Muscle Fish Audio Information
Retrieval (AIR) Datablade Module,
327–28
NEC TigerMark DataBlade Module, 329
and partner profiles, 324–31
Verity Text DataBlade Module, 331
Virage Visual Information Retrieval
DataBlade Module, 330–31
VXtreme Video DataBlade Module,
326–27
dynamic Web support, 323–24
information management, and rich
media content, 314–17
Informix Dynamic Server with Universal
Database Option and digital media,
320–22
partnerships, 332–36
Avid Technology-Informix partnership,
334–35
Bulldog Group-Informix for Digital
Media Management partnership,
332–34
Silicon Graphics (SGI)-Informix partnership, 336
relational vs. object-oriented, 318–20

N

NameTag DataBlade Module, 104–18
    access methods, 118
    advantages of, 105–6
    API and NameTag applications, 106–7
    architecture outline, 108–9
    client functions, 118
    components of, 106–7, 108
    Custom Name List, 106–7
    datatypes, 109–17
    defined, 104–5
    document storage/associated datatypes,
        109–17
    features, 109
    functionality, 109
    installation, 118
    Name Lexicon, 106–7
    NameTag datatype, 110–13
        secondary classification (SUBTYPE),
            110–13
        top-level categories (TYPES), 110–11
    NameTag Functions, indexing documents
        using, 110
    Pattern Data, 106
    processing model, 107–8
    provided functions, 113–14
    server functions, 114–18
        NAMETAG(parms), 114
        NTbatchConfigure, 114–15
        NTentityAttr, 118
        NTentityOffset, 118
        NTentityString, 117
        NTextractEntities, 116–17
        NTextractTag, 117
        NTinit, 114
        NTlastError, 115
        NTloadDocument, 115–16
        NTloadFile, 115
        NTnext Entity, 117
        NTprocessDocument, 116
        NTresetError, 115
        NTshutdown, 114
NAMETAG(parms), 114
NEC TigerMark DataBlade Module, 329
Neovista, 40
Netscape plug-ins, 10, 12
Network Computer Architecture (NCA), 15,
    65
Network environments, 181
Novell Network Loadable Modules (NLMs),
    10, 12

NSAPI, 187–88, 381
NTbatchConfigure, 114–15
NTentityAttr, 118
NTentityOffset, 118
NTentityString, 117
NTextractEntities, 116–17
NTextractTag, 117
NTinit, 114
NTlastError, 115
NTloadDocument, 115–16
NTloadFile, 115
NTnext Entity, 117
NTprocessDocument, 116
NTresetError, 115
NTshutdown, 114
Nulls, 185

O

Object Database Connectivity (ODBC), 318
Object identifier (OID), 27
Objectives, 82
Object Management Group (OMG), 348
Object mapping, 50
Object-oriented database management sys-
    tems (OODBMSs), 2–3, 319
Object-oriented design and implementation,
    54–55
Object-relational DBMSs, architectural
    options for, 11–16
Object-relational DBMSs (ORDBMSs):
    and DataBlade modules, 66
    functionality of, 3, 4–6, 17
    marketplace architectures, 11–15
        IBM DB2/6000 Common Server, 14, 16
        Informix Dynamic Server with
            Universal Database Option, 14–15,
            16
        Oracle 8.0, 13, 15
        Oracle 8.1 and 8.2, 14, 15
        Sybase Adaptive Server, 11–13, 15
    performance of, 3–4, 6–11
        degree of coupling, 9–10
        loose coupling, 4
        loose integration, 3
        tight coupling, 3–4
        tight integration, 3, 6–9
    See also Database extensibility
Object request Brokers (ORBs), 10, 348–50,
    351, 363–64
O'Connor, Craig, 179, 395
ODBC links, 364